High, Wide & Lonesome

HIGH, WIDE & LONESOME

Hal Borland

The University of Arizona Press   Tucson

The University of Arizona Press
Manufactured in the United States of America
♾ This book is printed on acid-free, archival-quality paper.

94 93 92 91 90   5 4 3 2 1

LIBRARY OF CONGRESS CATALOGING-IN-PUBLICATION DATA
Borland, Hal, 1900–1978.
  High, wide, and lonesome / Hal Borland.
     p.   cm.
  ISBN 0-8165-1177-2 (alk. paper)
  1. Borland, Hal, 1900–1978—Homes and haunts—Colorado.
2. Borland, Hal, 1900–1978—Biography—Youth. 3. Authors,
American—20th century—Biography. 4. Naturalists—United States—
Biography. 5. Frontier and pioneer life—Colorado. 6. Colorado—
Social life and customs. 7. Colorado—Biography. I. Title.
PS3503.0563Z467   1990
818'.5203—dc20
[B]   89-78516
                                                               CIP

British Library Cataloguing in Publication data are available.

To Barbara

Who is my love, my song

Foreword

By an accident of time and place, I grew up on an American frontier. I was born in 1900, ninety-six years to the day after Lewis and Clark left St. Louis on their expedition across the newly acquired Louisiana Purchase; but my formative years were spent under circumstances not far different from those my great-grandfather knew in western Pennsylvania a century earlier, when Conestoga wagons were still hauling freight over the Alleghenies into the raw, new Ohio country. In that sense, I was born old. I am a kind of bridge between an almost legendary past and a fabulous but often worrisome present. In a way, I am my own grandfather, or even my great-grandfather. In terms of social history I have lived close to one hundred and fifty years, simply because I grew up on an island of isolation in eastern Colorado.

As a result of strange eddies in the migration of a restless people, eastern Colorado and western Kansas were virtually untouched by the whole nineteenth century. After Lewis and Clark, the trappers and traders ranged the whole area from the Mississippi River to the Pacific Coast. Then the Army, following the trappers' trails and often guided by the trappers, "explored" that country. In 1836 a ragged frontier army won freedom for Texas. A decade later another motley army won a war for California. Gold discoveries set off a series of mass migrations, to California, to Montana, to the Denver area. The Mormons made their stark trek to Utah, not for gold but for

7

land and freedom from persecution. And after the Civil War the Texans, cattle-poor and rawhide-tough, trailed their longhorn herds north across hundreds of hostile miles to the railroad pushing its way westward across Kansas.

In their haste, these rushes and treks and trailings detoured or leap-frogged vast areas, some of which became virtual islands of isolation in a shallow sea of settlement. Those islands, isolated geographically and doubly victims of the time and culture lag, east to west, which was so pronounced before the era of national magazines, newspapers and radio, became our last frontier. Eastern Colorado was one of those islands.

That high, wide and lonesome land is roughly two hundred miles square, an arid, treeless, short-grass upland with few live streams. To the north lies the Platte River, along which emigrants followed the Oregon Trail. To the south lies the Arkansas River and the old Sante Fe Trail. To the east is central Kansas, long accepted as the western limit of feasible agriculture. To the west is the barrier of the Rocky Mountains.

No major emigrant trail ever crossed that area. It was too dry, and the Indians were too fanatically hostile. For years a large part of it was an Indian reserve, and it was the range of one of the last great buffalo herds. In 1877, the year after Colorado was admitted into the Union, President Rutherford B. Hayes called those high plains an unsalable desert, unfit for human habitation, and recommended that it be set aside as a grazing reserve, to be tamed by the stockmen if they ever needed the grass enough to undertake the job. His recommendation was ignored, but the area's character had changed very little when my father decided, in the spring of 1910, that he wanted to take a homestead there.

We arrived on that "unsalable desert" by a route that sums up a good deal of frontier history. My father's people came from Scotland to America before the Revolution and settled in New York State. After the Revolution they moved to the frontier in western Pennsylvania. My great-grandfather, who came to be known as Old Will, was taken from there to Ohio as a child. In young manhood he moved, with his wife and basic possessions, to frontier Indiana. His son, my grandfather, who was known as Young Will, in turn moved west, fording streams and hacking his way through the forests. But by then the frontier was moving swiftly westward; Young Will went all the way to Nebraska. He settled not far from a secondary trail which crossed the Missouri River at St. Joseph, Missouri, and angled north to the Oregon Trail on the Platte.

Young Will Borland, my grandfather, was only casually a farmer; he was by trade a blacksmith and millwright. After a few years on the frontier farm he moved to Sterling, a new community on Nemaha Creek, and set up his forge and built a mill. He was a small bull of a man, five feet six and close to two hundred pounds. He had lost one eye in a boyhood accident, but he was a crack shot with a rifle. He made nails and hinges for the village church, built wagons that would last a farmer's lifetime, fed, clothed and schooled a big family, and died in his fifties. Two of his sons became blacksmiths, two became railroad men, one became a teacher, one the local sexton, one an editor.

My father, still another Will Borland, was the editor. He started to learn the blacksmith's trade, but after a year of it he walked out of the shop and apprenticed himself to the village printer. He became a master printer and, eventually, a part owner of the weekly newspaper where he had learned his trade. But he, too, had the westward urge and dream of his father and his father's father. So we went to Colorado, that spring of 1910, and settled on a homestead almost thirty miles south of the Platte valley town of Brush.

By 1910, railroad promotion and the depression of 1907 had persuaded a good many marginal farmers in the Midwest that free land, even on the forbidding high plains, was worth a gamble. They were willing to bet Uncle Sam, as the saying went, that they could live on those dry plains five years—later

9

reduced to three—without starving out. If they won the bet, the land was theirs. If they lost, all they lost was their time and a little labor. So there was a fringe of homestead settlement all around that arid area when we arrived. My father chose a homestead out beyond that fringe.

Our homestead was as far from Brush, both in distance and in travel time, as Hillsdale, Ohio, had been from Chillicothe in my great-grandfather's day. It was as far as my grandfather's homestead near Vesta, Nebraska, had been from Nebraska City. In terms of horse travel, the means they used and the means we used, it was a good five hours each way even in good weather. In spring mud or winter snow it was a long all-day trip each way. There were telephones in our day, but the nearest one was twelve miles from the homestead. So was the nearest post office. The nearest doctor was thirty miles from us. And our closest neighbor was two miles away.

Looking back from this age of atomic power, our life on the homestead seems almost as strange as life in Medieval England. Yet the grandfathers would have been at home there. They pioneered in timbered country, but the plains would not have baffled them for long. Lacking logs, they would have built a sod house, as we did. Lacking firewood, they would have burned cow dung and sheep dung, as we did. They would have made do with what they had until they could provide better. They would have hunted their own meat, ground their own corn, tended their own sick, buried their own dead, and persisted. And all without heroics; with only that dogged determination, that persistence in the dream, which is a bright golden thread through all of America's history.

In a sense, this book is a fragment of American history. It is the story of the frontier and the pioneering I knew. As a nation, during my own lifetime we have had to face bitter questions about our purposes and our basic philosophies. Many of the answers, when we face the questions squarely, lead back to the frontiers: to men and women in a wilderness, whether it is a bleak Atlantic shore, a savage woodland, or a lonely, distant prairie; to men and women stubbornly trying to make a safe home, security for themselves, a better world for their children.

Colonial New England is far away and long ago, and Dan Boone's Kentucky is a misty legend. But the Old West is just over the horizon, a frontier which in many ways summed up three centuries of American pioneering and growth toward maturity. Reaching for a remembrance of it, trying to understand this heritage of ours, we sometimes catch only false heroics and false melodrama, but now and then we do capture enough of its reality to recognize our enduring purposes. No matter where we came from or when, the pioneers were our rootstock, our source, our beginnings. They shaped the pattern for America.

H. B., 1956

1

When father and I started out, that late April morning, it was like the dawn of creation, so sweet and clean and crisply damp-cool. All along the first two miles south from town the black-birds in the big cottonwoods *ka-cheed* among the jade-flake leaves, leaves no bigger than a ground squirrel's ear. The blackbirds themselves were like gems, jet set with ruby and gold, the red-wings and the yellow-heads, all *ka-chee*ing in the sun not half an hour high. And in the roadside alfalfa, silvery blue-green in new leaf and dew, was a jack rabbit in from the sand hills for breakfast, the sun making his long black-tipped ears pink as rose quartz. It was all spring and new beginnings, a morning to be alive and laughing.

I wanted to laugh and shout when the jack rabbit in the alfalfa swiveled his ears, stood on his haunches, knee-high to a tall man, and wriggled his nose at us. Then Father did laugh, and Dick and Shorty broke into a trot, snorting and eager and full of life, and the rabbit hopped away. The wagon, loaded with lumber and roofing paper and sections of galvanized well casing, jolted on the gravel road, creaking and rattling.

Father let the horses trot a little way, then drew them down to a walk again and handed the lines to me while he rolled a Bull Durham cigarette. Already Nebraska was "back east" and we were Coloradoans. Father, who had been a printer since he was fourteen, was going to be a ranchman, or at least a farmer.

"If I'm ever going to make a change," he'd said two months

13

ago, "I'd better make it now, or I'll wake up some morning and find that I'm an old man." Father was almost thirty-two years old. So he came to Colorado alone, from the little Nebraska town where he was born less than thirty miles from the Missouri River, and he found the land he wanted and filed on it as a homestead. He went back to Nebraska, sold his share of the weekly newspaper, sold the house where we lived, and told Mother and me we'd move just as soon as winter was over.

Winter began to break up in March, hurried as though just for us by an early spring. Mud and melt crept along the Missouri River bottom lands and up Nemaha Creek, and Father helped us with the first packing. Then he left the rest of the packing to Mother and me and came to Colorado, to rent the little green house in Brush for a temporary home, to buy a team and wagon and a couple of cows and a dozen chickens. He even set two broody hens so Mother would have a flock of chicks for summer frying. And, ten days ago, Mother and I came out to Brush, eighteen hours on the cindery green-plush train, eating from the big box of picnic food, napping in the stiff-backed seats, talking to the friendly conductor and brakeman. The brakeman said to me, "Why, at almost ten, you're big enough to ride a bronco and shoot a coyote!" And I couldn't wait to get to Colorado.

Now we were on the way to the homestead, Father and I. Mother had seen us off, breakfasted and eager. Father had said, "We'll be back within a week or so, ten days at most. We'll get a house up and dig a well; then we'll come back for you." And she had kissed us both and waved goodbye, slim and dark-haired and a little misty-eyed. Mother would be twenty-nine in the fall. She was still standing there in the dooryard, watching, her hands wrapped in her apron, when we turned the corner at the depot and waved. She waved to us, then turned and went back to the little green house, and we headed south along the road lined with tall cottonwoods just leafing out.

Two miles from town we came to the end of the cotton-wood lane. Ahead was the first range of sand hills. We turned east, skirting them. We were climbing out of the Platte valley, going toward the high flatlands. Behind us the valley was lush with trees and irrigated fields. Ahead, where we were going, the hills rolled gently all the way to the horizon without a tree in sight. We skirted the sand hills another mile to the east, then turned south again, and the hard road ended. The horses began to strain as the heavily laden wagon's wheels bit into the sand track.

I watched the front wheel on my side, the left, as it turned in the sand, felly-deep. The sand lifted with the wheel and fell back in a little cascade that glistened in the sun and made a soft, singing hiss. The hub rattle was muffled. Only the puffing of the horses and the creak of harness where louder than the singing hiss of the sand at the wheels. I looked south and asked, "Is that where we're going, to that hill?"

"Farther than that," Father said. And when we had crossed the next hollow there was a new farthest hill. We were going farther than that one, too, much farther.

We crossed the sand hill strip and were on hard road again. The sun was halfway toward noon. The horses were sweating, and the smell of sweat and warm leather was a Nebraska smell. It was a Grandpa smell, Mother's father, who was a farmer and teamster. I would always remember him for the smell that was upon him, a clean farm smell of hay and horses, not a barn smell. Grandpa was a gentle man, a man who never had a cross word for horses or dogs or small boys. The other grandfather, Father's father, I never knew. He died before I was born. He was a blacksmith and a millwright. There was a profile picture of him that hung in an oval frame in Grandma Borland's house. It showed only one side of his face, and one eye; he lost the other eye as a boy. He had a face like Father's, except that Grandpa Borland had a full black mustache. All grand-fathers had mustaches. Grandpa Clinaburg had a brown one, except when he had been hauling flour for the mill; then it was white, and so was his hair. Sometimes Father told stories about Grandpa Borland, but not this morning.

We topped another rise and I pointed again to the farthest hill in sight. "Farther than that one?"

Father laughed. "That hill is this side of Gary, and Gary's just about halfway there."

So I watched the meadow larks on the fence posts at the side of the road, saw the yellow of their breasts and the spotted brown of their backs and the lengths of their bills. I watched the funny way they flew on their stubby wings. As I listened to their songs it seemed they were saying, "This is the time to see the world!" and "Hello there, boy!" And I watched the striped-backed little ground squirrels and asked Father what they were. He told me and I said they couldn't be squirrels because the squirrels along Nemaha Creek back in Nebraska had long, bushy tails. These, I said, were squinneys, and Father said, "You'll see lots of squinneys."

It was eleven o'clock when we reached Gary. Gary wasn't really a town; it was a store and post office, a big, rambling frame building with a wide porch and a long hitch rack. Father tied the team at the hitch rack and we went inside. It was dark and cool and smelled of coffee and leather and calico and coal oil. Tom McDowell, the tall, lean, lesiurely storekeeper, wore a blue work shirt and a vest open down the front. He drawled when he said, "Warm morning for April, ain't it?" Then he glanced out the big front window, saw our wagon and its load, and he asked, "Homesteaders?"

Father said, "Yes. We're going down in the corner of the county. Just going out to build the house."

Mr. McDowell said, "Well, good luck. That's down on John Gerrity's range, isn't it?"

I was edging down the long brown counter, looking at the yellow coils of lariat rope, the leather work gloves, the bibless overalls, the high-heeled boots hanging in pairs from the ceiling. At the few bolts of calico on the shelves, the rolls of table oilcloth, the square, slant-topped, lacquered bins of coffee and tea, the glass-topped bins of ginger snaps and pink-iced cookies. There was a glassed case with boxes of cigars and bags of smoking tobacco and a pile of long brown slabs of chewing tobacco. And at the back of the store, in the corner, was a cubbyhole of a post office with its barred window and its squares of mailboxes. Beside the mailboxes stood big burlap bags of Mexican beans and white hundred-pound sacks of sugar.

Father was buying cheese and crackers and sardines. Mr. McDowell was saying, "That's down south of Gerrity's main camp. Up at the head of Ketchem Holler."

"I don't know that name," Father said.

"That's the big valley just west of the school section," Mr. McDowell said. "They used to use it to hold the herd when they had roundup, the big ranches."

"I guess that's it," Father said. "We're just west of the school section. On section seventeen."

Mr. McDowell nodded and put the things in a paper sack. "Good hay land in there. Well, I'll probably be seeing you some more. Expecting any mail?"

"Not yet," Father said. He paid the bill and we went back to the wagon. There was a watering trough beside the store, so we watered the horses before we drove on.

Three more miles south, past a few farms and alfalfa fields, and we came to another range of sand hills. We drove to the top of the first hill, pulled out of the main track, and unhitched the horses. Father slipped the bits from their mouths and set out a tin pail for each of them with a couple of quarts of oats.

We sat in the shade of the wagon and Father opened the package of cheese. He cut a slice with his pocket knife, laid it on a big square cracker, and handed it to me before he opened the can of sardines. I took a bite, caught the cracker crumbs with my tongue, and sucked the warm, tangy cheese and felt the crispness of the cracker. I held it in my mouth, just tasting it, before I chewed it. Father cut another slice of cheese, put it on another cracker, and lifted a mustard-drippy sardine on his knife blade. He put the sardine on the cheese and handed the whole wonderful thing to me.

Crisp cracker, tingly cheese, and mustardy sardine! It was even better than Nemaha Creek catfish and bread and butter! The oozy mustard filled your mouth, there was the crunchy taste of cracker and the warm sardine taste, and there was the clinging cheese taste, all combined. Cheese and crackers are good food on any hilltop; cheese and crackers and mustard sardines are a banquet.

We banqueted till there wasn't a crumb of cheese left or a drip of mustard in the sardine can. Then we lay in the shade under the wagon and watched two sand lizards no longer than my hand, lizards with green and sand-colored backs and yellowish white bellies and white throats that pulsated as they breathed. The horses snuffled, there was a breath of cool air in the shade, and somewhere in the distance a hawk on the wing screamed a faint, echoing challenge.

Off to the south was another high hill, faint green and gleaming sand-gold in the sun. I sat up and pointed, and Father smiled and said, before my question came, "Still farther than that, son." We hitched the horses to the wagon and went on.

There were no more fences, now. On a distant hill there was a house, a lonely house without even a barn. Then, as we drove on and on, that last house was out of sight.

The road had become a trail, two faint ruts in the greening sand grass. Then we came to the far edge of the sand hills and hard land was under us again. There we left the wagon tracks, turned southwest onto a high flatland. We climbed a long gentle slope and were alone in a vastness and a distance that that were like nothing I had ever seen or imagined. In all directions I could see the horizon, not a hill between that interrupted the smooth, round bowl-rim of blue. It was like being a very tiny ant on a table under Mother's very biggest mixing bowl, a blue and silver bowl and a tablecloth all greeny-tan and full of little wrinkles.

Father drew up the horses for a moment and just sat and looked. There was an expression on his face that I had seen only once before, the first time he came home from out here and told Mother and me about the homestead he had filed on. But now it was even brighter, that look, and it had a kind of smile deep inside that didn't show on his lips but only in his blue eyes. I looked at him, and I looked again at the distance, and I felt a kind of smile, inside myself, and a sense of awe that made me not want to say a word. It was so big, so vast, so new, so wonderful.

Father took a deep breath and we drove on. It was like driving into a world nobody had ever seen before except God, a world God had just made, like the world in the Bible before there was an Adam or an Eve. Even the sounds were all new. The hub rattle of the wagon was muted in the deep mat of curled buffalo grass. The creak of the harness was not much louder than the squeak of a cricket in your pocket.

We went on across the upland and came to a prairie dog town where the grass was thinned away and there were hundreds of pockmark holes and pimple mounds where the brown little prairie dogs, fatter and bigger than Nebraska squirrels, sat and yipped at us and jerked their skinny tails and dived down their burrows when the wagon came near.

We came to a broad, shallow lake, melt from the winter snow and drain from the spring rain, that would shrink to a little mudhole in another month or two. It hardly looked like water, it was so clear, and under the water the grass was growing, much greener than the flat all around it. Ducks were there, scores of teal and mallards and even canvasbacks, swimming on the clear water over the green grass as though they were swimming in the air. And around the edges were brown curlew and snipe, with their long grotesque beaks and fat stubby bodies. And killdeers, with their black coats and white shirt fronts, running along in the shallows and bobbing and leaping into the air and crying *kill-deer, kill-deer, kill-dee, dee* as they flew a little way and settled again.

We came close to the water and the ducks quacked in excitement and flailed the water and rose on beating wings, dripping so much that for a moment there was a flash of rainbow in the spray. They rose and circled and came back to land with outstretched feet and cupped wings, in a new rush of spray.

Then the lake was behind and the meadown larks were singing, "Hello there, boy!" And little horned larks went spiraling up, right under the horses' noses, singing as they flew high in circles. And when we came down a little slope into hidden hollow there was a rush of small hoofs and a flash of white rump patches as a herd of pronghorn antelope, surprised at their grazing, bounded away, stiff-legged and breathtakingly swift. They ran to the next hilltop, circled, came back behind us and, full of curiosity, followed the wagon for half a mile.

Midafternoon and we saw another wagon coming toward us. Just the sight of it was startling. I felt the way Robinson Crusoe felt when he saw the footprints in the sand. We had been all alone in this tremendous world, and now there was someone else.

The wagon was drawn by a black team, a shiny, black, arch-tailed team of horses, and on the wagon seat was a little man with a round face and stocky body and a grin that was a welcome itself. He drew alongside and stopped and shouted, "Hello, strangers! Where you heading?"

Father said we were going out to our homestead to build a house.

"Where you located?" the little man asked.

"Section seventeen," Father said. "North half of seventeen."

"Good!" the little man exclaimed. "I'm just a couple of miles from you. My name's Farley, Jake Farley." He reached in the pocket of his bibbed overalls. "I've got a house built and you can stay there till you get a roof up. I'm going to town a week or so. Here's the key." He tossed it over and Father caught it. "Make yourself at home!" and Mr. Farley relaxed the lines and his black team took off at a fast trot, the empty wagon rattling over the grass.

We drove on, now following Mr. Farley's wagon tracks, the only mark on that whole expanse of grass.

The hills were covered with buffalo grass or buffalo mixed with grama, and the draws, or valleys, were carpeted with bluestem. Here and there were clumps of yucca with their stiff, evergreen, bayonet leaves; and now and then we came to a hollow where sheep had grazed the grass away and cut it out with their sharp hoofs and sagebrush had taken over, sage and greasewood. And here and there were big beds or scattered clumps of cactus, the flat-leafed gray-grizzly ones full of vicious thorns and the greener, less spined prickly pears. But even the yucca and the sagebrush and greasewood and the cactus were lost in the vastness of grass, the highest sagebrush wasn't as high as the hubs on the front wheels of the wagon.

"Good soil," Father said. "That grass has been here forever. Even the sagebrush doesn't do too well, because sage likes poor soil. The grass takes over even from the sage, when it gets half a chance."

At last we came to a hill that sloped down to Mr. Farley's house, and we were at the end of the day's journey.

Mr. Farley's house was set on the gentle hillside above a valley of bluestem already ankle-high with new growth. It was a long low building still new-pine yellow and smelling of pitch. Just down the hillside was a pump on a little wooden plaftorm, a green pump so new the paint was still on the handle.

We unlocked the door in one end of the house, the end with two windows. There was a partition across the middle. One end, the end we went in, was the house. It had a cookstove and an iron bed with brown blankets over a blue-striped mattress and a bench built under one window to eat from and a bench beside it to sit on. The other end of the building was the barn, with big doors and no windows and no floor and a manger built against the partition.

We unhitched the horses and put them in the barn. Father took our box of groceries into the house and I went for a pail of water. Father built a fire in the stove with cow chips, dried cow dung, from the pile in the corner behind the stove. He opened a can of beans and fried a pan of bacon, and we sat down at the bench beneath the window and ate our supper.

The sun set. We grained the horses. We walked to the top of the hill west of the house and Father pointed to the third hill beyond and said, "It's over there, son. That's where our homestead is."

We stood there several minutes, looking. Father undoubtedly was thinking of Nebraska, of the job he had given up, the home town he had left, the warnings spoken and unspoken that had accompanied the goodbyes. A man with a job was supposed to stick to it, and a man in business for himself was honored and respected. For a man who left school at the age of thirteen, Father had done well. One of his brothers, I learned long later, had said he was a fool to pack up and leave. But then, he had been called foolish to quit the blacksmith shop and become a printer. He had gone his own way, following his own dream; and now that dream had turned to the land, to land of his own in a new country. He had worked nineteen years for someone else. Even as part owner of the paper back home he had been under a boss, the editor who taught him the printer's trade and who would, as long as they worked together, always be the boss. He wanted to own himself, be his own boss, work out his own destiny. These things must have been heavy in his mind, as well as a sense of responsibility for a wife and a son, who had been uprooted from home, friends and security. He had moved from one job to another the eleven years he had been married, had lived and worked in half a dozen places including Omaha and Nebraska City before he returned to his home town. But always it had been a move from a good job to a better one, and always there had been a weekly pay envelope. Now he had quit a job to move to a new land, to take his chances there. But it was his choice, his and Mother's.

We watched the flare of the sunset and we looked out over the endless rolling plains. Then we went back down the hill, and even I felt that Nebraska was a long, long way from there. I looked at the horizon to the east, but I couldn't see beyond the plains. In the eastern sky, maybe half as far away as Nebraska, was a long thin cloud all pink and lavender with reflected sunset. I wondered if they could see that cloud in Nebraska.

We went down the hill and Father lit the coal oil lamp in the bracket over the table. The horses, just beyond the partition, were eating hay. I could hear the *crunch-crunch* as they ate, and old Dick snuffled as loud as though he was right there in the room with us.

"Tired, son?" Father asked. "You should be. So am I. It's been a long day, and we'll have a busy day tomorrow. Let's turn in."

I sat on the bed and took off my shoes. I unbuckled my overalls and unbuttoned my blouse, thinking that next year I would be old enough to wear shirts instead of blouses. Shirts like Father's, that you had to take off over your head.

Father stood at the doorway, looking out at the dusk. "Your grandpa," he said, talking half to me and half to himself, "went all the way from Indiana to Nebraska in a covered wagon. With an ox team. He took a homestead, over near Vesta. Built a house and a mill, and fought wolves and Indians. Your grandpa was a crack shot, even if he did have only one eye. He used to shoot deer from his cabin door, they say.

And they say he killed an Indian once, with just his hammer and a hook-nosed hoof knife. . . . I guess it's in the blood to keep moving west. But of all his kids, I'm the only one who got west of Nebraska."

He turned to me, still sitting on the bed in my underclothes. "Get under the covers, son. . . . I suppose you'll grow up and move on, too." He sat down on the bench and took off his shoes. He sat there, wriggling his toes in his black cotton socks. He looked at me. "Your name should have been Will too, like mine and your grandfather's and his father's. Kind of slipped up, I guess, when we got to you. Your great-grandfather was from Ohio. Born in western Pennsylvania, but they moved to Ohio when he was a baby. When he grew up he moved to Indiana. That must have been back in the eighteen thirties or forties. . . . And now we're away out here. Out here in Colorado."

He yawned and stood up and blew out the light, then came over and got into bed with me. I hugged him.

"Lonesome, son?" he asked. "Miss your mother?"

I did, but I said, "No." I snuggled against him and drew up my knees and closed my eyes. Just beyond the head of the bed old Dick was snuffling and Shorty was eating hay and rattling his halter rope against the manger.

Later, much later, I wakened. Outside a whole pack of wolves were howling. Howling and snapping and snarling right there at the door. I was in Nebraska, and there was a pack of wolves, and Grandpa Borland wasn't anywhere around to kill them with his hammer and his farrier's knife.

I wanted to cry out, but I couldn't. Then the wolves were quiet for a moment and I heard old Dick snuffle. I knew where I was, right here in Mr. Farley's cabin in Colorado. Miles and miles from town. I was alone here in this house, and it was dark, and there were the wolves again, howling and trying to get in the door.

I was frozen with fright. Then the wolves were quiet and I

heard Father's deep, slow breathing, almost a snore. I forced a hand to reach out and clutch him.

He wakened. The wolves were howling again. I was crying. Father sat up. "Son! Wake up! You're having a bad dream!"

I clung to him, sobbing. "The wolves!" I whispered.

Father put an arm around me and listened. Then he laughed. "Those aren't wolves, son. They're just coyotes. Two coyotes can make more noise than a dozen tomcats. They won't hurt you."

I listened, and they weren't wolves. And they weren't at the door. They were coyotes, up on the hill. The panic eased away.

We lay down again. Father put his arm around me and, knowing security, I went to sleep again.

2

We left Jake Farley's cabin the next morning to the song of meadow larks and with the bright sun of a new and wonderful day. We drove over the hill and across the flats, and jack rabbits leaped from the bunch grass and went galloping into the distance. One of the jacks looked as big as the antelope we had seen the day before. He wasn't, of course, but Father said he must weigh at least ten pounds. He ran in great leaps, and every sixth or eighth leap he went higher than before and turned his head and looked back at us.

We drove two miles west and came to the long slope that was the east side of Ketchem Holler. The broad valley began just there to our left and wound in a big sweep to the north. It was so deep that the morning shadow still lay on the blue-stem at the bottom. Beyond, to the west, another long slope marked the far side, and at the top of the slope the land flattened out again in a high tableland.

We paused on the hillside and Father said, "There it is, son. That's our land. Our east boundary runs along the far edge of the valley. Our land lies east and west, half a mile wide north and south and a mile long. A half section, three hundred and twenty acres of these old plains."

I had no conception of acreage or distance. To me, that whole expanse of hillside across the valley and the tableland beyond were ours. Father felt a kinship with the plains, but to me they were a personal possession. What are the boundaries of boyhood, anyway? That land, as far as I could see, belonged to me. The school section, with its great beds of cactus, were to become mine, and so were the flats off to the south, with their huge prairie dog town. So was the whole of Ketchem Holler, even John Gerrity's big sheep camp where the prickly poppies grew lush in summer and the doves haunted the empty sheds in winter. So were the sand hills still farther to the north. The boundaries of boyhood, as I knew them for a time, were that thin, distant line of the horizon; and even that did not bound the dreams and the imagination. Long later, when I first saw the red stone house where Daniel Boone was born in the red hills of Pennsylvania, I understood why he had to go and see far places. That red stone house was set in a cup of hills, every one a challenge. Those who live with a far horizon in their boyhood are never again bound to a narrow area of life. They may bind themselves, but that is a different matter.

As we went on down the slope and around a shoulder of the hill we came in sight of a windmill, the tall four-legged tower, the big, many-vaned wheel and the silvery fan. Beside the tower was a low, broad, galvanized watering tank. It was John Gerrity's windmill, at his upper camp. Nearby were half a dozen big brown squares, the manure beds where the sheep pens had stood last season. Gerrity leased the school section as a base for his upper camp and the flock based there grazed all the hills around.

The windmill wasn't running. It had been shut off and the pump pulled last fall, when the board-panel pens were taken away for the winter. Soon they would be back, as soon as lambing was over, and the mill would be running again.

We drove past the quiet mill and the empty tank and on across the valley. The windmill, Father had been told, was several hundred yards east of the section line. We drove a little way up the farther slope and were sure we were on our own land.

We got down and explored the hillside on foot. The buffalo grass, just beginning to show spears of green through its curled brown mat, was a thick carpet. Cattle had been there this spring, for there were cow chips everywhere. And there were bleached bones, buffalo bones, and a few buffalo skulls with the peeling dark gray horns still on their bony cores. The blue-stem in the valley was ankle-high and green as young rye. There wasn't a tree, a shrub or a bush in sight. We hadn't seen a tree since we left the farms near Gary, and even there they were cottonwoods that had been planted near the houses.

Coming down from the high flatland to the west was a shallow draw that widened as it reached Ketchem Holler. Father and I walked up the north side of this draw. Father was appraising, talking aloud to himself. "A house here on the south slope will have the hill at its back for shelter in the winter. Water should be fairly shallow, for the well, here at the edge of the draw."

We went up the hillside a little way, to a flat little bench-land. There on the bench was an old buffalo wallow full of rain water, a saucer-like hollow ten feet across and a foot and a half deep. Buffalo once had wallowed in the mud there to drive off the flies and gnats, but in the years since the last buffalo were killed the wallow had grassed over. As with the lake on the flats, the grass under the faintly brown water was bright green. Father cupped a handful and tasted it. "It's all right," he said, and I got down on my belly and drank from the pool itself. It tasted like rain water.

"Bring the team and wagon," Father said. "We'll build the house right here."

I brought the wagon and we unhitched the horses and un-harnessed them and hobbled them so they wouldn't wander too far. We put down boards on the grass beside the wagon for a floor and leaned boards against the wagon for a lean-to roof. We had a camp. We stowed the blankets and the box of groceries in it and Father took a spade and made a plains-style fireplace, a narrow trench with the sod piled on each side to support the skillet. Then we gathered a pile of dry cow chips and we had our camp complete.

Father squinted at the sun and got his directions straight, and then he cut a stake and drove it for one corner of the house. I held the tape and we laid out the other corners, square with the sun. The house was going to be fourteen feet wide and twenty feet long, with a narrow end to the north and with the door facing the east and the sunrise.

When we had it all laid out, Father took the posthole auger and dug a hole at each corner. In each hole we set a split cedar post, four feet down and well tamped in, to anchor the house against the wind. Then we laid out the sills and the floor joists, Father nailed them into place, and I held the corner studs while he nailed them to the cedar posts.

Noon came. We ate cold sandwiches and drank water from the buffalo wallow. We worked all afternoon, I fetching the saw, the square, the nails, holding the studs while Father toe-nailed them to the sills. By sunset we had a rough framework up and braced, the beginnings of a house.

Father put down his hammer and flexed his fingers. Shadows were already darkening Ketchem Holler. I was almost too tired to stand. Father looked at me and at the shelter there beside the wagon; then he looked at the horses and he asked, "Well, son, shall we catch up Dick and Shorty and leave the wagon here and ride back over to Farley's cabin for the night?" He waited for an answer, leaving it to me.

I looked at the deepening shadows and at the skeleton of the house and at the makeshift lean-to, open at both ends. I thought about the little green house in town, and about Mother, and about the coyotes last night.

I slowly said, "Let's stay here."

"Fine," Father said.

I said, "I'm not afraid of coyotes." I said it very firmly and resolutely.

Father peeled potatoes and set bacon to fry. Then he sent me for a pail of water.

It was getting dark. The buffalo wallow was at least fifty yards from the lean-to. I walked all the way there. Then I began to see shadows moving, which weren't shadows at all, or anything but imagination. I sloshed the pail quickly into the water, got it two-thirds full, and ran. I ran halfway back, then walked, my heart pounding.

Father had opened a can of beans. He took the pail of water from me without a word, started to pour some into the coffee pot, then reached for a flour-sack dish towel. He held the towel over the lip of the pail and strained the water into the pot. Then he showed me a dozen tiny, wiggling things in the dish towel.

"Wiggle-tails," he said. "I guess you might call them mosquito tadpoles, because they'll grow into mosquitoes."

"Do they bite?" I asked.

Father laughed. "Not till they turn into mosquitoes. I've probably drunk a quart of them, one time or another. But they don't make the coffee taste any better. Next time push the top water aside and dip the pail deep. The wigglers are always on top."

It was full dark before we ate. Our only light was the last glow of the cow-chip fire and the faint gleam of the early stars. Far off across the valley a turtle dove was *hoo-hoo*ing.

I was almost too weary to eat, but Father finished everything. He even wiped out the bean pan with a slice of bread. Then he poured another cup of coffee and rolled a cigarette. I sat there beside him while he smoked.

"Asleep, son?" he finally asked.

"No."

"Tired?"

"Um-hmm."

He tossed the cigarette into the fire trench. "Let's go bring in the horses for the night, just to be sure they're here in the morning."

As we left the lean-to almost all the stars were out, bright as candles. The night wasn't really black at all, with all the stars.

The far hill, the other side of Ketchem Holler, was a black shadow, but the faint tan of the grass here on our hillside was almost shimmery, catching and reflecting the starlight. I could see the horses, heads up, watching us as we approached.

The night wasn't strange or frightening. It was home, our new home. I let go of Father's hand and walked alone.

We caught the horses and took off the hobbles and led them back to the wagon and tied their halter ropes to the wheels. As we went around the wagon to the lean-to Father pointed to the sky. "See the Dipper up there? Away high, this time of the year, and tipped over, the bowl upside down."

I found the Big Dipper.

"There are the pointers, those two stars at the end of the bowl. Down where they are pointing, halfway to the horizon, is the North Star."

I found the North Star.

Father looked at the framework of the house, outlined against the hillside, and measured it against the North Star. "Just about right," he said. "Just about true north and south."

We went into the lean-to and sat on the blanket pallet to take off our shoes. "Same stars we had in Nebraska," Father said. "Even out here you needn't ever get lost, if you can see the sun or the stars. You'll know your directions. You can always count on the sun and the North Star."

We crawled between the blankets. Father put an arm around me. I lay there for several minutes. Then from far down Ketchem Holler came a faint *yip-yip-yip, yowrrr-yowr, yip-yip*.

I held my breath and listened. At last I said, "It's just an old coyote, isn't it?" I whispered it.

Father said, "Yes, just a coyote."

I listened again, and I said, "I'm big enough to shoot a coyote."

"Um-hmm."

I lay stiff and tense. The coyote kept on yipping. Then I began to relax. That was the last I remembered.

The sun wakened us, streaming in the open end of the lean-to. The air was chilly. Outside, just down the slope, two meadow larks were singing, trying to outdo each other. I sat up and listened, then kicked the blankets off. Off of Father too. He opened his eyes and growled, but I knew it wasn't a scolding growl. I laughed, and he grabbed me and began to wallow and tousle me. We made a rat's nest of the bed, and then Father rolled me right out into the cold, wet grass.

After the first wet surprise it felt good. I shouted and leaped and flapped my arms and crowed at the sun like a rooster. I ran down into the bluestem and back, my underdraws flapping around my legs, breathless.

Father was tucking his shirt into his overalls. He grabbed me and carried me, squealing, under his arm to the buffalo wallow. But he didn't duck me. We washed our faces in the cold, clear water, and I ran back and dressed while Father built a fire and mixed pancake batter. I hobbled the horses and turned them loose to graze, and we ate breakfast.

We floored the house and we put shiplap lumber on the walls, leaving gaps for the door and windows. We put up rafters for a curved roof that made the cabin look like a squat railroad car. And the night we got half the roof boards on we moved inside. We finished the roof, put on roofing paper, and framed the doors and the windows.

It was just a shell of a house, but Father planned to lay up sod around it and put sod on the roof for winter warmth and summer coolness. And the night we finished the roof I made my own separate pallet of blankets.

So we had a house. It had no door and no window sash, but it was a house, our house.

Then we dug the well.

Father chose the site, just down the slope from the house at the edge of the draw. We moved the wagon to the place and Father bored a hole with the posthole auger. He went down four feet, as deep as he could go, a hole eight inches across.

Then he unscrewed the handle from the auger, put on an eight-foot length of pipe, put the handle on again, and had an auger twelve feet long. By standing on the wagon bed he could go on digging with it.

We had to lift the auger every time it filled, and I emptied it; then Father put it down the hole again and went down another auger-length. We went down and down, a foot at a time, and the pile of soil beside the well became bigger and bigger. At first the soil the auger brought up was brown. Then it was fine yellow clay. We were still in the yellow clay, but we were down almost twelve feet at the end of the first day's digging.

The next morning we put on another length of pipe and started on down. It was slow going, because we had to lift all that length of pipe every time we had an augerful. We had gone down only about four more feet by midmorning when we saw a bay team and a spring wagon down in Ketchem Holler. The team turned and came up our draw.

A big red-faced man was driving. He had two big rough-coated dogs in the spring wagon with him, and alongside, trotting in the grass, were four long-legged hounds, dark-coated and sleek-tailed as though they had greyhound blood.

The man drove up beside us and the hounds came and sniffed at me. The man said, "Hello," in a deep, gruff voice.

Father greeted him and the man said, "Homesteader?"

"Yes," Father said. "I've taken the north half of section seventeen, here."

"I'm John Gerrity," the man said. "My camp down there," and he waved a hand toward the windmill in the hollow. "Got water yet?"

"Not yet."

Gerrity smiled. "Likely you won't. Water's spotty in this country. If you do get it, it won't be good water. And it'll dry up in a dry summer. This land's good for nothing but grazing. You won't stay."

"Maybe not," Father said, "but we'll sure try."

Gerrity smiled. "They come, and they go. Maybe you noticed this country is still pretty vacant."

"I noticed there was lots of room," Father said.

"Good country," Gerrity said, "for coyotes, and jack rabbits, and sheep. You'll find out!" He gathered his reins and called to his hounds. "I'm running coyotes today," he said. "Cleaning up the range before I put the sheep out." He looked at the well again and shook his head. Then he turned his team and drove back down the draw.

John Gerrity had come to Colorado twenty years before, a young laborer working for the railroad. He was a big man, a tough man. He had plenty of tough company in the railroad crews of that day. But whereas the others were content to lay ties and spike rails all day and drink and fight in resounding brawls most of the night, John Gerrity had a gnawing personal ambition. He was going to get ahead. He saw opportunity in this raw, new country. He didn't know what he was going to do, but he knew he wasn't going to be a pick and shovel man all his life.

He quit the railroad and took a job as roustabout in a livery stable. There he listened to the casual talk of the cattlemen who came to town, and he began to understand things about this short-grass country that he had only vaguely sensed before. He began to see where he wanted to go.

This was grass country, a land of free grass. The man who moved in and took that grass, and was strong enough to hold it, became a cattle baron. Once you had a range you could buy cheap cattle in Texas or in Mexico, trail them north, fatten them on the grass, and sell them at a most satisfying profit.

There were various ways to get the range. It was government land, widely conceded to be of no value except for grazing. Technically, it was open to anyone who would homestead it. Practically, it was not considered farm land and hence not desirable homestead land. The farmer of that day would not give it a second look. So, by forfeit and economic practicality, it was left to the ranchmen to use as they would.

A ranch generally started with a homestead at a strategic point, a place where there was natural water, a stream or a pond. Since water was scarce, if you controlled the water you controlled all the grass for miles around. So the ranchman homesteaded and took title to a home place with water on it. Then he persuaded a few of his chosen cowboys to homestead the other strategic plots on his range. As soon as they proved up on those plots, they sold them to the ranchman for a few hundred dollars. Thus, by owning a few hundred acres and controlling the water, the ranchman came to control thousands of acres of grass.

These things John Gerrity learned. And he planned ahead to the time when he, too, would be a cattle baron. But chance and weather changed his plans. A drought struck in New Mexico, on the sheep ranges. Desperate sheepmen shipped their flocks north, looking for grass or buyers. John Gerrity, a provident man, had a few hundred dollars. Hearing about the grass-starved sheep, he went to Denver and bought all the sheep he could get for cash and credit, a flock of five hundred head. He knew little or nothing about sheep management, but he had a knack with animals, and he had this driving ambition. He had his sheep delivered to a way station east of Denver, unloaded them, and took to the hills with them.

All that summer John Gerrity, with nothing but a bedroll on his back and a rifle in his hands, roamed the hills with his flock. He fought off the coyotes, avoided the major cattle ranges, and somehow pulled more than four hundred head of that flock through the summer. He had them sheared on shares and made a few hundred dollars from the wool. And that fall he drove them to market and sold them for four times what he had paid. John Gerrity was in business.

He spent that winter looking for range he could appropriate.

He found the place he wanted in Ketchem Holler, an area that was on the fringes of three different cattlemen's ranges. There was no water on it, but he hired two men and drilled test wells. Once he found plenty of water within easy drilling distance, he homesteaded the spot, built a sod house and put up two windmills. And in that move he proved his shrewdness. The cattlemen had passed up that land because it had no natural water, no stream or pond. John Gerrity reached into the earth for water, found it, and harnessed the wind to pump it. Then he went to New Mexico, where the drought was abating but still pinched, and he bought a thousand head of sheep. He hired two herders and drove the sheep overland to his new homestead. That year he sheared his own fleeces, had his own wool money, and sold his crop of lambs for more than he had paid for the whole flock. And he had a herd of ewes which he wintered and held for another crop of lambs. By the time the cattlemen woke up to what was happening, John Gerrity was a sheep ranchman with control of five thousand acres of grass. A few more years and he controlled ten thousand acres by the simple expedient of drilling more wells and building more windmills.

From that point is was a simple and inevitable step to buy a ranch nearer Brush, a place of only about a thousand acres, where he could grow huge crops of alfalfa, build acres of feed pens, fatten his own lambs for a premium market price, and hold his flocks of mother ewes over the winter. John Gerrity never became a cattle baron. He became a sheep baron, thanks to a drought in New Mexico and enough imagination to drill a well. On such simple turns of fate and personality does the history of an area often hinge.

For ten years, after John Gerrity had become a sheepman of consequence, with half a dozen flocks on the range each year, he made his periodic rounds of the whole area, acquainting himself with the occasional homesteader, discouraging him if possible, talking him into failure. John Gerrity had no liking for violence. He had long ago outgrown his brawling. Why knock a man down when you could talk him into pulling up stakes and going away quietly?

So he made his rounds of the range every spring, with his pack of hounds, looking for coyotes. But he never overlooked a dugout or a soddy or a frame shanty, or even a man with a wagonload of supplies making his way across the unmarked flats. It hurt John Gerrity's heart to see a man wasting his time trying to tame that land, particularly if the land he choose to tame was on John Gerrity's sheep range.

He had thought he had our land properly under control. Among the public lands of the West, certain sections—two out of every thirty-six—were set aside as school land. These plots could not be homesteaded. They were reserved for the support of the public schools. They could be leased, and the lease money went into the state's school fund. The section just east of our land was a school section, one mile square, 640 acres. John Gerrity had leased it and put down a well on it and built a windmill. It was the site of his upper camp, where he based one flock every summer. By ranch tradition, Gerrity's sheep camp on that leased land should have effectively controlled all the public land, the free range, for several miles around.

Now we had homesteaded land adjacent to Gerrity's leased land. And John Gerrity, making his annual inspection, had seen us, talked to us, given us warning. Not that he would drive us out, but that we would starve out, dry out, discourage out.

We watched him go, then lowered the auger into the hole again. When we pulled it up to empty it, Father said, "So that's Gerrity. Well, he's entitled to his opinion, I guess. But he doesn't know us." And we went on digging.

By midafternoon we were through the yellow clay and into

fine yellow sand. The third augerful of sand was damp, I shouted to Father that we were getting close to water, and he grinned.

A few more augerfuls and the first gravel came up, gravel big as marbles. "Now," Father said, "we're getting there."

Down again, and down some more, and finally the auger came up with a load of gravel that was dripping water. We kept on four or five augerfuls. Then we pulled up the auger and laid it on the ground. Father dropped a pebble in the hole. It splashed, far down there at the bottom. Father laughed and I shouted and Dick and Shorty, grazing in the draw, looked up to see what was happening.

"So the water's spotty around here?" Father said. He punched a hole near the top of an empty bean can and tied the chalk line to it and let it down the well. He jounced it up and down and brought up a canful of muddy water.

We put the auger in again and went down a little farther, but when the water measured five feet on the auger shaft Father said, "That's enough."

We took the galvanized sheet-iron tubing we had brought and put it down the hole, section by section, the perforated section at the bottom. Our well was finished. We had been two days digging it. "Now," Father said, "we'll let it settle overnight and see if it's good water."

The next morning when I let down the bean can on the chalk line it came up full of clean, clear water. Father tasted it and said it was good, icy cold and sweet and good.

"Now," he said, "if you'll get about half a pail of it we'll see if it's hard or soft."

I bailed up half a pail of water, one canful at a time, and Father tried it with a bar of soap. Cold as it was, it made a quick suds. And there was no scum around the edges. Father said it was better than the water we had back in Nebraska.

We had a house. We had a well. Now we could bring Mother out to the homestead.

The audacity of man is matched only by the simplicity of his basic needs. There we were, strangers to that land, a man and a boy who had never before built a house or dug a well. But we needed a house, so we built it. We needed a well, so we dug it. We had only a hazy understanding of the blizzards that would test that house and we knew nothing at all about where water might be. But Father said, "We'll dig here." In effect, he said, "Let there be water." And there was water.

It was as though we expected that land to be hospitable. The fact that it was hospitable, to a degree, was sheer accident. And yet, all through history man has been saying, "I shall live here," and finding the means to live where he chose. Either this earth is a remarkably habitable place or man is a favored creature. I would rather believe in the habitability of the earth, because when man comes to believe too much in his own favor he achieves an unhappy arrogance. The earth has its own pulse and rhythms, and the wise and fortunate man leans with the wind, sows with the season, and searches for water in valleys where water flows.

That afternoon Jake Farley came over to see us. "I see you've been working," he said, walking over to the house and squinting at the corners to see if they were plumb. They must have been; he made no comment. He went inside and he said, "What did you floor your barn end for?"

"There isn't any barn end," Father said. "It's all house. I'm going to build a separate barn."

Mr. Farley frowned, then grinned. He had a red, round face and a long thin nose. "That's right," he said, "you've got a woman. Women don't seem to like the smell of a barn, though I never could see why." He laughed. "I was born in a barn. You a farmer?"

"Printing's my trade," Father said.

"I been a farmer all my life. Till last winter I always worked for somebody else. One day last fall out shucking corn back in Ioway, I says to myself, 'Jake, you fool! Shucking corn and freezing half to death, for fifteen dollars a month and keep, and for someone else. Time you got some sense,' I said. And I climbed in the wagon and drove back to the house and drew my wages. Decided, just like that, to come out here and have my own place."

"You came out here last fall?"

"Came out to Brush. Worked in the livery stable there all winter. Filed on my claim in February. . . . See you're digging a well."

"It's all dug."

"Get water?"

"Plenty. Good soft water, too."

"How deep?"

"Struck water at seventeen feet, then went on down a ways. We've got about six feet of water in the well now."

"Good thing Gerrity didn't come around and tell you you couldn't get water before you dug it," Farley said.

"He came while we were digging," Father said.

"Tell you what he tells everyone? That you can't get water, and if you can it'll be no good, and if it's good it'll dry up."

Father grinned. "That's what he told us."

Mr. Farley laughed. "I guess you'll make a farmer yet," he said. "Get your woman out here to tend house and you can get busy with your breaking plow. One thing about this country, you can plow it. No stumps and no stones. Just set the plow in the ground and go. And that reminds me. I'm going to plant sod corn next week or so. Thought I might borrow the boy for a few days."

Father shook his head.

"No work to it," Mr. Farley said. "Just follow me down every other furrow and drop corn. I cover it with the next furrow and the planting's done." He turned to me. "Does that sound like work?"

I didn't answer. Father said, "Not this year. I need him myself."

"I'd pay him a quarter a day. And his dinner."

"No," Father said.

Mr. Farley turned toward his wagon. "Well, I better get back home. Just stopped by to say hello. Good to have a neighbor. You're going to have neighbors, pretty soon. A lot of 'em."

"Who's that?"

"Gerrity's herder and a flock of sheep. They'll be moving to the camp down there in a week or two." He was loosening the lines from the front wagon hub where he had tied them so that if the team started away the hub would wind the lines, windlass-like, and check them.

"Why don't you stay and have supper with us?" Father asked.

Farley hesitated, looked at the trench fireplace and the pile of empty bean cans. "Thanks. Some other time, when your wife's here to do the cooking." He grinned. "I've got enough beans at home."

I watched as he drove away. I felt a little bigger, a little older, than I had an hour ago. Jake Farley had wanted me to work for him. He was willing to pay twenty-five cents a day. That was a dollar and a half a week! And Father had said no. Father had said he needed me to help him.

It was almost sundown. Father laid a length of board over the well casing and piled dirt on it, to keep ground squirrels from falling in and drowning and spoiling the water. He finished it and said, "Well, I guess we'll have to eat alone." He looked at me with a hidden smile. "What shall we have?"

I knew what we were going to have. We had one last can of beans and four slices of bread and just enough flour to make pancakes for breakfast. Tomorrow morning we were going back to town.

"Let's have beans," I said, carefully keeping my own grin out of sight.

"Beans it is," Father said. There was a twinkle in his eyes. "How about gathering a few dry cow chips while I get some water and wash out the coffeepot and the skillet?"

41

3

The farther we got from it, the more the homestead house diminished in size, in workmanship, and in potential comfort. Back in town, it seemed thoroughly inadequate. Father reconsidered. He said to Mother, "You'd better stay here for another week. We'll go back and finish the house and get the well in working order."

"Stay here another week," Mother said, "with you two out there batching? I should say not!"

"We haven't got the door in yet," Father said.

"You've got a roof on, haven't you?"

"Yes. But the windows aren't in. And there's no pump in the well."

"I guess," Mother said, "I can get water to wash my hands from the buffalo wallow. And if you made coffee with that water, I can. . . . Oh, Will, there's no use talking. I'm going along."

It was a long, slow trip. The wagon was loaded high, with more lumber, with the door and the window sash, with the pump and pipe for it, with the beds and the stove and the dining table and the barrel of dishes, with the two chicken crates tied on top of the load. And with the two cows tied to the tailgate.

The cows were the most trouble, but we had to take them along and the only way to take them was to lead them. You can drive a cow, but a cow is constitutionally opposed to a lead rope. Especially a lead rope tied to a wagon. She objects at the start, she gives in momentarily, then she gets confused. As you proceed, you are alternately leading her and dragging her. She never braces her legs, as a balky mule would, and she never leaves her feet. She plods, she stumbles, she groans, she strains halter and lead rope to the breaking point. She disapproves of the journey, and she shows her disapproval at every step.

Our two cows, with bovine consistency, alternated in their objection. One of them was always holding back, groaning, trying to halt the wagon. When she gave in and led almost docilely for a little way, the other held back. By the time we reached the first sand hills Father said, "I'm not going to put up with this all day." He handed the reins to me, took the buggy whip and got out to drive the cows. They were still tied to the wagon, we were still leading them, but with someone walking behind them they had some dim notion of independence. The lead ropes slacked and they walked along almost contented.

A mile of that and Father got back in the wagon. "I guess they'll lead now," he said. They did. For just about a hundred yards. Then the groaning, the stumbling, the straining began again. I got out and walked behind them. They looked back, saw me there, and with maddening innocence they stepped out and kept pace with the wagon once more.

There is a long-standing fiction that milk cows are docile creatures without an ounce of guile or malevolence in them, but it is sheer fiction. The most friendly and tractable cow will deliberately put her foot in a milk pail, waiting till it is at least half full. She will switch her tail when there isn't a fly within a mile of her, cruelly lashing the milker's face. She will demand human company, on foot, when she is being led anywhere. And she will do all that with a placid and guileless eye upon you all the time. No wonder cows are sacred in India. They brought passive resistance to a point of maddening perfection centuries before Mahatma Gandhi was born.

Between us, Father and I walked all the way from Brush to

the homestead that day to humor those two cows. We started before sunup and Mother packed a picnic lunch so we wouldn't have to stop at the Gary store, but it still was late afternoon before we reached Ketchem Holler.

As we drove up the last slope from Ketchem Holler, the house we had built looked like a little shanty set out in the middle of nowhere. We drew up beside it and Father helped Mother down from the wagon. We stood there looking, all three of us, and Mother said, "It looks kind of lonesome, doesn't it?"

Father said, "When we get the barn up, and chicken house built—" He just couldn't say any more.

Mother drew a deep breath. "I want to see the inside."

We went in. Mother looked at the bare board walls with all the studding and rafters showing, at the holes where there were going to be windows, at the roof so low she could have stood on a chair and touched it with her hand. "Why," she said, "it's a very nice little house. Big enough to live in and not too big to take care of. I like it!"

And, just like that, it was wonderful.

"We'll put the stove here," she said. "We'll curtain off the north end for the bedrooms. I'll need shelves beside the stove when you get to it. And when I get curtains up— Bring in the beds and set them up. And the stove."

So we unloaded the beds and set them up. We set planks for a skid from the wagon to the doorway and eased the cook-stove into the house and set it on its base. I got the stove pipe and Father set it into place, up to the ready-made sheet-iron chimney on the roof. Mother began unpacking the dishes and the cooking pans. I went out and gathered cow chips.

There was so much to do, and dark came so fast. Mother lit the lamp in the house and got a lantern ready for us to use outside. Father milked the cows, though they hadn't much milk after the long day's trip. I picketed the cows for the night and hobbled the horses. We unloaded the pump and made a shelter in the wagon for the chickens, still in their crate, so the coyotes wouldn't get them. I brought a pail of water from the buffalo wallow, carefully dipping deep to avoid the wigglers.

Then Mother said we'd done enough, and supper was ready anyway. We went inside and Father set the door against the door frame, and it was home. The beds were made with their familiar patchwork quilts. The table was set with the blue-checkered cloth. Three places were set with the plates sprigged with pink rosebunds, and the cut-glass spoon holder and sugar bowl were in the middle of the table. The coffee pot was simmering on the back of the stove and there were fried potatoes and canned corn and fried round steak. There was a fat brown loaf of home-made bread Mother had brought from town. There was even a glass of red currant jelly from the bushes back in Nebraska.

We sat down and Mother dished up the food. She set the pail of water on the stove to heat for the dishes. She said, "It isn't very much, and it probably isn't very good. These cow chips don't make a fire like cobs or kindling. I'll have to get used to them. But I guess we won't starve."

It looked like home; it smelled like home, for all the pitch smell of the new pine lumber; it even sounded like home, with Mother making little of a good meal.

The next day we hung the door and put in the window sash. It took longer than we thought, so it was the middle of the afternoon before we got to the well. We threaded the pipe into the cylinder and hooked up the pump rod and we lowered them into the well and fastened the pump on top. Father sawed two planks for the pump to sit on till we could build a platform. It was almost dark, but when I went to work with the pump handle we had water, well water, to wash the dishes in that night.

Mother said her men were wonderful. "You've built the house, you've dug the well and got the pump working. I guess we'll make out."

We decided the barn could wait a while, but we had to

have a chicken house or the coyotes would get all the chickens. Father said this was as good a time as any to learn how to cut sod and lay it. "If it doesn't turn out right," he said, "I guess the chickens won't mind."

So we took the chalk line and four stakes and laid out a six-foot square, and that was the floor plan. We hitched the team to the breaking plow and went down to the edge of the draw and plowed a deep furrow in the tough grass. The sod turned in a thick, root-matted strip. Father plowed half a dozen furrows, then took the spade and cut the strips of sod into chunks a foot and a half long.

We brought the wagon and hauled a load of those sod strips to where we'd laid out the chicken house, and Father laid a line of sod around the chalk line, leaving a gap for the doorway. Then I helped lay the next layer, grass side down and seeing to it that the joints didn't match up, so each sod overlapped on the two pieces below, like bricks. We put on layer after layer till we had the walls up three feet, then made a door frame out of two by sixes and set it into place. We plowed more sod and went on up with the walls until it was high enough for Mother to stand inside. Then we put the rafters on and nailed the roof boards, leaving wide eaves to keep the rain from washing down the sod. We put a layer of sod on the roof, and it was finished except for the door, which we built out of shiplap. We hinged the door into place, and there was the chicken house, a shed-roofed little building like an old-time fort except it didn't have any loopholes through which you could shoot at the enemy.

Father looked at it and said, "There's probably lots of better chicken houses, but I never built a better one."

Mother said, "The walls aren't quite plumb and it isn't exactly square, but it ought to keep the chickens in and the coyotes out. Now if you'll just run the plow through that patch where you took the sod I'll have a place for a garden."

Oh, there was so much to do and there were so many things

to see! Sunrise was the most beautiful thing in the whole world, with a few clouds in the east every morning, just waiting to be pinked and gilded. Sunset was full of purple and red and sometimes silvery and even yellow halfway to the top of the sky. Night was full of coolness and stars, and there was a new moon there in the west that got higher and bigger every evening. The hills turned greener every day, and in one little hollow not a hundred yards from the house I found a patch of yellow violets, tiny golden violets that I picked and carried to Mother. She said they were the prettiest flowers she'd seen since we left home, and she put them in a water glass and set them on the window sill. Up the slope back of the house I found the grass twinkling with sand lilies, little white stars on stems like wild onions. I picked a bouquet of them, but they wilted before I got to the house.

Every morning the meadow larks sang, "See this fine world!" and "This is a time to be alive!" I knew that's what they sang because the words fitted their notes so well. And every evening the bullbats, wide-winged night hawks, came swooping and sailing just about sunset, sailing like hawks, then beating their wings quickly for a few beats, then sailing again; and now and then swooping toward the earth in breath-taking dives with an echoing bull roar of air through their spread wing feathers. They were wonderful birds, even though their cries were nothing but a scratchy kind of complaining *eeep-eeep!* Sometimes a dozen of them would gather over our draw and sail and dive there for an hour or longer.

Down Ketchem Holler the coyotes yipped almost every evening, and it always made me shiver just a little, because they were almost-wolves. But when a night came that they didn't howl it seemed almost lonesome because the night was so still, so quiet. I would lie awake and listen for them, and wait, and wait and listen and listen, and finally I would fall asleep still listening. And the next thing I knew it was morning again and the meadow larks were singing, "This is a time to be alive!" and

47

I got up and pulled on my overalls, very quietly, and went outdoors to watch the sunrise.

One morning there was the sound of men and wagons down in Ketchem Holler, half a mile from the house. John Gerrity's men had come to the camp with loads of panels for the sheep pens. They unloaded the long wooden panels and set them up, fastening them together with baling wire, and they put the pump in the well and started the windmill, to pump water into the big watering tank.

They got the camp all set up, and the next morning they brought the herder's wagon and left it on the hillside beside the pens. That afternoon the herder came with a big flock of sheep, and there was the din of blatting ewes, bleating lambs, bass-voiced rams, and sheep bells. From that time on, till the sheep went back to the main ranch for the winter, I seldom heard coyotes at night. I went to sleep to the sound of the sheep blatting and the sheep bells clanging across the valley.

The herder's name was Louie, and he was a little man with a thin voice and a kind of frightened smile and the smell of sheep all over him.

Sheep herders of that day were strange men, as different from cowboys as a sheep is from a steer. It was said that all sheep herders were crazy, that they went around talking to themselves and blatting like their own sheep. Some said the loneliness of the herder's life made him crazy; others said only a man not quite right in the head would take a sheep herder's job. Most of them were simple men in every sense of the word, child-like and even tetched a little. It took a man with a hermit's inclinations to herd sheep, for he spent months alone, seeing only the commissary man who made his rounds every couple of weeks to leave fresh supplies and see that all was well with herders and flocks. Some herders were gruffly antisocial, some were merely uneasy in the company of other people, and some were almost pathetic in their need for occasional human contacts. All of them had dogs for helpers, and the best of the herders were as fond of their dogs as they might have been of their own families. Louie was such a man.

Louie came originally from the Ozark country, where his father was a farm hand. Grown, Louie drifted west, calling himself a cobbler but really one of those unskilled and only mildly competent men who do life's drudging tasks which call for no imagination or initiative and little ability beyond a willingness to follow the simplest of orders. Actually, sheep herding was an upward step for Louie because it demanded a certain amount of initiative and put upon him the burden of responsibility for the flock. A flock of sheep represented an investment of several thousand dollars, and it is still a mystery to me why the sheepmen entrusted their flocks to herders who were generally regarded as a grade or two below a farm hand.

But Louie, and so far as I know most of the other herders, did have both a love of sheep and a simple devotion to the job. They knew how to handle sheep, which are unbelievably stupid and seem to have an instinct for self-destruction. Louie would doctor a sick lamb for a week, using the simple medicines he used on himself, epsom salts, permanganate of potash, and a black salve he called "tar." Louie would have died for his flock, I am sure, if the need arose. Yet he would ignore Gerrity's specific order to move his flock to a range Louie didn't like, and I am sure he ignored Gerrity's order to pasture them on our land.

Until we knew him, Louie had worked for Gerrity the year round, as a farm hand and roustabout at the home ranch in the winter. That was when he had a wife and a son to look after. After we moved in, Louie talked occasionally of taking a homestead of his own, but he never did. As soon as the lambs were sold in the fall he drew his wages, got on the train and vanished. The supposition was that he went to Denver, and sometimes he hinted at marvelous adventures during his winters off, though they probably were largely imaginary; they never had any specific locale and they never were recounted in any detail.

With the first breath of spring, Louie was back, to help with the lambing, to separate the flocks, and to return to the upper camp.

Some sheepmen had houses at their camps. Gerrity used the wagon system. Each herder had a canvas-topped wagon fitted out as a compact home. In the earlier days the herders each had a team of horses, tended their flocks on horseback, and moved their wagons when they pleased. But now the horses had been taken away. The herders' wagons were taken to the camp site and left there, and the herders tended flock on foot.

Louie's wagon had sideboards built out like benches, with the canvas top accordingly wider than the wagon bed. The bench on one side provided a bunk on which Louie slept. On the other side were storage bins and shelves for his gear and for his groceries. Near the front was a tiny stove whose chimney poked through a tin shield riveted to the canvas tilt. It served as a cookstove and it also provided warmth on frosty nights of spring and fall. At the back of the wagon was a set of steps that could be swung upward into the wagon at night or when it was on the road.

The wagon always smelled of fried potatoes and rancid mutton tallow and coal oil and cow chips. The only light it had at night was a coal oil lantern. I never visited Louie's wagon without seeing his cobbler's tools laid out. It was as though those tools represented something, some facet of his personality, that he could not ever relinquish; it was almost as though he told himself every day of his life that he was not really a sheep herder, he was a cobbler. He had a trade. Yet never did he come back from his mysterious winters off to talk about working in a cobbler's shop. They were a symbol of a part of his life which he never outgrew, which he never quite understood and which he still could not turn his back upon.

The second evening he was there, Louie came over to our house to get acquainted. He came to the door and took off his hat and said who he was, and Father invited him in. But Louie said, "I'll just sit out here." So he sat there on the step, a strange little man who smelled, as Mother said later, "like the billy goat Uncle Gus used to keep."

But Louie was a polite little man. He said "ma'am" to Mother and he called Father "mister" and he kept his hat off all the time he was there. Father asked how many sheep there were in the flock, and Louie said there were close to fifteen hundred head of ewes and every ewe had a lamb. Father said that many sheep would eat a lot of grass. Louie said, "They keep eating, all right. But I'll do my best to keep 'em off your land."

Then he saw me. "I got a boy of my own," he said, "just about his age."

"Where is your boy?" Mother asked.

"Up in Denver with his mother. She up and left me. Run off with the cook from the main camp. He's a short-order cook up in Denver and I guess they're making out pretty well." He looked at me. "You got a dog?" he asked.

I said no.

"I'll give you a pup," Louie said.

"What kind of a pup?" Mother asked.

"Sheep dog. Best dog there is, ma'am. My little Fido dog, she's the mother. Father's Gerrity's big collie. Mighty fine dog, he is. The boy ought to have a dog, ma'am."

"We'll see," Mother said.

"They're only a week old," Louie said. "Ain't got their eyes open yet." He was silent a long moment. Then he asked, "You got any shoes need mending?"

"Are you a shoemaker?" Father asked.

"That's my trade," Louie said, and there was pride in his voice. "Learned it in reform school."

I saw Mother stiffen. Father asked, "Where was this?"

"Back in Missouri," Louie said. "My mother died when I was six and my pappy couldn't care for me. He put me in the school to learn a trade. I got a good education there, for a poor boy." He stood up. "Nice knowing you, m'am. And you, mister." He looked at me. "You come pick out the pup you want. There ain't but three of them left. You can take him soon's he's old enough to wean." He turned and walked away, his black hat still in his hand, down the slope and across the valley to his little house on wheels.

I said I wanted the puppy. Father said he thought it might be a good idea. Mother said we'd wait and see. She didn't want to be obligated to a man like that, who'd been to reform school. Father said it didn't sound as if he'd been a boy who had to be sent to reform school, but more as if his father put him there to be rid of him. Mother said anyone who smelled that way ought to be put somewhere. Father said he supposed anybody around sheep all the time smelled like sheep. And then to change the subject he said, "We'd better plant corn tomorrow, if we want to have a corn crop this year. And when we get that done we've got a barn to build."

The next morning he hitched the team to the breaking plow and laid out a field on the slope back of the house. He plowed two furrows around it, then went back to the house for the sack of seed corn he'd brought from town. He brought a bucket and put corn in it and showed me how to plant it, walking down the furrow and dropping a kernel every foot or so and stomping the kernels in the ground with my heel so the birds and ground squirrels couldn't steal it all before he got the next furrow plowed.

And that's the way we planted our corn. We plowed and planted all morning. When we went back to the house for dinner Father said it would take us two days to plant that field. "And," he said, "even counting on the ground squirrels and the birds getting their share, if we have a good season we'll have a plenty for the winter."

So after we'd eaten we went back to where we'd left the plow and hitched the team to the doubletrees and Father looped the lines around his shoulders and took the handles of the plow and said, "Hup, Dick, Shorty! Let's go." The horses lea..d into their collars, the plowshare sang as it clipped the grass roots, and the sod rolled in a broad ribbon off the curving rods that a breaking plow has instead of a moldboard.

I walked along behind the plow, dropping corn and heeling each kernel into the ground. It was like walking down a narrow brown road, step by short step. The sun was warm, the birds were singing, and the warm, brown, springy smell of the soil was everywhere.

We were halfway to the upper end of the field, where the team would turn and come back down the other side, when old Dick snorted and tossed his head and reared, and Shorty bunched his feet and jumped to one side. They almost overturned the plow. Father shouted, "Whoa there! Dick! Shorty!" and he let go the plow handles and grabbed the lines.

Then I heard the buzz. A high, rattly buzz, like a big grasshopper flying. Then it got faster and sounded like a big bumblebee, a mad one. And I saw the snake in the furrow just ahead of the horses.

It was a rattler. It lay in an irregular coil, its wedge-shaped head drawn back and its tail lifted just above the coil and vibrating in a blur. Its glistening, scaly body was thick as my arm and a dusty brown color, not much darker than the yellow-tan of old buffalo grass, but across its back were dark brown oval patches. Except for the shine and the ripple of its muscles it looked almost like a big cow chip lying there in the furrow.

The horses had shied over onto the plowed ground. Plains bred, they knew rattlesnakes. Quivers of excitement ran down Dick's dark bay back. Shorty was rearing and stamping and snorting. Father stepped to the plow beam and pulled the clevis pin, releasing the doubletrees. He stepped across the beam and drove the horses to one side, where they stood, watching the snake and tossing their heads against the restraint of the lines.

"Go back to the house," Father ordered, "and bring the spade. And watch where you step!"

He didn't need to say that. I ran, my heart pounding, but I

watched every foot of the furrow in front of me. And when I came to the end of the furrow I ran across the grass in big bounds, dodging every cow chip and bunch of grass.

The spade was in the wagon. As I turned to run back with it Mother called from the house, "What's the matter?"

"A snake!" I shouted. "A great big snake!" I didn't have time to say any more. I ran back, feeling braver now with the spade in my hands. But I kept to the furrow, where I could see what was ahead of my feet.

Father held the spade toward the snake, and it struck so fast I could hardly see its head. It struck the spade blade with a ringing bang, and before it could coil again Father jabbed at it with the sharp edge and cut it half in two. The snake began to writhe and Father swung the spade like an axe. It didn't take many blows. He stunned it and then he cut off the head, which lay there in the furrow convulsively snapping its ugly mouth.

Father called me to him and poked at the severed head with the blade of the spade. "There," he said, prying the mouth open, "are the fangs." They looked like thick cactus thorns, two of them, in the front of the upper jaw. "He strikes with those fangs, and that's how he puts the poison in whatever he hits."

He began to dig a hole in the furrow. "Now you know what a rattlesnake looks like. Don't ever forget. You saw the way it struck at the spade. A rattler will strike at anything in reach. The poison from those fangs will kill you. Don't ever fool with a rattler. If you haven't something to kill it with, something long enough so you are out of reach of the strike, go away and leave it alone."

He buried the head there in the furrow and he tossed the body, still twitching, over onto the plowed ground. He hitched the team to the plow again and we went on plowing. But every time we came to the place we'd killed the rattler the horses shied and Father had to grab the lines and haul them back.

"I guess," he finally said, "we don't have to worry too much about running onto a rattler without knowing it as long as Dick and Shorty are around. They'll let us know. Some say a western horse can smell a snake, especially a rattler."

That evening Louie, the herder, came to the house again. As before, he stayed out on the step. He said, "Those pups are getting to look pretty nice. They favor their father. I thought maybe the boy would like to come down and pick out his."

Father said, "That sounds like a good idea." I saw him look at Mother, and I knew they had talked it over, because she didn't shake her head. "Wait a minute till I get my hat and we'll go look them over."

So Father and I went back with Louie. On the way Father told Louie about the rattler. Louie said, "I kill lots of them. Got a whole cigar box full of rattles. One's got twenty rattles, biggest one I ever heard of."

"Did you ever get bitten?" Father asked.

Louie looked at him as though he'd asked if the herder had ever shot himself in the head. "If I had," Louie said, "I wouldn't be here. One of the herders got bit on the hand last year, and when Gerrity found him he was black as coal and swelled up like a sheep with the bloat."

"He was dead?" Father asked.

"Dead as if he'd blowed his brains out. . . . No, mister, I never been bit, and I ain't going to be. When I die I want to die white and not all bloated full of poison."

As we went up to Louie's wagon a shaggy black and tan dog came toward us from the pens, barking and wagging its tail. Louie said, "These are my friends, Spot," just as though he was talking to another man, and he made a gesture with his hand and the dog went back and sat down beside the pens. Louie led us up the steps at the back of the wagon. In the half-dark I saw a small brown dog, not much bigger than a fox terrier, on an old blanket beside the stove. Huddled against her belly were three little white and tan puppies. The mother lifted her head and tapped the floor with her tail.

Louie knelt beside her and said, "This boy is going to have

one of the pups, Fido," in the same tone he had used with the other dog. Fido licked his hands and looked at me, as if she had understood every word. Louie picked up the three pups and laid them in a row on the blanket. They were fat and their pink noses quivered. Only one had his eyes fully open. They all began to whimper at once. Two of them crawled back toward their mother, but the one with its eyes open got up on its legs and looked at me and stopped whimpering. I held out my hand and it came over and sucked my finger.

"I want him," I said.

Louie grinned and nodded approval.

Fido licked the other two puppies. I picked up mine and held him a minute. He had a white nose and a white stripe up his face and brown ears and a white line around his neck. I held him up to my cheek and rubbed the fine, soft fur with my face. He licked my cheek. Then, finding nothing to suck, he began to cry. I put him down beside his mother. The other two pups were sucking greedily, but my puppy pushed one of them away and took the dug and settled down to his meal.

"He'll take care of himself," Louie said.

"When can I have him?" I asked.

"Soon's he's ready to wean. Two–three weeks."

We left the wagon and Louie showed us the sheep pens and explained that the black sheep in the flock were counters, one for every so many sheep, so you could look at a flock and count the black ones and know how many sheep there were in the flock. He pointed out the big old rams, with horns and deep voices and eyes that looked almost red. And then Father said we had to get home.

On the way back he said, "Well, son, you seem to own a dog. What are you going to call him?"

I thought just for a minute; then I said, "Fritz."

"Fritz? That's a funny name for a dog."

"I like it," I said.

"Who did you ever know named Fritz?"

I couldn't tell him I knew Fritz Strubel, back in Nebraska. Fritz Strubel was a ne'er-do-well farmer, a red-faced, loud-mouthed drunk. Once Fritz came staggering down the street and saw me and gave me a whole dime to buy candy. I had never told anybody, and I couldn't even tell Father now.

I said, "I just want to call him Fritz."

Father said, "He's your dog. Call him whatever you want to."

4

The corn came up in such fine long rows of bright green spears that we wanted to gloat over it. But you don't gloat over sod corn any more than you do over grass growing or baby meadow larks hatching in the nests on the flats. Sod corn always comes up and does well with the moisture held at its roots by the grass turned under. Sod corn is not a personal achievement. Besides, there was little time to gloat over anything. We had a barn to build, we wanted to lay sod up around the house, we had to get some fencing done, and we would soon have to cut hay.

Father went to town and hauled out lumber and posts and barbed wire, and he bought a mower and a hay rake. It must have been about then that he began to count his money. The farmer who moved to the plains from a rented place in Iowa brought along basic farming equipment, even though it might have been old and worn. He had a plow and a harrow and a disc, and he had a mower. He had hand tools. He had the tools of his trade. The tools of Father's trade, a set of compositor's rules and a make-up rule, could be carried in his pocket. They were of no use at all on a farm. He had a blacksmith's son's knowledge of farm machinery, he knew how to use carpenter's tools, he knew a tug from a hame strap. But he had to buy the machinery. He was starting from scratch.

We laid out a frame barn that we would sod up later, and we began building it the way we had built the house, except that it had no floor and the roof was a shed roof with its low side to the north. But the hay came so fast that we had the barn only half built before we had to start cutting.

A valley of bluestem is as pretty a sight as anyone can ever hope to see, especially on a sunny day with a light breeze and a few big clouds floating high. The breeze ripples the grass like wind on water and the cloud shadows are like blue and purple light playing on it. A valley of bluestem, on a day like that, is like a deep, deep lake rippling and dancing in the sun, never still a minute.

Bluestem is a common name for any one of many species of grass which grow tall under favorable conditions, make good hay if cut at the right time, and are a godsend to arid regions. The family includes the hated Johnson grass of Texas, but it also includes such cultivated fodder crops as Sudan grass, kafir corn and even broom corn from which household brooms are made. The bluestem of the plains is a lesser member of the family which sometimes grows five feet high, has a bluish-silver color and thrives with a moderate amount of moisture.

Bluestem is a valley grass. By then the hills were green with buffalo grass, curling tight even before it was ankle-high. Buffalo grass got its name because its curly mat looked somewhat like the shaggy pelt of a tawny buffalo to the first men who came to those plains. It greened in spring, then cured where it grew by early summer and provided feed for grazing animals all fall and winter. Buffalo grass grew on all the hills, and up on the high flats the grama grass was like a lawn, already getting ready to send up its strange seed stems, crooked at the top like little shinny sticks. But in all the draws, and especially in the draw by the house, the bluestem rippled and flowed, so tall it hid the horses' legs when they walked through it. In another week or so it would begin to head and get tough and woody.

We stopped work on the barn and Father hitched the team to the mower. He started at the outer edge of the draw and cut a swath around it. The mower clattered and clicked its metallic *click-click-click* at the corners, and the grass fell in a sparse swath there at the edge. Then he went around a second time and the grass was thicker. The third time around it made a regular waterfall as it fell behind the clattering sickle bar, a green waterfall that lay in a long green stream behind the mower. After an hour there were long green lines of cut grass all around the valley.

By noon the hot sun and the dry breeze had begun to cure the grass and the sweet hay smell was everywhere. On those high, dry plains hay cures quickly. We let it lie in the sun that day and the next morning Father said I could rake it. He hitched the team to the high-wheeled rake with its long curved teeth and I climbed into the iron seat, which was much too big for my bottom. I could just reach the pedal to trip the rake teeth. He handed me the lines and said to keep the windrows straight, and he watched while I went around the field the first time.

Haying wasn't work, not to me. Raking hay wasn't, at least. There I sat on the high seat, the lines in my hands. Dick and Shorty knew the job better than I did, so I concentrated on making straight windrows. When I had a rakeful of hay I kicked the trip pedal. The long, curved teeth lifted, the hay was left in a neat long pile, the teeth dropped and began gathering hay again. The horses went around the field and I tripped the teeth time after time, and we had a whole series of long, low piles of hay. The next time around I added another length to each pile, and the windrows grew.

The sun was hot. The hay smell was all around me. Every now and then a cottontail rabbit scurried out of the hay in front of the horses. Once I caught a prairie chicken in the rakeful of hay, and when I tripped and dumped it the prairie chicken burst out right beneath me and went zooming into the air, startling me so that I almost fell off the rake.

By noon I had the whole valley raked.

Since we hadn't had time to build a hay rack we put the sideboards on the wagon and used it to haul the hay. We couldn't haul half the load we could have put on a rack, but you have to do with what you have. We hauled hay in the wagon and built the first stack just back of the barn, where it would give some protection from winter storms and where it would be handy to fork into the barn.

Building a haystack is an art. You put down the first layer in the shape of the finished stack, making sure there is more around the edges than in the middle so the hay won't slide out as you put more on it. And you have to build it with the hay lying right, the ends pointing toward the middle. You build it carefully, forkful by forkful, always building the edges first, keeping the sides straight and tromping the middle down good and tight. Father had helped stack hay several times, when we visited Grandpa Clinaburg, who was the best hay stacker in Nebraska, and Father remembered how. But building a stack alone isn't easy. I forked it off the wagon and Father built the stack.

Because we had to make so many trips with the wagon, which held so little hay, it took two days to build that first stack. We didn't build it very high, because I couldn't pitch the hay very high from the wagon; besides, if we kept it low we could be pretty sure it wouldn't lean and eventually fall over. But we finally got it finished and topped off so it would shed the rain. Then we started another stack alongside the first one.

We got two good stacks of hay from that draw beside the house, and then just to be sure we had enough we went over into the next draw to the south and cut enough for two more stacks. Before we got it all in Father said we'd have saved a week if we'd taken time out to build a hay rack, because half our time was spent just coming and going with those little wagonloads. But we got it in and stacked.

Then we did the first fencing. We built a fence around the haystacks, because the cows, when we turned them loose to graze, went right to the stacks. With all that fine green grass to eat, they went right to the stacks. We were trying to finish the barn, but I had to spend most of my time driving the cows away from the hay. Cows, I said angrily, are the laziest critters alive; they won't even eat grass. Father laughed at me. "Cows," he said, "aren't so different from other creatures. Including man. If a man finds a way to get his groceries free he's not likely to sweat himself too much working for them."

So we built a fence around the stacks. Then we finished the barn. And after that Father said we'd better get some sod up around the house because winter was coming, sure as sunrise. So he plowed the sod, tough sod in the edge of the draw, and I cut it into strips, and we hauled it in and started sodding the house.

We'd been at that job just two days, and we began to have trouble with the flying ants. We put up a pole and tied an old shirt at the top and most of the ants swarmed there. But we still had to fight a few of them, and between fighting ants and laying sod we were pretty tired. We went to bed early, and we went right to sleep. It must have been around midnight, because the full moon was bright outside, when I waked up hearing Mother say, "Will! Will, there's something out in the yard!"

Father was a sound sleeper. He muttered something, but I was out of bed and at the window before he even sat up in bed. Out there in the moonlight was the biggest herd of animals I had ever seen. They were all around the house, and for a minute, because I was still half asleep, I thought they were buffalo. Father and I had been talking about the buffalo herds, that afternoon, the buffalo that used to graze that whole country and who had left all the bones and skulls and horns still there on the hills.

Then Father was up, in his nightshirt, and at another window. "Cattle!" he exclaimed. "Cattle all over the place!" He reached for his shoes and his overalls.

I was dressed as soon as he was. He looked around for a club or some weapon. The only thing he could find was a buggy whip. He tossed it aside and picked up the .25-20 rifle and began loading it. I grabbed the buggy whip. Father stepped outside onto the step and yelled at the cattle.

I squeezed out the door and onto the step just as he fired the first shot over the cattle. The roar seemed to be right there beside my head. All the bells in the world began ringing in my ears, but I still could hear the rush and rattle of horns and click of hoofs as the cattle surged away from the house. Father followed them and I was right behind.

We ran around the house and saw cattle around the hay stacks. Father fired two more shots and I yelled and the cattle bawled and there was the creak and snap of barbed wire stretching and breaking, the crack of a fence post being broken off. The cattle bellowed again and ran up the hillside.

Mother was with us now, armed with a broom. She ran ahead of us and Father shouted, "Sarah! Come back here! They're range cattle and they'll charge you!" But she didn't stop.

One of the steers turned and started toward her. Father snapped the lever, reloading the rifle. Mother shouted, "Get out of here, you dirty thing!" and she swung the broom. The big red steer bellowed and turned and ran, tail high.

But the flight of the rest of the herd had slackened. They had reached our cornfield. We charged them, all of us shouting, but they didn't run. They were eating green fresh corn-stalks, which by then were waist-high. Mother ran among them, flailing with the broom. I lashed out with the buggy whip. Mother was sobbing in anger. Father fired two more shots over them. Then they began to run again. Father fired another shot and they kept on going.

We slowly walked back through the cornfield. In the moonlight it looked as though they had tromped half our corn into the ground. It wasn't a beautiful cornfield any more; it was a bleak and sorry sight.

Father said, "Go on back to the house, you two. Go back to bed."

"What are you going to do?" Mother asked.

"Stay here. They'll probably be back, now that they've had a taste of corn. You two go back to bed."

"I want to stay," I said.

Father said, "All right. But go get the rest of your clothes on. And bring my shirt and that old brown coat. And some more shells."

"I'll stay too," Mother announced.

"You," Father said, "are going back to the house and get some sleep."

Mother and I returned to the house. She lit the lamp and I put on my shirt and got a coat. I put two handfuls of cartridges for the rifle in my pocket and picked up Father's brown coat. As I left the house I noticed that Mother was starting a fire in the stove.

Half an hour later Mother came out to us, there on the hill beside the cornfield, with a pot of coffee and bread-and-butter sandwiches. We ate them and Father sent her back to the house.

The cattle came back twice, once about three o'clock and again just at dawn. We drove them off both times, and at dawn they drifted up Ketchem Holler to the south.

We had breakfast just after sunup, eating with one eye out for the cattle. Father said, "The loss of that corn is going to hurt. I'd thought we could buy a few more head of cattle this fall, but without fodder or corn and with the hay we lost when they got into the stack yard we won't have enough feed." He glanced at Mother. "We can't afford to buy feed. The money won't hold out forever."

Mother said, "Whoever owns those cattle will have to pay for the corn."

"I don't know," Father said. "I don't know whose they are, anyway."

"Oh," Mother exclaimed, "I wish you'd shot one! Then we'd at least have had some beef steak to show for what they ate!"

We went back to the cornfield. By daylight it didn't look quite as bad as it had by moonlight. Lots of it had been eaten off and a good deal knocked down, but we could straighten up some of it. We started to work, trying to save what we could.

Late that morning we heard the cattle again, off to the south, bellowing and making quite an uproar. Father picked up the rifle and we waited to see what was going to happen.

The cattle came over the hill to the south, a herd of maybe two hundred head, closely bunched. Then we saw that there were horsemen with them, three horsemen driving the cattle. They came over the hill into sight of our house, and one of the horsemen loped around the herd and headed them east, toward Ketchem Holler. They got the herd turned and one of the riders left them and came toward us at a fast trot. The other two kept the herd moving down the big valley.

The rider was a youngish man in a wide-brimmed black hat and blue work shirt and bibless overalls. His horse was a leggy sorrel with white mane and tail. He rode up the slope toward us, there in the cornfield, the bit chains jingling, still trailing a long end of the lariat he had been using as a whip. He rode straight in his stirrups, the reins in his left hand. He was the first cowboy I had ever seen.

He drew his horse to a high-headed stop at the edge of the cornfield. "Howdy," he said. "I didn't know anybody had moved in here."

None of us said a word. Father still held the rifle in the crook of his arm. The cowboy wasn't wearing a holster or a gun belt, but under his left leg was a saddle scabbard with the dark stock of a carbine in sight. His saddle was very dark leather, worn and sweaty, and it creaked as the horse moved.

The cowboy sat there smiling. He looked at me and his smile became almost a grin. He must have seen the look in my eyes. He looked at Father and Mother again and said, "My name's Clothier, Jack Clothier. I'm from the Lazy Four over north. Sorry about the steers. Looks like they got in your corn patch."

"Yes," Father said gruffly, "they got in the corn." He glanced around at the field. "You can see what they did."

Jack Clothier nodded. "I'm sorry," he repeated.

"You're going to have to pay for this!" Mother exclaimed.

"No," the cowboy said, shaking his head. "You didn't fence it."

"Do you mean to tell me," Mother demanded, "that when your cows ate our corn—"

"That's exactly what I'm telling you," the cowboy said. "Unless it's fenced, there isn't a thing you can do about it. That's the law."

"Who made the law?" Father flushed angrily.

"The state legislature." The cowboy swung down from his saddle, dropped the reins on the grass, and the horse stood as if tied. The cowboy came over to us. "That's the law," he repeated. "When land is not under fence it's technically open range. You should have fenced your corn, mister."

"We haven't had time," Father said.

"I know." The cowboy's voice was sympathetic. He walked out into the cornfield, shaking his head. "You had a good stand of corn," he said sadly. "I hate to see any crop destroyed."

"Then keep your cattle away from here," Father said firmly. "Next time they get in my corn you'll find some dead steers."

The cowboy's mouth tightened. "Don't do that, mister. For God's sake, don't shoot any cattle! That's almost as bad as shooting a man, in this country. Sure, it's your homestead, and around it, it's open range. Even your crop land."

"It's not right!" Mother exclaimed.

"I'm not talking about right and wrong," the cowboy said. "I'm talking about the law. Some day there'll be enough homesteaders in here, maybe, to change the law. But that's the way it stands now, ma'am." He turned to me. "How old are you, son?"

I told him.

"You like it out here?"

"Yes."

"Where do you come from?" he asked Father.

"Nebraska."

"I got a sister who lives at Broken Bow."

But nobody wanted to talk and visit. He knew it. He went back to his horse, flipped the reins over its head, caught a stirrup in one hand, thrust a plain boot toe in it and swung into the saddle in one easy movement. He reined the dancing horse around and said, "Sorry to meet you folks this way, but I'm glad to know you, just the same." He looked at me with a special half smile. He said to Father, "I'll try to keep these steers down at the lower end of the range, but if they drift up this way again, just drive them off. And get a fence up. Please, mister, get a fence up."

He reined his horse around and loped down past the stacks and the house and down Ketchem Holler after the cattle.

Jack Clothier was in his late twenties. He grew up in eastern Kansas, a farmer's son, and at fifteen he went to work for a cattle buyer. At seventeen he went with a visiting ranchman to western Kansas and took a job on a ranch. Before he was twenty he was a top cowhand and an expert rider. He drifted into Colorado and worked for half a dozen ranchmen, breaking horses to the saddle, spending his money as he made it. Those were his free and easy days, when he worked a few weeks or a few months on one job, wearied of it, quit, moved on to another ranch and another string of unbroken horses. He worked from Texas to Wyoming, never settling, a typical cowboy. Though not a gunman, he took part in a couple of range wars, fighting, brawling, but never killing a man. Few of the cowboys were killers, and most of them detested the professional gunman. Their job was tending cattle and keeping order on the range, not starting or perpetuating feuds.

But, like most horse-breakers, Jack wearied of it after a few years. He saw old riders who hadn't known when to quit, aging men with gimpy legs, gnawing hernias and battered features, and he decided he'd had enough broken bones to last him for a while. He'd begun to outgrow his young daredeviltry. He took a job on the Hashknife, down south of our area, as a straight cowhand. And, two years before we arrived, he moved up to the Lazy Four, a top hand who drew almost as good wages as a foreman. He had settled down to learn the cattle business.

He rode back down Ketchem Holler, that day, and we went back to the house. Mother started cooking dinner and Father and I repaired the fence around the haystack. We had to put in two new posts and stretch all the wire and staple it to the posts again. Father didn't say much, but I kept thinking about Jack Clothier and his sorrel horse and his smile.

Mother called us to dinner. We ate, hardly saying anything. We were all tired and sleepy and feeling hurt and angry about the corn. Finally Mother said, "I don't care what he says, it just isn't right."

Father said, "Apparently there's nothing we can do about it except put up a fence."

"There ought to be!" Mother said.

That afternoon we hauled a load of posts up to the cornfield and Father and I began digging postholes.

5

I carried my puppy home in the crown of my hat when he was six weeks old. He cried half the night the first night I had him, and I thought Mother would tell me I had to take him back. But Mother must have remembered all the dogs I'd had and lost one way or another—by poison, or by being kicked by a horse, or by distemper; and she also probably knew that, since I was the only small boy in the whole area, I needed companionship. Anyway, she was patient with him and with me, and after the first two or three nights Fritz was one of the household.

Louie had said my pup was a "smart one, maybe even as smart as Fido." He'd said I could teach him anything. "All you have to do is tell him what you want and make sure he understands."

I wasn't sure what Louie meant, but Louie's dogs were the only ones of all those among Gerrity's herders who would obey hand signals, and Louie taught them. He would stand on a hillside, the flock scattered all over the valley, and say to his dogs, "Go bunch 'em." The dogs would trot down the hillside and around the flock, urging the strays back where they belonged, pulling the flock together; and they would stop and look at Louie, even a quarter of a mile away, and he would gesture with his hands and they would go back and find a stray hiding in a hollow or a clump of soapweed. It was uncanny, the way they understood. But then, Louie talked to his dogs just as though they were people. Maybe he knew dog language. Folks said all sheep herders were at least a little crazy, and maybe Louie was crazy that way.

At first Fritz was all feet and tail, so awkward he would fall down in the middle of the floor. Then he began to catch up with himself and grew into a well-proportioned dog. He looked like an undersized collie, with a collie coat and collie markings, but with the broad brain-box of a back-country sheep dog and with broader shoulders than most collies.

And he was, as Louie said, a smart pup. He learned to bring the cows in to the barn when I told him to, and he even learned to herd the chickens into their house when a thunderstorm came up. One young rooster squawked at him and tried to outrun him, and Fritz grabbed it and killed it. I scolded him and said he was a very bad dog, and he sulked for a whole day, wouldn't come near me; but he never killed another chicken. He spent hours trying to catch squinneys, then learned that if he chased one in a hole and lay quietly waiting, the little ground squirrel would eventually come out of the hole and he could grab it in one quick snap. He killed dozens of ground squirrels. Eventually he used the same tactics with prairie dogs and was one of the few dogs I ever knew who could catch a prairie dog. And he became a snake killer. But that was later.

That first summer, while he was just a growing pup, we wandered over the whole country within two miles of the house, Fritz learning how futile it was to chase jack rabbits, how stupid it was to go running through a cactus bed, and how silly it was to try to catch a meadow lark. I think the meadow larks, especially those close to the house, liked to tease him. He would see one in the grass and would start creeping up, like a coyote stalking a mouse, step by slow step. The meadow lark would go on walking slowly about, looking for insects but keeping one bright, dark eye on the dog. The bird would move slowly away, keeping at least four feet between them, and the pup would creep ahead, slow step by step. This would go on maybe five minutes, sometimes ten, the bird always keeping just far enough away; and at last the pup would lose patience, make a lunge. The bird, as though expecting just that, would leap into the air, fly a little way, then come back, as though deliberately tantalizing, and light again not ten feet from the frustrated pup. And the futile stalking would start all over again. Fritz spent hours at it, and never to my knowledge did he catch a bird.

In our wanderings I began to find stone arrow points. I learned to look for them in bare places where the spring rains had washed the ground. And at last I found a gravelly hillside half a mile west of the house where an Indian point-maker evidently had had his workshop. Fritz and I spent hours there, Fritz trying to dig out ground squirrels, I sifting through the heaps of flint chips.

That had been Cheyenne Indian country. The Cheyennes were a plains tribe with a northern background, a fierce-fighting people who once were farmers in Minnesota but were driven south and west by the Sioux. They became plains wanderers and buffalo hunters, ranging that whole area between the Platte and the Arkansas rivers. When Bent's Fort was built on the Arkansas in 1832 the tribe divided into a northern and a southern group, but they continued to hunt buffalo all across the High Plains. And until trade iron was available from which to make arrow heads they used the old, old flint points. The point-maker, a skilled craftsman who knew how to flake flint, set up shop wherever there was a supply of good flint and replenished the tribe's supply of ammunition. The plains were not very liberally salted with flint outcroppings, so when a source of supply was found it was remembered. The point-maker returned there periodically to shape blanks for future use or, if he had time, to make a fresh supply of finished points and knives for butchering.

My hillside was the only place in that whole area where the gravel outcrop had large pieces of flint in it. The flint chunks there were seldom larger than my fist, and they were mostly a smoky gray with an occasional piece of bright, glassy, reddish-brown. It probably was a lesser flint bed for the Cheyennes to which they came while on buffalo hunts or to which they retreated when on a war expedition if they ran short of good arrow points. Most of the chips were of the smoky gray stone, indicating that the point-maker preferred that flint for his work. The chips were not much bigger than a man's thumbnail, and many of them were not much thicker than a fingernail. Sifting through them, I found several broken points, one of them obviously discarded when half finished. The point-maker had been part way through when the point flaked the wrong way, and he tossed it aside.

After I found that one I went through all the chip piles, and I found a dozen or more of those flawed points. I found only three or four good points there, but I turned up several oddly shaped pieces, sharp edged and obviously worked to a pattern, that I couldn't identify. Later I learned that they were knives and scrapers; but at the time they were only oddly shaped pieces of flint. I was interested only in arrow points.

Then one day out on the flats north of the point-maker's workshop I found a buffalo skull with some strange object imbedded in the eye socket. It looked like a piece of gray flint. I dug at it with my pocket knife, chipped away the leaching bone, and finally freed a perfect smoky-gray flint arrow point. When I compared it with one of the flawed points from the gravel bank they matched perfectly. They might have been made from the same piece of flint.

I sat back on my heels there in the buffalo grass, the hot sun all around me and the silence of the plains, and I wanted to lift my face to the sun and sing a primitive song of triumph. I didn't know exactly why, but I could almost feel a sinew-backed bow in my hands and smell the warm, meaty smell of a fresh-killed buffalo. For a little while, there in the sun, I was a young Cheyenne buck who had gone out with his first hunting party, who had been carried by his buffalo horse to a small band of buffalo, had been so excited he had driven his first arrow into the eye socket of the young bull, then had clung desperately to his horse as it leaped away from the pain-maddened bull's rush, had nocked a second arrow and driven it cleanly between the ribs, where it belonged, and had brought down meat.

I wanted to sing that primitive song, that ululating yelp of manhood and triumph, a song that hadn't been heard on the hilltop for at least forty years.

I made some kind of primitive noise, song or not, and Fritz began to howl. He stood there, a little way from me, and lifted his head, coyote-wise, and howled; and his hackles lifted and his tail drooped. Maybe the same thing got in him that was in me; maybe he reverted, somehow, to his own racial past. He howled, and I came back to the present, and I laughed at him and he barked at me. And we went back down the hillside, passed the gravel slope without stopping, and went to the house.

Father was building a shed on one end of the house, a sloped roof and three sides to keep off the rain and snow. It was a shed for fuel. I helped him finish it and he said, "I'm going to town in the morning. Want to come along? Going to leave early and make it there and back the same day. Have to get a load of coal."

I said yes, I wanted to go.

He said we'd get the chores done early and get to bed, because we'd get up away before sunrise.

At supper Father said, "The only thing about this country I don't like is there's nothing to do with. No timber, not even any rocks."

"There's sod," Mother said.

"Yes," Father said, "there's sod. And cow chips. Why, there's not even any old boards. Every thing you build has to be out of new lumber, and you have to buy it and haul it all the way from town."

"I know," Mother said. "It seems like every time you turn

around you have to spend money. But I guess it's the same anywhere when you have to build something from the ground up."

Father nodded, but he seemed blue about something. "If it was a farm back east," he said, "there'd at least be an old shed, or something, you could use for lumber. I keep forgetting that there isn't even an old rusty nail out here. Nothing!"

Mother thought for a moment. "We could burn sheep chips. Louie said some people burn them."

Father smiled wryly. "Louie said they keep you warm two ways, building the fire and carrying out ashes. Oh, we'll try them, but we'd better get some coal, just the same. Sure you don't want to come along to town?"

"No," Mother said. "It'll be a long, hot trip. I've got things to keep me busy. By the way, you'd better get some more coal oil. We're down to the last gallon. And a couple of lantern globes. One of them is cracked, I see."

We got up at three-thirty. It was so dark outside I couldn't even see the barn at first. We went out and curried the horses and grained them and Father harnessed them. Then we went in and had breakfast. And we hitched to the wagon by lantern light. We put a lantern in the wagon, thinking we might need it before we got home. We left the house just about four o'clock.

It was the dark of the moon and the stars weren't very bright. They never are, the last week in August. But before we reached the floor of Ketchem Holler my eyes had adjusted so that I could see the horses' heads and even make out the light gray mass of Louie's flock in the pens against the dark shadow of the far hillside. Louie's dogs barked at us until we were around the first bend of the valley. Then we were alone with the night, and not even a coyote yowled.

The horses, full of life as they always were in the early morning, and with only the empty wagon to pull, trotted along as though they could see every step of the trail. They undoubtedly could, for horses have excellent night vision. We went down the valley about a mile, then climbed the slope to the ridge and began angling northeast. That way we avoided the sand hills just north of Gerrity's main camp.

Dawn came there on the ridge, at first just a faint lightening on the eastern horizon, a line of milky blue beneath the deep, deep blue embedded with stars. The milky blue spread upward, and lower stars in the east faded and vanished. The light increased till we could see an occasional clump of soapweed. Then there was a pinkish tinge that began to spread upward. Clouds that hadn't been visible at all caught the light and hung there across the east, just above the horizon, like opalescent veils, pink and amber. Now it was almost full daylight, with the sun not yet up.

Father tapped my leg and pointed off to the west. I looked, and there, not a hundred yards away, was a coyote, trotting along parallel to us almost like a dog. Now and then he would turn his head and look at us. He was neither frightened nor wary. How long he had been there, traveling with us, I don't know; but he trotted there, always the same distance away, for at least a mile. Then he stopped and watched for several minutes and turned west, away from us, and vanished down a hollow. That was the first time we had seen him. After that we saw him almost every time we went to town in the early morning. Always he was in the same place, on that particular part of the ridge, and always he trotted there about a hundred yards from the wagon, until we came to that little hollow, where he turned back. But—and this is a strange thing I never did understand—if we had the .25-20 with us, the rifle with which we might have shot him, he never appeared. If there was no gun along, he was almost always there. Whether a coyote can smell a gun, I do not know; all I know is that that coyote never showed himself, even out of gun range, if we had the rifle in the wagon.

Soon after the coyote left us, that morning, the whole

eastern sky blazed with light. Long rays shot up from the horizon, like the conventional sunburst, and that strand of clouds was shot through and through with silver and gold and red and even purple, colors that shifted so quickly they could hardly be identified. And then the first blazing rim of the sun tipped the horizon and the colors faded. Even that filmy veil of clouds seemed to vanish.

Sunrise on the plains was always like that unless the whole east was clouded. It blazed with color, then burst into blinding light. And never were the colors the same twice. Some mornings it would be pink and gold, other mornings it would be vivid red, or orange, or a kind of purplish bronze. But always it flamed and flashed and exploded into light as the first rim of the sun appeared. And always the sun seemed to leap upward, once that first rim was in sight. Five minutes, and the whole sun was there. One minute you were in that unearthly pink or cerise light, the whole world hushed; five minutes later it was a blaze of white light, dazzling, and every meadow lark on the plains was singing.

Until the coyote appeared I had been almost asleep, dozing on the spring seat and leaning against Father. But with sunup I was wide awake. By then we were crossing the little thumb of sand hills where we had eaten lunch that first day, on the way out to build the house, and as we crossed the sand and started the last three miles of hard road to Gary the horses began trotting briskly. We passed the Gary store before Tom McDowell was up. Father's watch showed that it was only a few minutes after six.

It wasn't quite nine o'clock when we came down the last slope south of Brush and saw the Platte valley ahead of us. It was the first time I had been to town since we moved to the homestead, and to my eyes, accustomed to the limitless expanse of the treeless plains, it seemed that the whole valley was filled with trees. As we drove up the aisle of cottonwoods where the blackbirds had been so songful that last week in April I thought I had never seen such tall trees. They were enormous. Strangest of all, they seemed to close in around me. I was already getting the sensation of the plainsman, who feels uneasy in a wooded country. He can't see, he says; everything is closed in around him.

Brush seemed like a big town. Its buildings were so tall. The three-story buildings near the depot were like skyscrapers. I had been looking at a house whose eaves were only seven feet above the ground, and even the windmill down at Louie's camp wasn't much higher than the top of the second-story windows in those buildings.

And the street was busy. Several drays were at the depot, loading freight and express. The hitch rack at the post office had a dozen teams and four or five saddle horses. People were walking on the sidewalks, dozens of people. People in store clothes. I hadn't seen so many people in weeks.

We left the team at the hitch rack beside the post office and walked down the street, stretching our legs and looking in the store windows. There was a newspaper office on the west side of Main Street and when we passed it Father hesitated, almost stopped, then went on. Down past the bank on the corner, and then across the street and past Nelson's general store. And back toward the post office across from the depot. At last we went down a side street to a lumber yard.

The man behind the desk turned to us and Father asked him the price of coal. The man mentioned a figure. Father shook his head. "It seems pretty high," he said.

"Good coal," the man said. "The best Colorado coal."

Father said, "It's gone up since last spring."

The man nodded. "Always goes up this time of year. And there's another increase coming."

We went to another lumber yard. The price was the same there. Father reminded the man that he'd bought lumber from him a few months ago, and posts and barbed wire. The man said, "Oh, yes," but he obviously didn't remember. He didn't bring the price of his coal down a nickel.

We went back to the wagon. I was hungry, so we got out the

lunch Mother had packed for us and each ate a sandwich. Then we drove down the street to Nelson's store and Father ordered a list of groceries Mother wanted. "They should be cheaper in town," she had said. "The Gary store's convenient, but you have to pay the freight from town on everything you buy."

I listened as Father gave the order. When he had finished I tugged at his sleeve and whispered, "Sardines."

"We've got lunch with us," Father said.

I tried not to show my disappointment.

We left the grocery clerk to fill the order and went to the clothing department, where Father asked the price of work shirts and overalls and winter coats and overshoes. He didn't buy anything. We went to the notions counter and he bought several spools of thread and a packet of needles. Then we went back to the grocery counter. Father paid the bill, counting the change carefully. He picked up the box of groceries, then glanced at me and set the box down again. He reached in his pocket and drew out a handful of change and turned to the clerk. "And a can of mustard sardines," he said. He put a nickel and five pennies on the counter and dropped the sardines in the grocery box.

We drove back to the first lumber yard and Father bought a ton of coal. The man said, "Just one ton? That won't last you very long."

"It'll do for a while," Father said. "Winter's not here yet."

"Price is going up," the man said.

"One ton will do." Father took a deep breath, as though he wasn't sure but he hoped he was right.

We got the coal and started back toward the depot to turn south and start home, but when we got to the post office hitch rack Father drew up. "Before we go," he said, "let's stop at the newspaper office for a minute."

As soon as we opened the door of the newspaper office there was a familiar smell, printer's ink, benzine, lye water, paper. It smelled just like the print shop back in Nebraska. Up at the front, near the door, was a roll-top desk with its wire-braced chair, the desk piled with galley proofs and billheads and loose envelopes and letters and penciled notes and out-of-town newspapers. Back of that was a long make-up stone with its overhead racks of lead and slugs; on the stone were iron chases, newspaper page size, with ads in them and vacant columns for news. Along one side was a row of type cases. On the other side were two job presses, one a big Gordon. At the back was a flatbed newspaper press, a two-page Miehle, and a Fairbanks-Morse gasoline engine to drive it. The walls were hung with yellowing farm sale posters and old calendars. The back windows were smudged and fly-specked till you couldn't see through them.

A tall, dark-haired man was on a stool at the type cases, setting type. He looked around and asked, "Something I can do for you?" Then he recognized Father. "Oh, it's you! Hello, there, farmer!" He set his composing stick down and came to greet us.

Father and he shook hands. Father said, "This is the boy. Thought I'd show him a Colorado shop."

"Good," the man said. "Well, how's it going?"

"Going fine," Father said. "We're all settled. Got the house up and the well dug and a crop of corn in."

The man shook his head. "Lord, how I envy you. I was going to ask you to lend me a hand for a week or so, but I know it's no use. My man's out sick, so I'm having to handle it all alone."

Father looked around the shop, then shook his head. "I'd like to help you out, Ed, but I've got a lot of farm work to do."

"Needn't apologize," the man said. "If I ever get away from here, I'll never come back." He laughed. "If I had the sense God gave a goose I'd lock the place and walk out. But I can't afford it. Between trying to keep a printer and trying to make ends meet, I'm always in hot water."

"You've got a good man, though?" Father asked.

"Good enough. He goes on a spree about every six months, but when he's sober he's a crackerjack. Usually he waits till there's a tramp printer in sight to take his place before he buys a bottle, but this time he couldn't wait. Sure you can't give me a week?"

Father hesitated. Then he shook his head. "No, Ed, I just can't do it now. Some other time, maybe."

"Well," the man said, "you know your own mind. I'll make out. I always do. But if I get stuck again I may call on you."

Father said, "Maybe I'll see my way clear, next time."

"Good." The man went with us to the door. "Stop in the next time you're in town."

We went back to the wagon and started for home. Father didn't say anything till we were in the first range of sand hills, just out of sight of town. Then he said, "I quit it once. But it's good to know I could go back if I had to." And a little later he said, "Son, I want you to learn a trade, when you're a little older. I don't care what it is, even the printer's trade. Once you've got a trade you'll never have to starve."

It was a hot afternoon and the load was heavy. The horses had already come thirty miles and they had the same distance still to go. They didn't have any hurry left in them.

We didn't even stop to eat. We got out the sandwiches Mother had sent with us and Father opened the can of sardines and we ate while we drove. The sardines were good, but not nearly as good as they had been with crackers and cheese in the shade of the wagon that April day. And I suppose a part of the savor was missing because Father was so deep in his own thoughts.

We watered the horses at Gary. The sun had almost set. We had just reached the sand hills when dusk came on with a cool that spread quickly over the plains. Turtle doves began to coo in the distance. And then, as we passed the sand hills and were on the big hard-soil flats and the first stars came out,

Father seemed to settle whatever problems had been gnawing at him all afternoon and he began to talk about Grandfather Borland.

"He must have had some pretty tough times," Father said. "He went all the way from Indiana to Nebraska in a covered wagon. With a wife and several kids. Probably hacking his way through the woods a lot of places. And even when he got to Nebraska he had to start from scratch.

"He built a house, with his own hands, and he built a mill. Built his own water wheel and ground corn. And set up a blacksmith shop. He made out. He must have done pretty well, for those days.

"There were seven children," he said. "And then his wife died. And there he was with a family and nobody to take care of them. So he got on a horse and rode back to Indiana and married my mother. She was the younger sister of his first wife. The first wife was Deborah. Everybody calls Mother Anna, but her name was Angeline. Angeline Sexton. He married her and brought her back to Nebraska."

I had never known this. All I knew was that Grandfather Borland came from Ohio or Indiana originally, and that Grandmother Borland was always called Anna. She was a tall, thin woman with a big nose and eye glasses and a firm mouth, and she and Mother never got along very well.

"He brought her out to Nebraska," Father was saying, "and they had nine children. That made sixteen children, altogether. I was the third child of the second family." He chuckled. "About all I remember, when I was a little boy, is that we never seemed to have enough shoes or enough butter. Dad just couldn't keep us in shoes. And Mother couldn't make enough butter. We kept cows, and we grew most of what we had to eat. Mother and the older girls made most of our clothes. I didn't have a pair of store pants till I left home. But somehow Dad kept a roof over our heads and we never really went hungry.

"He was quite a man, your grandfather. One day when I was eight or nine, it must have been, I was in the shop with him and he was building a wagon wheel. Out of hickory he had cut and seasoned himself. He'd turned the hub on a lathe that he made, and he was trimming spokes with a broadaxe, a short-handled broadaxe. He was very particular about his tools. They had to be razor-sharp. He was trimming this spoke, and the axe hit a small knot, or something, and glanced and came down on his left wrist.

"I heard him grunt and I turned around and saw the blood spurting all over him. He dropped the axe and grabbed his left hand with his right one and I saw that he'd cut it almost off. He shoved his hand up against the wrist and held it there, and he said, 'You watch the shop while I go see the doc,' and he walked out the front door and up the street. He went two blocks, dripping blood at every step, and in half an hour he came back, his arm all bandaged up. He was white as a sheet, but he said, 'Go get Walt and Milt and tell them to come run the shop.' He took a big chew of tobacco and when I didn't run he picked up a pair of tongs and threw them at me. I got Walt and when we got back Dad was heating a plow share in the forge. He made Walt hold it on the anvil while Dad drew an edge on it, grunting with pain every time he struck a hammer blow. Then he quenched it and went out back of the shop and vomited. But he never missed a day at the shop, and when the arm healed it was so strong he could lift an anvil by the horn with that hand. It was always crooked, because the doctor had to tie the tendons, so he never could open the fingers more than enough to grip a pair of tongs."

Just imagining the pain, I felt faint. I thought I, too, was going to vomit. But I gripped my hands hard together and breathed deep, and the chill night air began to clear my head.

We were almost to the long slope down into Ketchem Holler. The horses, knowing they were near home, wanted to hurry. The stars had begun to glitter.

Father said, "I guess we're not so bad off, out here. Dad made out. And I'm the only one who had the nerve to get out of Nebraska. I guess we'll make out."

He had been talking to himself as much as to me. There's small comfort in having someone else tell you that your problems are dwarfed by those of another, but when you tell yourself those things you aren't lecturing, you aren't drawing comparisons which make you look like a weakling. You are rallying your own pride and your own strength, reaching back for some of the fortitude that was the mark of your own people. You are rallying yourself, standing up to circumstance in the way of your kind. It is a human impulse and a tribal necessity. When a man, or a people, forget where they came from and no longer look back with pride on their beginnings and confidence in their own blood and sinew and belief, that man or that people is doomed.

We were in Ketchem Holler, at last. Down on the flat valley floor the horses wanted to trot, and Father let them. We came to the place where we could hear the windmill and the blat of the sheep and the clang of the bells at Louie's camp. Then we went up the slope toward the house. There was a light in the window. I saw the door open for a moment, and I heard Fritz barking. It was a friendly, welcoming bark.

We drove into the dooryard and Mother came out to meet us. She hugged us and kissed us and said, "It's been an awful long day. I'm glad you're home." Fritz was pawing at me, licking my hands. Mother said, "Get unhitched and come in to supper. I've kept it warm for the last hour. I thought you never would get here."

Father said, "Its been a long trip. But we got what we had to have." And we began unhitching the horses. It was after nine o'clock.

6

We cut the corn before the heavy frosts came. We had only half a crop, after what the range cattle had done to it, but it made a big rick in the stack yard. We cut it instead of husking it there in the field so we would have some fodder as well as the grain and so that we could sow rye in the cornfield. The rye was sown by hand, broadcast, and a rain came the next day. It came up and made a bright patch on the hillside, twice as green because the grass was all bronze and tan by then.

We built a corn bin in the barn, and it was my spare-time job to snap the ears and husk them. I got the bin about half full before I found that from up on a haystack I could watch fall coming.

We'd built a short ladder to use in building the barn, and by getting on the roof of the barn and using the ladder I could get on top of the nearest haystack. From up there I could even see the wind.

Most of the wind was from the northwest, at that time of year. Away off there, Father said, more than a hundred miles away and clear over the horizon, were the Rocky Mountains. I hoped that from up on the stack I might see the mountains, but I couldn't. All I could see was the wind that came from them. It would come sweeping over the flats and down the hillside, and the bronzed buffalo grass would shiver. Then it reached the rye, which was just about ankle-high, and the rye would lean and wave. Then it rattled the dry corn leaves down below and ruffled the loose hay on the ground. About then I would close my eyes to slits and see the wind itself. It looked a little like summer heat waves, except that the waves didn't shimmer in the fall. They just waved there on the hilltop and low in the sky, cool and quiet and very deliberate.

Some days there would be clouds, big puffy clouds blue around the edges, and the clouds always made the sky a deeper blue. I would lie on my back and watch the clouds sail over and feel the biting chill when their shadows struck me. If I sat up and watched those cloud shadows on the plains they went ten times as fast as the clouds moved when I lay on my back and watched the clouds. And the cloud shadows weren't blue or purple as they had been all summer; now they were gray or black.

In the summer there had always been a hawk or two sailing in the sky. Now the hawks were gone, and even the bullbats had left. But every few days I would hear a faint distant gabbling and if I looked closely I could see a thin, wavery pencil line much higher than the hawks ever flew. They were geese, Canada geese, going south. Every time I saw them I felt a kind of inside sadness and at the same time a joy at seeing those big birds away up there. They could see the mountains, and they probably could even see Nebraska. But every time I saw the geese I also knew winter was coming, and I always went down from the stack and back to work snapping corn and husking out the ears.

Then one morning it was raw-cold and there was white frost. A few days later Gerrity's men came with wagons and extra herders and moved Louie's flock down to the main camp. Before Louie left he told Father which of the old pen sites would be best to plow for sheep chips. And after the sheep were gone the men took down the pens and shut off the windmill. After that I would wake up in the night and lie listening and wonder what was wrong. Sometimes I would lie awake a long time before I knew nothing was wrong at all; it was just the silence.

There weren't any sheep blatting on the other side of Ketchem Holler, and there weren't any sheep bells clanging. You get so used to sounds that you don't even hear them until they aren't there any longer; then you miss them.

A few days after they took down the pens and hauled them away we went over to the sheep camp with the plow and wagon. Father picked out the old pen sites, as Louie had said, where the pens had been two or three years ago. The sheep manure, trampled hard, had dried all that time and when we plowed it up it came out in big chunks, brown and dry and hard. Father said it looked like cheap lignite coal. We hauled a load of it home and tried it. It burned all right and it held fire twice as long as cow chips. So we hauled enough to fill the fuel shed right up to the roof, and after that Father didn't seem to worry quite so much. A person who grew up in timbered country just can't get used to seeing winter come without having a big woodpile beside the house.

After we got the sheep chips in, everything seemed easier, the way it always happens when you do something for yourself that you didn't think you could do. Like the evening when Mother and Father sat down with the Sears, Roebuck catalogue to see what we had to have for the winter. Father kept stopping at this thing, or that, and Mother kept saying, "We don't really need that."

Finally Father said, "The boy's got to have warm pants."

Mother said, "You've got two old pairs that are frayed around the bottom but still have lots of good material. I can make him warm pants."

"How about shirts?"

"I can cut down some of your old ones."

"You need a new coat."

Mother laughed. "I've got that brown one from five years ago. It's a little worn and out of style, but I've already planned how I'll make it over."

Father smiled. "All right. Now tell me you know how to make mittens and overshoes."

They both laughed. "I can make mittens," Mother said, "but I guess we'll have to buy overshoes."

So the Sears, Roebuck order wasn't nearly as big as they had expected.

And the same way with other things. Mother said that with all the corn we had, she'd like to have some corn bread. So she picked out a bushel of the best ears and shelled it by hand and ground it in the coffee mill. She blistered her hand doing it, because corn is much harder than coffee beans, but she had enough cornmeal, even after she sieved out the hulls, for a batch of corn bread and cornmeal mush for breakfast. It was so good that Father and I took turns and ground ten or twelve pounds of cornmeal and Mother stowed it away.

Then she took the bacon and salt-pork grease she had saved all summer and cooked it up with lye and made soap. Since we had chickens and eggs and milk and our own butter, about all we had to buy at the store was flour and salt pork and sugar and coffee. Mother said the only thing she missed was fresh meat. "If we only had a calf to butcher," she said, "or a hog!"

"Next year," Father said, "we'll have to get a couple of shoats. And if Bessie's calf isn't a heifer we'll keep it and fatten it and have young beef." Bessie was the big yellow cow. She'd been bred when Father bought her and she was due to calve in December. She had already gone dry. Father said, "How about some rabbit meat? Some of them, especially the white-tails, look pretty near as big as calves."

Mother said, "Get some. It's cold enough so the meat will keep."

So Father and I went out after rabbits.

There were two kinds of jack rabbits, the black-tails and the white-tails. The black-tails were the true jack rabbits, long-legged and lean and with very long ears. Their rather long tails were mostly black and their bodies were gray and their ears were black-tipped. The white-tails were really prairie hares. They were just as long-legged as the black-tails but they were heavier, had more meat on them. Their tails were white and their fur was much lighter in color. Some of them weighed ten pounds.

The jacks aren't burrowing animals. Even in the coldest weather they just huddle down in a little hollow in the ground or beside a sagebrush or a soapweed. When startled they run at top speed a little way, then stand on their hind legs for a moment and look around. Then they are off again. If you are hunting with a rifle you try to get them when they stop that first time. The only gun we had was the .25–20, which wasn't a rabbit gun. It was a coyote or antelope gun, and unless you shot a jack rabbit in the head or shoulders there wasn't much left to eat. Besides, shells for the .25–20 cost more than three cents apiece.

We went in the wagon, expecting to get a lot of rabbits. It was a good thing we did. We didn't get a load of rabbits but we went a long way, clear over to Badger Creek, six miles west. We saw lots of rabbits on the way over, but Father didn't have much luck. He tried to shoot from the wagon, and the horses always moved just as he was about to shoot, throwing him off balance. So he let me drive and he walked, finally, and he shot two rabbits. The first one he hit in the shoulders, and the back and hind legs, the meatiest part, was all right. He hit the other one in the back, and only the hind legs were worth saving. And he used ten shells. As he said, we could have bought round steak with what the ammunition cost.

But it was a pretty drive. Several times Father looked around and said, "Wonderful country! And millions of acres of it." Then about noon we topped a steep hill and down at the foot of it was the gleam of water. It was a water hole, a long, narrow pool lined with willow brush. It was Badger Creek, which was just a series of those long, narrow water holes except in spring when the snow melt and the rain made it a flowing stream.

We'd been on the flats so long by then that the sight of a pond of water and a line of willow brush was almost unbelievable. We went down the slope and back of the willows there was a thrashing in the water and a sudden rush. A flock of ten mallards went winging out of there, flying frantically. Father exclaimed, "Ducks! My gosh, just look at the ducks!" He just sat there watching them as they flew up the valley.

We stopped beside the brush at the edge of the water hole. It was all stunted brush, little willows not much taller than a man, but it was the nearest thing to trees we'd seen except in the Platte valley near Brush. We poked around in it and a cottontail rabbit jumped out and ran like mad, startling us so much that Father didn't even raise the rifle. The cottontail ran up the hill and into a hole. We thrashed around the pond and didn't see another living thing, though there were lots of hoof prints where horses had come down to drink.

We didn't know it then, but we were at the lower end of Pat Thompson's range. Old Pat Thompson was a horse ranchman, one of the real old-timers of that area. Pat had been raised a Texan, back in the early days. His father had been at the Alamo and Pat grew up as a brush-popper, married young and left a wife and several children to ride off to war in '61. When he came back in '64 his wife had died of the fever and his children had been parceled out among the neighbors. Folks expected him to marry again, settle down and become a Texas farmer.

Pat couldn't see it that way. He rode off to Mexico for a few years and came back just in time to gather a herd of longhorns from the brush patch that had once been his ranch, throw them in with a couple of neighbors' herds, and go up the trail north to the new railroad pushing its way west through Kansas.

Pat trailed cattle from Texas to the railroad several years, then spent a season as a hide hunter, killing buffalo. And after that he returned to Texas and took a trail herd all the way to Montana. On that trip he passed through this eastern Colorado area and marked it in his memory.

Pat had in him the restlessness of the old frontiersman. Hills were made for climbing and distances were designed to be explored. He had to go and do. He had to break trails, and what those who followed did with the new ground to which he led them was none of his concern.

Then something happened to Pat Thompson. It may have been a woman. It may have been remorse over the children he had never shouldered as his own responsibility when he came back from the war and who by then were grown and on their own. Whatever it was, Pat returned to Texas, gathered a little bunch of good mares, made his peace with one son, and started north. They came to the Badger Creek country, settled in a wide valley there with water for their horses, built a soddy and pens, and bred the mares to the stallion old Pat had ridden north.

They had their troubles. Pat was truculent, and twenty miles to the south of them was a cattle ranch whose boss resented intruders. Pat's son was shot and killed. Pat himself was shot through the hip. Rifle shots, not revolvers. Pat crawled to his house and healed himself in the way those tough old settlers handled emergencies, dressing his own wounds, knowing he would go through a time of fever and probably delirium, putting food and water within reach, then crawling into his blankets. Pat survived. And for five years he fought a single-handed feud with the cattleman to the south, finally losing his ultimate triumph when the cattleman died in his bed of pneumonia.

After that Pat began to mellow, as much as his kind ever really mellows. He settled down in his soddy, an aging man devoted to the one thing he had ever loved and not lost—horses. When he needed money he rounded up a bunch and drove them to market. Most of the ranchmen around used his horses for saddle stock. He glared at the homesteaders and called them damned fools. He lived in the past, perhaps a little mad, and the few strangers who encountered him smiled at his tales and warnings. Pat had known that land when it was young. He had seen men come and go. Mad or not, he had a sense of time and a sense, if not an understanding, of destiny.

There beside the water hole on old Pat's range, that day, Father and I washed what was left of the shot-up jack rabbit, spitted it on green willows, and cooked it over a fire of dead willow brush. There was little heat in the wood and we had to use ashes for salt, but we gnawed the bones, it tasted so good.

While we ate, Father talked about hunting trips when he was a boy. He had an old muzzle-loader shotgun but he never had enough money to buy both powder and shot, so he used pebbles for ammunition. One day, trying to shoot a goose, he put in a double charge of powder and a whole handful of gravel. The gun blew all to pieces. "All I had left," he said, "was the stock and part of the breech. I was lucky I didn't blow my fool head off."

I said I wished I had a shotgun. He said, "Some day. You're not big enough for a shotgun yet."

When we had eaten we gathered a wagonload of dead willow brush and started for home. We saw only two jacks on the way, but Father shot one of them right through the head.

I think Mother was more pleased with the wood than she was with the rabbits. We cut it to stove length and she used it to cook supper. She started to, that is. It was so dry it flamed and died right out, making little heat. Finally she reached for the cow chips and said, "I guess I'm getting to be a Coloradoan. You can have your old willow brush! *I* can't cook with it."

The rabbit she cooked that night was the best meat we'd had in a long time. She steamed it slowly and then took off the lid and browned it and made milk gravy. The meat was tender and juicy, and there was a lot of it. I thought it tasted like the drumstick of a chicken, but with more flavor. Mother said she thought the other rabbit wouldn't be quite so gamy if we let it freeze a few days; but she ate every bit of her piece.

The next Saturday we went to Gary for the mail and met Jake Farley there. He and Father talked about hunting and

Jake said he had a .22 rifle he never used. He offered to lend it to us, so Father bought two boxes of .22 cartridges and we stopped at Jake's place on the way home and got the gun. Shells for it were so cheap that Father let me practice with it, and the next time we went out after rabbits I shot one myself. It was a lucky shot, I guess, because I hit it in the head and it kicked a couple of times and was dead. But the next time we went out I shot one through the shoulders and it squealed and screamed like a baby. Father had to take the gun and kill it, and I was so sick I vomited. He said I should be glad I hadn't just broken a leg or wounded it so it got away and died in pain. He said killing a rabbit with a gun was a lot more painless to the rabbit than letting a coyote run it down. I knew he was right, but I kept hearing that scream. Finally he said the only way to kill a rabbit was to shoot it in the head; that way it was all over with in a hurry.

But it was weeks before I tried to shoot another rabbit.

The first week in November Jack Clothier came over to see us again. He sat on his horse in the dooryard and talked to Father and me till Mother came to the door and said, "It's too cold for you folks to stand there talking. Come on in."

We went in. The cowboy took off his hat and said to Mother, "I thought maybe you'd drive me off the place, after last summer." He grinned when he said it, and he had a nice grin.

Mother said, "Maybe we should." But she pushed the coffee-pot to the front of the stove. She wasn't giving an inch, but she was being nice.

"How'd your corn come out?" he asked. "I see you've got a good pile of fodder there in the stack yard."

"We got about half a crop," Father said.

"It could have been worse," the cowboy said. "It looks to me like you're all set to ride out the winter."

"We aim to," Mother said.

"Good. Too many homesteaders are quitters. I saw a lot of

them who just packed up and went back to live off the wife's folks when things got tough. That's what cleaned out this country ten–twelve years ago. Too many quitters."

"I didn't know this land was ever homesteaded," Father said.

"Not right in here. Over north, and east. A wave of home-steaders came in. Most of them lived in dugouts. They hit a hard winter and then a dry summer and they gave up."

"Not to speak of the range cattle eating their crops," Mother said.

"Well, yes, ma'am, that happened too. But the cattlemen couldn't have driven them out if they'd been stickers. They discouraged easy. They weren't the kind that stay."

Mother poured the coffee. "And you think we are?"

"You seem to be the spunky kind," the cowboy said.

"I don't know whether to take that as a compliment or not," Mother said.

Father smiled. "If your cattle come around this winter and break into the stack yard," he said "you'll find out how spunky she is."

The cowboy laughed and tasted his coffee. He looked at me and asked, "Do you read?"

I said yes, I could read.

He glanced around the room, saw no books or magazines. He said, "There's a bunch of old magazines at the bunkhouse, down at the ranch, you might like. If I'd been thinking I'd have brought them along." He turned and looked at Father, "You're not haying your cows, are you?"

Father said no, not yet.

"You won't have to, unless the snow gets deep. Newcomers think they have to hay their stock as soon as summer's over. But the grass is standing hay, cured right where it stands. Cattle will graze it all winter, just as long as they can get at it. Don't feed your hay till you're snowbound."

Father looked at him a moment, then asked, "Why are

you telling me that? The cattlemen don't want homesteaders in here."

The cowboy grinned. "I'm not a cattleman. I'm just a cowpuncher. The day of the big ranches is over, mister. Lots of cowmen won't admit it, but it's true. They keep squabbling with the sheepmen over grass, but it's folks like you who are going to put an end to the open range. One of these days they'll wake up and find you folks have choked them to death with barbed wire."

He stood up. He nodded to Mother. "Thanks for the coffee. You remind me of my sister, ma'am. She's spunky too." He grinned and put on his hat. Then he went out and got on his sorrel horse and rode away.

We all felt better after he left. Father and Mother kept discussing what he had said. It was both reassuring and a little challenging to know we weren't the first homesteaders. The others had been discouraged out. But we were the ones who were going to stick. Once Mother said, "I wonder if he was trying to say we might get dried out, too."

And Father said, "He didn't say that. He said the others were. He said we were the kind who don't get discouraged."

"Well, whatever he meant," Mother said, "we're going to stay."

A few days later he came back, with a bundle of magazines. He handed them to me without getting off his horse and said, "That ought to keep you busy for a while!" And he rode back down the valley.

The bundle was made up of copies of *Adventure* and *Top-Notch* and *Argosy* and *Bluebook*, dog-eared and with the covers torn half off. Mother went through them and saw that there weren't any swear words. She said that since there wasn't any school I could go to she guessed it would be all right if I spent my winter reading. That way, she said, I wouldn't be too far behind when I did get to go to school again. At least, I wouldn't forget how to read.

For Thanksgiving Day Mother killed a hen and stewed it with dumplings. We never made as much of Thanksgiving as New Englanders do. To us it was like a Sunday in the middle of the week. But we were more thankful than usual that year. As we sat down to dinner Father said, "I don't know about anyone else, but I think we've been pretty lucky."

Mother said, "So do I."

"We've been here almost seven months," Father said, "and we've accomplished a lot. We've built a house, none of us has been sick, we've got plenty to eat, and we've got our own land."

"I'm afraid the dumplings are kind of heavy," Mother said.

"That," Father said, "is what you always say."

Suddenly Mother asked, "You're not sorry we moved, then?"

"Sorry? Of course not. Are you?"

"You know I'm not, Will." Mother looked at her plate and tightened her mouth. I thought she was going to cry. She said, "Sometimes I wish we had more to do with, but I know we can't have everything at once. Sometimes I get homesick for the trees, but most of the time I don't miss them at all, any more." Then she said firmly, "I wouldn't move back for anything!"

Father smiled. "I guess Jack Clothier was right. I've got a pretty spunky wife."

Mother laughed. "I still don't know whether to take that as a compliment or not."

Years later I asked Mother if she hadn't been lonely and discouraged that first winter. She said, "Lonely, yes. But not too lonely. I had you two there with me. It was home. But I never was discouraged. I was blue sometimes, but I tried not to let your father see it." And I thought of the root meaning of the word "discouraged," and I knew she was right. She was never without courage. She missed the trees, as she said, and yet in later years when she visited in a heavily wooded

95

country she was ill at ease. The trees depressed her, she said. "I feel all closed in. I can't *see!*" And I knew that she was a plainswoman. There are times when I, even now, must get out of the valley, out of the woods, onto a hilltop where I can see a distant horizon. The New Englander loves his snug valleys, and the Easterner is often uneasy on the High Plains because he is so surrounded and even belittled by the vast distance and what he calls the overwhelming emptiness. But to one who grew up under that tremendous span of sky and on that endless expanse of plains, a land of lesser distances lacks one dimension.

That evening, after the chores were done, we all three played dominoes. Usually, when we played at all, it was just Father and me, because Mother always had sewing to do. But tonight she said the sewing could wait. She and Father laughed a good deal over the game, and neither of them really tried to win. It was one of the happiest evenings we'd had since we moved out there, one of the happiest evenings I could remember.

We had two more weeks of good weather, clear and cold but no snow, after Thanksgiving. Father and I went down to the sheep camp and plowed out more sheep chips and filled the fuel shed again. Louie had been right; we got a lot of ashes. But we'd hardly had to use any coal at all.

The first snow came in the middle of December. We thought it was going to be a real blizzard, but it turned out to be more wind than snow. It howled all night and until noon the next day, but only about an inch of snow fell. The wind blew it all off the hills and drifted it a foot deep in places. It was the first snow Fritz had ever seen. He ran around in it, barking excitedly and taking mouthfuls of it and trying to eat it, like bread. It must have nipped his tongue, because he was the most surprised dog you ever saw. Then he decided he liked snow and rolled in the deepest drift he could find and ran around barking like crazy.

I went up on the haystack to see if the winter wind looked any different from the fall wind, but it was so cold up there that all I could see was the tears in my eyes. I got down before the wind blew me down and broke an arm. Anyway, I could see the winter wind just as well from down on the ground. It was white, and it curled over the hilltop and came swirling down the slope. It made little whirlpools around the fence posts, and up high in the air it glistened like tiny spangles in the sunlight.

7

Christmas came on a Sunday. After that first light snow the weather had been clear and cold. The mail the Saturday before Christmas brought a letter from Aunt Eva, back in Nebraska, saying the folks were sending a box with presents for all of us, but the box hadn't come; so we went to Gary again the Saturday of Christmas Eve.

It was a long cold trip with a bright sun and a biting wind. We wore our heaviest clothes and we had horse blankets around us on the wagon seat and a lantern at our feet. By putting the blankets around our legs, with the lighted lantern under the blankets, we had some warmth.

Mother took along ten pounds of butter to trade at the store. Old Bessie, the yellow cow, had freshened just in time to give extra cream and Mother had saved it all and churned it. Bessie's calf was a heifer, a funny, wobbly-legged yellow calf. It came in the night, to Mother's relief because I had wanted to watch it being born. One evening old Bessie was very fat and restless and Father said he wouldn't be surprised if he had to be up in the night with her. But she had her calf easily and alone and when we went to the barn next morning she mooed softly and proudly and there was the calf, sucking and butting her bag, very much alive, its hair all curly where she'd licked it dry.

Lots of people were at the store, talking and laughing and buying Christmas things. They made way for us to get up close to the big round stove, the kind you used to find in all the railroad stations, to get warm. Everybody was talking to everybody else whether they knew each other or not. The store had only one little wreath at the post office window for Christmas decoration, but it looked very Christmasy with pails of ribbon candy and a crate of oranges and a keg of bright red cranberries and boxes of nuts and raisins and red and green frosted cookies. Somebody shouted, "Hey Tom, where's the mistletoe?" And McDowell, back of the counter, said, "In the living room. You didn't think I'd hang it out here in the store, did you, with all these pretty girls around!"

When we got warm Father asked Mr. McDowell about the mail and the express, but Mr. McDowell said there wasn't anything for us. I looked at Mother and she looked at Father, and it seemed that there wasn't going to be any Christmas. Father said, "There's supposed to be a box, from Nebraska."

Mr. McDowell shook his head. "Maybe," he said, "Con'll have it in his load today. He said there was a lot of stuff in town still to come out, and he took his big wagon to bring it all today. Want to do your trading while you wait?"

We waited. Con Hallahan was the stage driver who had the star mail route between Gary and Brush and hauled freight and express as well, and occasional passengers. Con lived near Gary, kept a pastureful of half-broken broncos, and every morning he wrestled a team of them into harness, hitched them to his wagon, and ran them all the way to Brush. In town he picked up the mail, freight, and any brave passengers, and he ran the broncs, almost tractable by then, all the way back to Gary. Each day he used a different team, so none of his horses ever were really tamed. When you were on the road and saw Con coming you pulled off to one side and gave him plenty of room. The best he could do with his horses was keep them between the fences. Often he made the fifteen miles between Brush and Gary, with a ton or more of load, in an hour and a half.

Mother said for Father and me to bring in her butter and then stay away and not be nosy while she did her trading. So we went over beside the stove and listened to the talk. Most of it was about the weather or about cattle or about hunting. One man, from over on Beaver Creek ten miles east, said it was going to be an open winter and a dry summer, because no snow meant no rain. Another said we would get all our snow in February. He said he'd killed a wild goose and examined its bones and feathers, and he knew. Still another said we'd have two feet of snow by New Year, and he quoted an almanac to prove it.

Mother finished her trading and Father asked if he shouldn't put the things in the wagon. She said no, she didn't want them to freeze.

"What did you get that's going to freeze?" he asked.

Mother laughed. "You'll see," was all she would say.

So we waited. It got to be half past three and the sun was low in the sky. Another half hour and it would begin to turn dusk. Somebody said Con must have found some Christmas cheer in town. Somebody else said Con probably had a big load, and all the men laughed.

Then, just before four o'clock, a man at the front window shouted, "Here he comes!" and almost everybody crowded to the front of the store. There came Con, his horses galloping and steaming, his wagon piled high with freight. He had two passengers on the seat beside him.

The door opened and most of the men surged outside. Con whooped and hollered and swung the team up beside the hitch rack and jumped down and snubbed them. Nobody else dared go near his horses, even after he had run them all the way from town. They stood there, eyes rolling, puffing steam like locomotives. And there was Con, a wiry little Irishman, a knitted red muffler around his head under his hat, icicles on his bristly red mustache. He handed his passengers down, two young women bundled to the eyes in coats and blankets.

They squealed and shouted greetings to the families waiting for them.

Con hauled down three mail sacks and carried them into the store, and a dozen volunteers began unloading the boxes. Con came back with a list in his hand and supervised the unloading, checking off each box and the name of the person to whom it was addressed.

Box after box came off, and we waited, hoping and holding our breath. Mother had just said, "I guess it didn't come. I guess—" when Con shouted, "Borland!" and Mother cried, "Will! There it is!"

Con laughed and said, "Just call me Santa Claus. Con Hallahan Santa Claus! And Merry Christmas to you, ma'am!"

Father went inside and signed for the box and we put the box of groceries in the wagon and under the blankets beside the lantern. We waited a few minutes longer while Tom McDowell distributed the mail, got two letters, and started home.

The sun had set. The wind had died down and the cold began to deepen. But the horses were full of life and we traveled right along. I thought the horses were almost as fractious as one of Con Hallahan's teams of broncs.

We played a guessing game for a while, guessing what was in the box. But Mother didn't approve of that. "Whatever they sent," she said, "I'm sure it's nice. And if you two keep guessing that way you'll just be disappointed when we open it." We had about guessed ourselves out, anyway. So Father began singing. Father had a good baritone and Mother was an excellent soprano, though neither had any training. Father sang "Two Little Girls in Blue" and "Just Break the News to Mother" and "In the Baggage Coach Ahead," and then Mother started "Daisy Bell." She never liked the sad songs like the one about the dead wife in the baggage coach ahead.

We all sang "Daisy Bell" and "Daisies Won't Tell" and "Under the Old Apple Tree." And finally Mother said, "It's

Christmas Eve." Very softly she began "O Little Town of Bethlehem" and Father joined her. We sang all the simple Christmas songs that were always sung at the Christmas Eve program in church back in Nebraska, when there was always a big Christmas tree with candles and a sack of candy for every child. We sang, and it was sad and beautiful, there on the plains with the stars brighter than the candles had ever been on the tree in church. And at last Mother sang "Silent Night" all alone. When she came to the end nobody said anything for a long time.

We crossed the last hill and went up Ketchem Holler to our own trail. As we went up the slope toward our house it was just a dark shadow against the hill with the other shadows of the barn and the haystacks beyond. Then Fritz barked, recognized us and barked a different note, and came running to greet us. Mother went in the house and lit a lamp and started a fire while we unhitched, and we went in and changed our clothes and did the evening chores.

The chores were the same as any other evening, but still it was a kind of special night. Father gave the horses an extra measure of grain and I got the very best hay for old Bessie. We finished the milking and I patted the yellow calf and looked at the manger and thought of all the Christmas songs and stories. And when we went to the house the stars were specially bright. It was a holy, silent night.

We opened our presents Christmas morning, our own presents first and then the box from Nebraska. Mother had put our presents on the table, wrapped in white paper and with our names on them. We each had an orange. That's what Mother had got in Gary and didn't want to freeze. Father and I each had a new pair of mittens, made of pants cloth and lined with flannel from one of Mother's old petticoats. I had a new cap, with ear flaps. And Father gave me two boxes of .22 cartridges, two whole boxes, a hundred shots! That was the most wonderful gift I could imagine. I was so excited I almost forgot the gifts I had made for them. Then I remembered and ran out to the barn, where I had hidden them. I had a braided horsehair hatband for father, made of hair I had pulled from old Dick's tail, and a butter paddle for Mother, whittled out of a piece of board.

The box from Nebraska had a fascinator and a pair of gloves and a shirtwaist for Mother. There was a necktie and a pair of socks and muffler for Father. And for me there were two pairs of black cotton stockings and a muffler and a book. The book had a light blue cover all scrolled in gold around a picture of a fairy tale prince and princess. The title was *Snow White*. Aunt Grace had started giving me fairy tales when I was five years old, and the age level never changed.

I wanted to throw the book across the room or put it in the stove. Mother was watching me. I put it down carefully, knowing I would have to write a nice letter and thank Aunt Grace and say I enjoyed it very much; but I wished just for once that I could tell her what I thought of the books she always chose for me.

The box also contained a peck of black walnuts and a jar of apple butter and two glasses of jelly, one of which had broken and spilled on Mother's shirtwaist. Mother said it didn't matter because she wasn't going any place where she could wear a shirtwaist like that. Father said, "You can wear it when I wear this red necktie." They both said it was a wonderful Christmas, and I agreed. I had a whole hundred .22 cartridges!

It was a bright, sunny morning, though the sun was a little hazy. It had warmed up overnight and there was a wind from the south. It hadn't got above freezing, but it felt almost balmy. After we had cleaned the barn and turned out the cows to graze and got the hay for the mangers I said I wanted to go hunting.

"Have you forgotten what day it is?" Mother asked.

I said it was Christmas.

"It's not only Christmas," she said. "It's Sunday." Mother

didn't approve of hunting on Sunday. She was a Methodist and all her family were Methodists, and Methodists were very strict about what you did on Sunday. Father had been a Campbellite, a sect favored by a good many of the Scotch-Irish, but he joined the Methodist church when he married Mother.

I said if I couldn't go hunting I wanted to go for a ride. I wanted to take old Dick and ride down to the big sheep camp. Father said he didn't see anything wrong with that, since it was such a nice day, and Mother said we'd have an early dinner and then I could go if I promised not to gallop old Dick. While I waited for dinner, she said, I could shuck some corn. Shucking corn was all right on Sunday.

I shucked corn for a while, then went up on the hystack. It was warm up there, with the south wind, but the horizon was all misty. Looking at the misty horizon off to the west I played that I could see the mountains. I'd never seen the mountains, but I thought they must be all jagged and very high and very rocky. In the mist that day I saw lots of mountains.

We had jack rabbit for dinner, and I said that if I could take the gun I would bring back a lot more rabbits. But it wasn't any use and I knew it. So I put the riding bridle on old Dick and mounted him from the manger and rode out of the barn. I always rode bareback because we didn't have a saddle.

Father said to take it easy. He grinned. "None of this playing like you're an Indian on a spotted pony chasing buffalo." Mother said that if I didn't promise I wouldn't let old Dick gallop she wouldn't let me go. I promised, and I called Fritz and we started down Ketchem Holler.

Father and I had been down to the big sheep camp but I'd never been there alone. It was the place that had been Gerrity's original ranch, situated where Ketchem Holler widened into a broad, flat valley with a long slope to the east and a steep cut-bank to the west. On the flat east of the camp was a small prairie dog town, and the cut-bank to the west honey-combed with holes where hundreds of bank swallows nested every summer.

The original sod house had vanished without a trace. The wells and windmills were still there, and in place of the old soddy there were frame bunkhouses, long, low buildings, to house the herders during lambing season in the spring and the shearing crews who took the fleeces in summer. And a couple of big open-front frame sheds had been built as shelter for lambing and to break the sunlight and heat for shearing. Fronting on the sheds were permanent pens, acres of them, built of broad panels much like those at the temporary summer camps except that those at the big camps were spiked to posts set deep in the ground.

The whole flat of the valley around the camp was grazed and hoof-cut till scarcely a spear of grass remained. In summer there were rows of prickly poppies along the pens, tall, gray-green plants whose stems and even their leaves were covered with small, sharp thorns. They were a weed plant, but they bore true poppy flowers several inches in diameter, big white petals with vivid yellow centers, and when you broke a stem it oozed yellow juice, as all poppies do.

The camp was a busy place every spring with flocks of ewes about to drop their lambs, with herders and wagons and camp tenders. Gerrity drove his lambing crews for days, pausing only to eat and catch a few hours of sleep. Lambing traditionally came at the worst time of year, usually with cold rain, some-times with late snow. Thousands of lambs were born, coddled when necessary, and often forced upon reluctant mothers. Then, the rush of lambing over, the sheep were divided into flocks and sent out to their various ranges. There they stayed until shearing time, when they were brought back to the big sheds and shorn, at first with hand clippers, later with power clippers driven by gasoline engines. The shorn sheep, looking unbelievably small and thin with their fleeces gone—looking, in fact, a little like small boys who have just had a close-clipped crew haircut for the summer after a winter of long, shaggy hair—were then taken back to their ranges to fatten until the first hard frosts.

Late October and all the flocks were gone again, back to the camp for sorting, then on to Gerrity's ranch, herded on foot every step of the way. There the lambs were fattened for market, the breeder ewes were penned and fed on alfalfa all winter, and spring brought the same round once more, camp, lambing, and the range again.

I took my time on the way down. It was a warm afternoon, so warm we'd eaten dinner with the door open. I had my mackinaw, but as soon as I was out of sight of the house I took it off and folded it and used it as a saddle pad. It was so mild it seemed strange that there were no meadow larks singing.

Fritz explored every clump of soapweed and bunch grass and routed out several jack rabbits. But he didn't chase them far. He knew he couldn't catch them, and they knew it too. They just loped off, running half sideways and looking back at him, and he yapped several times and ran them just far enough to prove that he wasn't taking any nonsense. I found a wash on a hillside that was worth searching for arrowheads, so I got off and looked for maybe half an hour. I found a rare pinkish-white point; and when old Dick wouldn't stand and let me shinny up his leg to get on again it didn't matter. I led him half a mile till I found a low cut-bank and could mount easily. It was one of those afternoons when time didn't matter at all. It didn't even matter that a gray cloud bank was rising off in the northeast.

When we got to the camp it was so warm the prairie dogs were out in the little dog town, yapping as though it was May. We went over there and watched them a while, and I poked into a big ant hill to see if any ants would come boiling out. A few of them did, but not many. And when Fritz got tired of trying to catch a prairie dog and went over to the sheds to chase cottontails I went along.

There were always cottontails at the camp. Fritz chased three out of the sheds and over to the burrows under the bunkhouses. He tried to dig in after them, but I stayed at the sheds watching the turtle doves. The camp was the only place around where the doves wintered, probably because they had shelter and food. Five or six pairs of them were there, away up in the crossbeams, cooing and fluttering, making that whistling noise with their wings when they flew. I tried to climb up and look in the old nests, away up there on the beams, but I didn't get very far.

Then Fritz and I went over to the cut-bank and looked at all the swallows' holes. Fritz found a hole at the foot of the bank that smelled of skunk and started to dig it out. But I didn't have a gun and there's no sense digging out a skunk if you aren't going to shoot it. On the way back to the sheds I found an old sheep bell without any clapper and a stockman's knife with one good blade, the little one, and the brown seed pod from a devil's claw which looked exactly like a goat's head with two long sharp horns.

The cloud bank in the northeast covered more than half the sky by then. And the wind had shifted and turned cold. The wind was in the east, now, and I put on my mackinaw. I climbed on the sheep pen and mounted Dick, but Fritz was still in the skunk hole. I had to go back and get him. I got off and pulled him out of the hole. Then I had to go back to the pens to get on Dick again.

The wind was in the northeast, now, and it had a bite to it. I buttoned my mackinaw and started for home. I hadn't gone a quarter of a mile when it began to snow. The first flakes were big and wet and they came so fast they clotted up like little snowballs. I shouted to Fritz, "Hey, it's snowing! I hope we get a foot of it!"

The wind increased. The big, wet flakes changed to little,

dry ones. Then the little flakes changed to hard pellets that hissed as they came down. They stung my ears and cheeks. I turned down the flaps on my cap and turned up my coat collar. The snow drove itself into old Dick's hair and stuck there.

Dick wanted to gallop. I didn't let him. I had promised. I let him trot. But a trot shakes you up a lot, riding bareback, especially if you aren't big enough to have long legs. The trotting warmed me up, though, and the wind was getting colder by the minute.

The wind was howling, coming in big gusts, and the snow was swirling along the ground, not sticking anywhere, just swirling and constantly moving. The sun was gone. The whole sky was gray. It was going to be dark early.

Old Dick wasn't a dark bay any longer; with the snow driven into his hair he was a light roan. And then, before I knew it, I couldn't see the hills at the edge of the valley. All I could see was a little world of swirling snow with a space maybe fifteen feet around me, a little circular world as though I was in one of those glass paperweights that have a snowstorm inside when you turn them over. I shouted to Fritz and pretty soon he came out of the storm and trotted right in front of Dick. Fritz was mostly white, too, with the snow pelted into his fur. He barked at me, then ran on ahead out of sight.

I knew how to get home. All I had to do was go right up Ketchem Holler till I came to Louie's windmill, then turn right, up our trail. All I had to do was stay in the valley, with the wind there at my left shoulder driving snow against my left cheek.

But pretty soon the wind was at my back. Then Dick was climbing a slope. I tried to rein him back to the left, where the valley should be, but he took the bit in his teeth and swung his head and looked around at me once or twice and kept right on the way he was going. And the wind got even stronger, right at my back.

After that I wasn't sure which direction we were going. I remembered that Father had said nobody needed to get lost out here. All you had to do was find the sun or the stars and you'd know your directions. But there wasn't any sun to look for, and there weren't any stars. There wasn't any sky or any earth, even. Just that swirling snow above me and beneath me and all around me. Dick and I were out in the middle of a whirling white nowhere, being blown along by that roaring wind.

I shouted to Fritz and kept shouting, and finally I heard him bark just ahead. I still couldn't see him. It seemed that we'd been going a long, long time since we left the sheep camp. Maybe we had missed Louie's windmill and gone right on south, onto the flats with the big prairie dog town. If we had, we could drift all night and not find any place to stop. My hands were cold. One at a time, I thrust them under my leg to warm them against old Dick's back. My cheeks were getting numb and my nose stung when I touched it.

Dick stumbled and I almost fell off. I grabbed desperately at his mane and hung on. If I fell off I knew I couldn't get back on. And he probably had stumbled in a prairie dog hole, and we were out on the big flats. Then Dick hunched himself and went up a steep bank, and I knew we weren't in the dog town. There weren't any hills over there. I didn't know where we were. I had a crazy idea that we had drifted over west and were in the breaks along Badger Creek.

Then Dick was hurrying and I knew we were going down a slope. Fritz began to bark just ahead of me. And suddenly, right in front of me, a house loomed out of the whirling snow. Fritz was there, barking. The door of the house opened, and it was a strange house because the door was on the north instead of the east where our door was. Then I saw Mother in the doorway, and it *was* our house! Suddenly the whole world turned around me and I had my directions straight.

I was there beside the step and Mother was shouting at me. I could see inside, the way the wind was making the flame in the lamp jump and flicker and smoke the chimney. Mother shouted, "Will! Will, he's here!" Fritz barked again, and I heard Father shout something. Then Father rode up on Shorty. He hadn't been out in the snow very long because Shorty's coat had only a little snow on it. Father rode alongside me and took the reins and shouted, "Get off! Get in the house!"

I slid off, so cold and stiff I could hardly stand. Mother led me into the house. She took off my cap and my mackinaw and began rubbing my hands and my nose. When Father came in from the barn a few minutes later she was taking off my shoes.

Fritz came in with Father and shook snow and water all over us. Mother didn't scold him. Tears were running down her cheeks.

Father said, "Is he all right?"

Mother said, "I think so. Get out of those wet clothes, son, and get into something dry." She put milk to heat for hot cocoa.

Father brought in a pail of coal and built up the fire. While we all had hot cocoa Father said the snow had struck at the house less than an hour ago. They kept waiting and waiting, thinking I would be there any minute. Then Father started down to Louie's camp on foot, but the snow was so bad that he knew he couldn't make it and came back and got Shorty. He was just starting out again when I arrived. "Old Dick," he said, "took a shortcut, I guess. He came right across the hills."

There wasn't much said, after that. We just settled down beside the stove and were thankful to be there. After a while Father took a lantern and went to the barn and did the milking. When he came back he said it was getting colder by the minute and the snow was still coming. Mother hung old quilts at the windows to keep out some of the cold. But there were cracks up at the eaves and when the wind blew especially hard the snow came in in white, shimmering plumes. Father took old rags and a table knife and stood on a chair and tried to plug the cracks, but he couldn't stop the snow completely.

"I guess," he said as he came back to the stove, "this is going to be a Colorado blizzard."

"Going to be?" Mother asked.

"Well," Father said, "if you ask me, it's just getting well started. Listen to that wind!"

It howled and the whole house shook. Then I knew why Father had set those cedar posts at the corners. I was glad we'd set the posts deep and tamped them tight.

Mother got supper, and while we ate she kept looking at me, then glancing at Father. Finally Father said, "What are you worrying about? He's here. Everything's all right."

"I'm not worrying," she said. "I'm just being thankful that you're here, both of you, not out there in that storm."

Father asked for another cup of coffee and rolled a cigarette. He held the match a moment after he lit it, then blew it out with a puff of smoke. "Well," he said, "we are here. All three of us." He looked at her, then turned to me. "I'm glad you were on Dick. I'm not sure Shorty would have had sense enough to come home. I know he didn't like to face the storm when I started out to look for you. He wanted to turn tail and drift with it. . . . Just listen to that wind! It's really nasty out there."

I listened to the wind, howling and swishing that icy snow against the windows, and I thought of that strange white world I had been in, where there wasn't any sky or earth or anything at all except Dick's snow-roan neck and his dark ears and blowing forelock and a little space beyond, and even that filled with swirling snow. My hands still tingled and my fingers were almost too stiff to hold a fork. But I was here, I was at home.

8

The blizzard lasted all the next day and the next night. We never did know when it stopped snowing because even after the sun came out the third day, away off to the south and looking only about half as big as it should, the wind kept on whooping and the air was still full of snow, most of it blown off the slopes. But by that afternoon the wind began to ease off and we could see that the sky was clear.

That night, the third night after the blizzard began, the wind died completely and the world was so still you could almost hear the silence. There was a half moon, dazzling in the white world, and all the stars in the universe were out and so close you could have reached up and touched them from a high hilltop. The cold settled down and I went to sleep hearing the beams and rafters creaking; but it was almost warm inside the house because the snow banked it and insulated it.

The next morning, the first morning we could really see around us, it was so dark in the house we didn't know when the sun rose. There was a drift at the south end so high that it covered the whole window, and the other windows were frosted so thick I couldn't scratch down to the glass with my thumbnail. But we knew the storm was really over because there wasn't any snowdrift on the floor beside my bed. The other mornings there had been a drift six inches deep from snow that drifted in through the crack at the eaves.

Outside it was a new, strange world. That drift at the south end of the house reached clear down to the pump. Back of the house was another drift so deep that only a few inches of the clothesline posts were visible. And if we hadn't known where it was we couldn't have found the barn. . . . There was a drift from the haystacks right over the barn roof, up to the eaves on the south side, which was all of eight feet high.

We wallowed our way to the barn, the snow over my knees even between the big drifts. It was so still the smoke from the house chimney went straight up as far as you could see. Wisps of steam crept out around the barn door, from the body heat inside, and plumed up and froze into shimmering little ice-crystal clouds.

We shoveled the barn door clear and did the milking. Then we had breakfast and started shoveling paths. We had to get to the haystacks and we had to get to the well. We'd filled the two water pails for the house the night before, but the one we left on the wash stand was frozen solid, the seam at the bottom forced open and the pail ruined. Mother said we'd have to remember to put both pails on the stove at night or we wouldn't have a good pail left. When we got a path to the well it took two tea kettles of boiling water to thaw the pump.

At dinnertime Mother said that after she did the dishes she was coming out and help. Father said there was no need of that, because we would just be getting to the stacks and that's all we'd try to do that day."

Mother said, "I'm tired of being cooped up in here."

"You can't get around in this snow," Father said. "It's up to your knees, even in the shallow places."

Mother smiled. "I'll get around, all right."

We went back to work. We had to cut through a drift higher than my head to get to the nearest haystack. Then Father had to get up on the stack with the hay knife and cut a slice down one end and pitch the hay down. We carried it into the barn, forkful at a time.

We were carrying the first forkfuls when Mother came out,

a red muffler around her head and wearing her long brown coat. The first we saw of her was when she was up to her knees in the snow beside the path. She shouted and waved, and Father almost dropped his forkful of hay. "Get back in the path!" he shouted.

Mother waved and waded into a drift up to her waist.

Father shouted, "Sarah! You'll catch your death of cold!"

She laughed and waded toward us, holding her coat around her. Father took his forkful of hay into the barn. When he came back she was there beside the path to the stacks, waiting. She flipped open her coat and laughed at him.

Father gasped. She was wearing a pair of his old trousers, stuffed and bulky with the underskirts she had tucked inside.

Women didn't wear slacks, in those days. Women wore skirts, long, full skirts, over lots of petticoats. Women didn't even reveal their ankles.

Mother drew her coat around her again and flushed. Then she tossed her head and said, "I told you I was coming out! You didn't think I would, did you?" She opened her coat again and looked at herself. "They're awful big," she said. "I had to tuck them all around the waist. But they're warm!"

Father started toward her, picking up a handful of snow.

"Will!" she cried. "Don't you dare!"

He tossed the snow at her. She tried to dodge and fell down. He picked her up and kissed her and carried her to the path to the house and set her down and brushed the snow from her coat.

They were both laughing. She said, "I don't care if it *isn't* quite decent! There's just the two of you here. . . . Now go back to work. I'm going to see if the hens laid any eggs."

Father shoveled a path to the chicken house for her while I carried the rest of the hay into the barn. Mother found four eggs, every one frozen solid. She fed the chickens and inspected all our paths. She said she'd been missing a lot by not getting out. Then she went back to the house and we finished the chores.

That evening we had ice cream. Mother thawed the eggs in a pan of water, mixed them with milk, added a little sugar and vanilla, put the mixture in a crock and set it in the snow beside the door. She stirred it several times to break up the big ice crystals, and it tasted like any ice cream made in a freezer. It was the first dessert we'd had in weeks.

It was bitter cold the rest of the week; then it began to ease off. The second week the sun cut through the places where the snow had blown thin on the high places. Father and I rode the horses between the drifts and made paths for the cows, and they found a little grazing and got exercise. Wherever they walked the snow began to melt, and by the middle of January there was plenty of grazing for them again. But the big drifts stayed on for weeks, well into February.

As soon as we could get out with the wagon we went down to Louie's camp and tried to plow out more sheep chips. It took us all day to loosen one wagonload, and the lumps were so full of frost they simmered and steamed in the stove a long time before they caught fire. But we were so low on fuel that Mother said we had to save what coal we had for cooking. So we burned soggy sheep chips.

We had only two more storms that winter, and both were more wind than snow. Late January was bitter and the cold didn't let up until February was half gone. But the last week in February a chinook came, a warm dry wind from the west, and all the snow went, even the last of that big drift between the stacks and the barn. Two days of the chinook and every hillside was trickling and the draws were soggy. Our rye, there in the cornfield, was green and shooting up.

We had raw weather after that, cold, damp days all through March, but the winter was definitely broken. We met Jake Farley at Gary one Saturday and he said he was going to start plowing in another week or two if the weather held. Another man heard him and shook his head. "No use plowing too much," he said. "It's going to be a dry year."

"Ground's in good shape," Jake said.

"Always have a dry summer after an open winter," the man said.

"Do you call this an open winter?" Father asked.

"One good snow, that's all we had. That Christmas snow."

"That was plenty," Father said.

But the man insisted. "One storm doesn't make a winter. Mark my word, it's going to be a dry summer." He walked away.

Jake said, "I'm going to start plowing week after next. By the way, are you through with that twenty-two? Rabbits aren't fit to eat now."

Father said we'd bring it back the next day.

"No hurry," Jake said. "But there's a pair of skunks under my house and I don't want them to have a family there. I don't mind two skunks, but five or six is one too many."

We took the rifle back to him the next day. He had skunks under his house, all right. Mother didn't even get out of the wagon. She said if it smelled worse in the house than it did in the yard she didn't see how Jake stood it.

Father said, "It smelled a little worse. But I guess Jake's used to it."

"Anybody who keeps horses in the house," Mother said, "wouldn't smell a skunk right under his nose. No wonder Jake never got married. No woman in her right mind would have him."

Jake was an odd person, neighborly as they come, shyly polite with Mother, and full of fantastic stories. Jake had a liking for the bizarre, the shocking, and he told his stories with a sly humor. He had known, or said he had known, more fantastic people than the manager of a freak show. He knew a man once, he said, who heard an uproar in his chicken house one night and went out to find a bobcat there. He caught the bobcat with his bare hands, choked it into submission, put a collar on it, and tethered it for the night. The next day he began taming it. It took quite a while, but this was a very patient man. He tamed the beast and taught it to hunt with him.

Taught it to point like a bird dog, in fact. It would point quail, standing with one paw raised and not a quiver except its bob tail, which signaled the man what kind of birds were there and how many. If it wagged its tail sideways, that meant quail. If it bobbed its tail up and down, that meant prairie chickens. And the number of twitches the tail made indicated the number of birds.

Things went fine and the man lived high for the better part of a year. He happened to be a bachelor, living all alone. Then the bobcat began to point redbirds instead of quail. This made the man mad. He cussed that bobcat till he was blue in the face. By then, of course, the cat understood human language, and he didn't like the names the man called him. He spat and growled and snapped and snarled, and one night the two of them had a fearful fight. Folks a mile away heard the uproar. The next morning they went to see what was going on.

They got to the house and there wasn't a sign of the man. The bobcat was there, asleep in the man's favorite chair. The man's shoes were on the floor, but not another sign of him. They folks who came to investigate didn't care for bobcats, so they shot him. After they'd skinned him out they opened his stomach to see if they could find any clue to what had happened. Inside that bobcat's stomach they found just two metal pants buttons, not another thing. And the coroner issued a death certificate: "Dead of unknown causes, probably et by a bobcat." And they buried the two pants buttons and put up a gravestone over them.

Jake also had a vast store of tales about hoop snakes, a kind of blacksnake that tucked its tail in its mouth and made itself into a hoop and rolled downhill. Jake's hoop snakes could do anything, from strangling a man to lassoing a stray calf. He knew a man who lost the tire from a wagon wheel out in the woods somewhere and didn't know how to get home, because without a tire the wheel would fall apart. Then he saw two hoop snakes. He caught them and teased them into grabbing each other's tails. They made a hoop just big enough to fit his wagon wheel, so he popped them on the wheel, jumped in his wagon, and drove away fast. The snakes' teeth got stuck in each other's tail, they couldn't let go, and he drove all the way home without a bit of trouble. But that night they worked their way loose, hooped themselves around his rain barrel, and the next morning when he went out they'd caved it in, squeezing the way they could. The poor man, with no rain water for his wife to wash her hair in, had a fight with his wife, she up and left him, and he went off to California and nobody ever heard of him again.

Jake also was an authority on exotic food, particularly on its effects. He knew a man who trapped muskrats for a living and one winter ate a few of them. First thing he knew, he grew a long rat-like tail and webs between his toes. Jake knew another man who, just to see what it tasted like, ate a bat. After that he couldn't sleep in bed; couldn't sleep a wink unless he hung by his toes from a rafter.

Jake barely escaped such a fantastic fate himself. One day he was riding his horse down a lonely back road and came to a dreary backwoods farm and stopped for a drink of water. The man invited him to stay for dinner, since it was around noontime. The place didn't seem too promising, since the man didn't have a chicken or a pig or even a cow, but only a lot of cats. But the woman said, "Ed caught a rabbit. You like rabbit, don't you?"

So Jake stayed and the woman fried the rabbit nice and crisp. Jake ate three pieces, even though it did have a kind of odd taste. Then he said his thanks and went out to leave, and on the barn door he saw a fresh cat skin stretched out to dry. That cat skin hadn't been there before dinner, and Jake remembered that while he and the woman were talking the man had gone outdoors to get "the rabbit, cooling in the well."

Jake felt a little queasy, but not quite enough to get rid of his dinner. But he didn't want to find himself crouched down in front of a mouse hole the next day or listen to himself purr every time he sat down in front of the fire, so he stuck his finger down his throat. That did it. "But," Jake said, telling the story, "for close onto a year I had to keep shaving off stiff hairs that tried to grow on my upper lip. Up till then I'd kind of thought I might look good with a mustache, but I didn't dare try to grow one after that. If I grew a cat mustache, no telling what would happen next!"

Jake told his stories with sly humor to Father and me. But never when Mother was around.

Quite a few new homesteaders moved in that spring. Most of them settled over east, beyond Jake's place. The strangest of the newcomers, and the one who roused the most speculation, was Emily Woods.

Miss Woods was middle-aged, had been a schoolteacher back east, and had decided she was going to have a place of her own on the plains. She came to Brush, hired a land locator, chose a low hilltop ten miles southeast of Gary, hired a man to haul lumber out, and built a house and a pint-sized barn for the sleek black buggy horse she bought. But the strangest thing about Miss Woods was that she had only one leg. There was ribald speculation among the men at Gary about where the leg was taken off, until the women heard echoes of it and put a stop to it. Miss Woods was a lady, a friendly soul, liked everyone, and within a few months everybody liked her. She hopped about the place on crutches, always had a laugh or a friendly greeting, and asked no favors.

Her house looked just like a little Illinois town house, gabled and trim and painted dazzling white. She built and painted it with her own hands. Then she added the crowning touch, which started the talk all over again. She put a picket fence all around the house, just as though it was a house in town with a fence around its fifty-by-hundred lot. She painted the fence white too. Then she planted petunias all along the fence and carried water to them every evening. They flourished and bloomed in a blaze of color that had every woman within miles envious.

There were rumors that Miss Woods had money, as the

saying went. She probably didn't have an income of more than fifty dollars a month, but any kind of cash income which one could depend on, regardless of markets or weather, was in a sense wealth. Several of the single men, including a couple of cowboys, made awkward efforts to court her, but she seemed quietly amused and after a time they all gave up. Miss Emily just wasn't interested.

The only settlers who came over our way were the Bromleys. They came out from Fort Morgan, the next town west of Brush, and they homesteaded a place on the high flats between us and Badger Creek. It was months before we met them, but meanwhile we heard stories about them.

They came from Chicago. She had worked in a library. He had been a clerk, or something like that, and he hadn't the first notion of what homesteading meant, or even of how to run a farm. They brought a whole emigrant carload of things, furniture and farm machinery. The farm machinery was all second-hand, a moldboard plow, useless for turning sod, and a springtooth harrow, which was never used on sod, and a corn planter of a kind used only on well-turned soil, and a two-wheeled cart. He also brought a lawn mower, which was very funny. He had a team of big bony work horses, both of them spavined; the story went that he had bought them as discards from the Chicago Street Cleaning Department. He had a .45-70 rifle, a relic of the Spanish-American war which shot a cartridge as big as a man's finger. That, folks said, was to shoot buffalo. Or maybe Indians.

And the questions Mr. Bromley asked were just as funny as the things he brought. "Which way does the wind blow out here?" And "How deep do you dig a well?" And, "How do you get the dirt to stick to the side of a house so you can plant grass in it and grow a sod house?"

It seemed that every time we went to Gary we heard a new Bromley story. Then, in mid-April, John Kraus arrived and we forgot about the Bromleys.

The first time we saw John Kraus was when he drove down the slope back of the house, from the north, with a buggy and a livery team. He stopped in front of the house and shouted. Mother went to the door. He said, "I want to see your man."

Father and I were out at the barn. Mother sent him out there. He drove into the barnyard and sat in the buggy all the time he talked. He was a big, red-faced, light-haired man and he spoke with a heavy German accent. He was from Cincinnati he said, and he was going to make a fine farm out here. Not just a little homestead—and he looked around at our place with a superior smile—but a big, fine farm.

Father said, "Yes?"

John Kraus was filing on the land just north of us, he said. High flat land. Up where he could see. He liked to see a long way.

Father made no comment. The horses were restless and John Kraus jerked angrily at the reins, hauled them back on their haunches, and cursed them. He turned to Father again. He wanted to know where our north line was.

Father told him, approximately. John Kraus asked if we'd had it surveyed. Father said no, but he knew where the corners were. John Kraus said we'd better have it surveyed so we didn't fence any of his land. Father suggested that Kraus have his own land surveyed.

John Kraus grunted. He asked about Gerity's sheep. Father said they weren't much of a problem. John Kraus said they'd better stay off his land or he'd eat mutton. He asked about range cattle. Father said he'd have to fence the cattle out.

John Kraus laughed. "I fence when I please," he said. He winked. "I like beef, too."

The horses were restless again. John Kraus jerked the reins, slashed at them with the buggy whip. The horses reared, jerked around, and threatened to upset the buggy. John Kraus slashed again with the whip, hauled the horses up snorting and quivering. "I got to go," he said. "This damn team is no good. When

121

I buy horses I'll buy horses that stand when I tell them stand."
He loosened the reins, brought down the whip, and careened
out of the yard and down the draw. The horses were still running when he rounded the shoulder of the hill and headed
toward town.

When he had gone, Mother came out and asked, "Who was
that?"

"Our new neighbor," Father said. "He's filing on the land
just north of us."

"I don't like him," Mother said.

"You don't have to like him. I doubt that we'll see much of
him." Father smiled. "He's a big farmer, he says, from Cincinnati."

"I don't like him," Mother repeated. "What's his name?"

"Kraus. John Kraus. He's a German."

Mother bristled. "What's being German got to do with it?"

"Nothing," Father said.

Mother's lips tightened. "Pa's German," she said firmly.
"And Pa's not like that." As one of Father's sisters used to
say, much to her annoyance, Mother had her Dutch up.

Grandpa Clinaburg was, as Mother said, a German, but I
never knew a gentler or more soft-spoken man. His parents
came from Germany in the 1850's and settled near relatives in
Missouri. Both parents died in a cholera epidemic when
Grandpa was a small boy, and his aunt, Sarah Buerstetta, for
whom Mother was named, took him to raise. When he grew
up he went to Nebraska and married Clara Atkisson, who was
Mother's mother.

Father never again spoke of John Kraus as a German. But
we saw little of Kraus. He built a small white house at the
north side of his land, almost a mile from us, then put up a
barn and began plowing and planting. We saw him only now
and then, usually at Gary, where he was stiff-necked and
truculent with easy-going Tom McDowell in the store.

Anyway, we were busy with our own problems. Our fuel,
even including the soggy sheep chips, barely lasted through the

winter. As soon as the warm days came we had to gather cow chips for cooking fuel. It took lots of chips, because we were eating beans almost every day and beans took a long time to cook. And we had to build a new chicken house. The first one was too small, and the sod walls we had laid up began to crumble. The cows found the corners of the chicken house a fine place to scratch their backs, and finally they caved in one whole corner. And we had to think about plowing and planting that year's sod corn.

We had to find a new place to get the sod for the chicken house because the place we had taken it last year had begun to gully out with the fall rains and had washed with the spring melt. It was a gully and a mud hole fifteen feet wide and four feet deep. So we went up the draw and plowed the new sod, and when we built the new chicken house we set posts at the corners to protect it from the itchy cows.

For the cornfield Father wanted to plow new sod alongside the old patch, which now was in rye. Of course we would have to fence it, and Father spent hours figuring out just how big we could make it. He had just so much money to spend for fence posts and wire. He got it all figured out, right down to the staples to fasten the wire, and we laid out the field all ready to start plowing.

Then came that Sunday afternoon.

It was one of those fine spring days, shirt-sleeve weather, and we ate dinner with the door and all the windows open. After we'd eaten we all walked up to look at the rye and see where we were going to plant the sod corn, and I found a handful of little yellow violets for Mother. Then she said, "It's such a nice day, and a Sunday, why don't we hitch up the team and go for a ride?"

Father said, "Fine! Son, you go get the horses."

I asked if I could ride Dick, and Father laughed and said, "I'll bet you can't catch him."

"If I catch him," I said, "can I ride him in?"

"Go ahead," Father said.

The horses were out grazing on the flat half a mile south of the house. I took the riding bridle and went after them. They were full of life and they never were easy to catch out in the open, but I took along an ear of corn. Usually old Dick would come to me if I lured him with corn. But that day both Dick and Shorty were frisky. I chased them all over the flat before Dick gave up, came to get the corn, and let me bridle him.

I climbed on, triumphant. But Shorty was still fractious. I had to chase him up and down for half an hour before he headed for the house. We started down the slope toward the barn, and Dick took it into his head to race. He caught the bit in his teeth and took out after Shorty. I couldn't stop him. Shorty wasn't going to be caught. He went down the slope on a dead run. Dick not fifty feet behind him.

I was whooping and hollering like an Indian, having a fine time. Then I saw that Shorty was heading for the mud hole, the gully where we took the sod last year. And Dick was going to follow him. I could no more stop Dick or veer him off than I could have stopped or turned a locomotive.

Shorty bunched himself and cleared the gully in a beautiful jump. Only a moment later I felt Dick gather himself and jump. We were in the air. I could look down and see the dark mud, the water still rippled from a clod Shorty's hoofs had flipped into it. I felt Dick's feet strike the far bank. Dick had cleared the gully too! Then the bank crumbled, loosened by Shorty before Dick hit it. Dick's head went down. His rump struck me in the back. I was thrown over his head. But Dick somersaulted and rolled, and I was under him.

I heard Father shouting. I saw Dick scramble to his feet and trot toward the barn, the reins dragging. Father shouted again, running toward me. I cried, "I'm all right!" and got to my feet and started to run toward him. A white-hot pain shot up my left leg. I felt myself falling. That's the last I knew.

I came to on my bed in the house. Mother was wiping my face with a cold wet cloth. Father was holding my left leg. The whole left side of my body throbbed with aching pain. I opened my eyes. Mother exclaimed, "Will! He's coming to!" I tried to sit up. Mother pressed me back. Father said, "It's all right, son, stay where you are." Father had taken off my shoe and stocking. He was probing my ankle with his fingers. I cried at the pain. He probed at my knee. There was no pain in the knee. "It's the ankle," he said.

"Broken?" Mother asked.

"I don't know. It's swelling like a balloon."

Mother put a cold compress on the ankle. I squirmed and tried to sit up and was so dizzy I almost vomited.

Mother said, "You'd better go put the horses away, Will. Now that they're in, don't let them out again."

"I'll hitch up," Father said. "We'd better get him to the doctor."

Mother shook her head. "It's almost four o'clock. And a Sunday. We'll wait till morning." Mother got another cold compress.

I must have been in mild shock. I slept fitfully the rest of the afternoon. But I got little sleep that night. Nor did Mother.

We left home before dawn. Even the jolting of the wagon was painful. The ankle was swollen as big as Father's two fists. It seemed we would never get to town. But we did, we were in Brush just before ten o'clock.

There were two doctors in Brush. One was a young man who had an office over the drug store. The other was an older man who had practiced there for years, had taken out appendixes on ranch house kitchen tables, and had probably taken half his pay in quarters of beef and tons of hay. The older doctor had the only hospital in town, a few rooms on the first floor of his house equipped with hospital beds and tended by a trained nurse and the doctor's wife, who had been a nurse before he married her.

We couldn't see that I needed a hospital, so we went to the young doctor over the drug store. Father carried me up the stairs and the young doctor gave me an injection which eased the pain, then examined the ankle. He announced that it was broken in two places. He splinted and bandaged it. When I could sit up on the table he said, "You're lucky, young fellow, to get off so easy. You'll be all right in a few weeks. Young bones knit quickly." He poured a dozen pills into a white envelope and told Mother, "Give him one of these if the pain gets too bad. And bring him back a week from today."

"Can I walk?" I asked.

"On crutches, yes. But you won't want to walk much for a few days."

Father paid him and carried me downstairs. On the street he asked Mother, "How about a cup of coffee before we start home?"

Mother said no, and we drove out of town, past all the houses, and Mother got out bread-and-butter sandwiches and we breakfasted on them, washed down with water from a windmill and stock tank in a roadside pasture.

Father made crutches for me from strips sawed out of a slat taken from the corn bin in the barn, plain sticks with crosspieces at the top. With them I could hobble around the house and the yard.

When we went back the next week to have the bandages changed, Father left Mother and me at the doctor's office and went to see Ed, the man who ran the newspaper. He met us at the wagon. Mother asked, "Well, how did you make out?"

Father shook his head. "It's the slack time. Maybe later, when the farm sales start. Did the doctor say he would wait for his money?"

"I paid him," Mother said, "from the butter money."

Father frowned. He started right for home, but Mother said, "Go on over to the lumber yard and get the posts and wire you need to fence the corn."

Father said, "You can't live on beans forever."

Mother smiled. "We've got corn bread and mush, too. Go get the posts and wire."

Father drove over to the lumber yard.

9

I wasn't much help for the next month. I spent most of my time hobbling around the nearby slopes, but as soon as I learned to use the crutches I got around well enough. Instead of looking at the far ridges, though, and trying to see the mountains, I had to take my time and look at things right under my feet.

Down the draw a little way I found two meadow lark nests and watched them every day to see when the eggs hatched. When the babies were out of the shells I tried to feed them. The old birds didn't want my help, and I couldn't seem to find the kind of bugs the fledglings ate, so I let the parents feed them. I tried to weave baskets out of grass stems, patterning them on the meadow lark nests. But I wasn't skillful at all, not nearly as good as the birds were, though I couldn't see why a bird's beak should be better at that job than my ten fingers.

In the evenings I often went up the draw to a place where the giant evening primroses opened big white and pink and lavender flowers at sundown. The flowers were broad as my hand and very fragrant. Just at dusk the big hawk moths came to hover over them and feed, and I thought they were hummingbirds until I trapped one under my hat. Then I saw the moth wings, instead of feathers, and the strange coiled tongue under its snout which the moth could thrust out like a long beak and use to suck the nectar from the primroses.

On hot afternoons I watched the big red ants that lived in

conical mounds a foot and a half high. They cleaned off all the grass in a big circle around the mound, and often there were ant wars going on there, as though they were broad, flat battlefields. The wars were usually between the red ants who lived in the mound and big black ones from somewhere else. There were furious battles, the ants biting off each other's feelers, and even legs, and then running around in circles, as if blinded. If a big black ant got up near one of the entrances to the mound, a whole swarm of red ones would attack him at once; and sometimes they rolled down the mound, a ball of red ones with the black one in the middle.

If there was no war going on, once in a while I poked a hole in the mound just to see them swarm out and go to work repairing the damage. But when I did that I had to get away fast because some of them always came to attack me, and their bite was like fire. If there wasn't a war and if I didn't poke a hole in the mound, I could lie and watch them and they would crawl over my hand, just exploring, and not bite at all. Then I could watch how they worked, three or four of them together moving a big pebble or hauling in a dead grasshopper and taking it inside the nest.

And once in a while I found a few Indian beads on the mounds, small blue or red beads that they must have brought up from somewhere down below with the fine gravel they used to pave their mounds.

I couldn't help plant the corn, but I could sort the best ears in the corn bin and shell them by hand for seed. Mother helped with the planting. She said she got tired being cooped up in the house all day and this was a chance for her to get out. Before they finished, she and Father planted a long row of pinto beans in the cornfield.

And as soon as the corn was all in, Father did a day's plowing for a new homesteader over east of Jake Farley's to pay for having Bessie bred to the new man's bull. I wanted to go along, but Mother said that, crippled as I was, I'd better stay at home. I saw Father give her a look, as though he thought that wasn't much of a reason, but she shook her head and that was that. I hadn't been allowed to go along last fall, either, when he took Daisy to a bull near Gary and paid five dollars for it.

Louie came back to the upper camp with a new flock of ewes and lambs, and when he saw Fritz he said he'd grown into a very fine dog. He said he wished he'd kept Fritz, because the pup he kept wasn't worth his keep. "Favored his father too much," Louie said. "That old collie ain't worth powder and lead to blow him up. Like some men you meet, regular dudes for looks but don't know enough to come in out of the rain."

Then, when the corn began to come up, Father and I built the new fence around the field. I couldn't dig postholes, but I could tamp the posts in after the holes were dug. We were stringing barbed wire the afternoon that Jack Clothier rode over with a new bundle of magazines for me. He saw my crutches and asked what happened, and he said, "And they didn't let you go to the hospital?"

I said I didn't want to go to a hospital.

"Hospitals," he said, "are wonderful places. A couple of years ago a locoed bronc shied at a tumbleweed and went over a cut-bank with me. Broke my leg in three places, and I had the time of my life in the hospital. Had the nicest nurse!"

"Which hospital?" Father asked with a smile.

"The one at Fort Morgan." The cowboy grinned. "But she's gone now. She's up in Cheyenne."

"What's a locoed bronc?" I asked.

"Loco," he told me, "is a Mexican word meaning crazy. Loco's a weed with a flower kind of like a sweet pea. But it's poison. If it doesn't kill a horse, it makes him crazy. But it's not as bad as death camas."

"What's death camas?"

"That's a weed too. It looks a little like a wild onion, but it's got a greenish-white flower. It's especially bad in a dry year because it stays green after the grass quits. If you see any, dig it up. It's bad, bad stuff. . . . I see you've got a new neighbor."

He and Father discussed John Kraus, and the cowboy said, "Well, I guess a man looking for trouble can always find it. . . .

"You," he said to me, "had better learn how to get off a horse. . . . I got to be going. So long."

After that I looked for death camas as well as arrowheads, but I didn't find any. All I found were sand lilies and wild onions, and there was no mistaking either of them.

Fritz was always with me while I was cricketing around on my crutches. He chased ground squirrels and tried to catch meadow larks and now and then flushed a jack rabbit. Usually he knew enough not to try to catch a jack, but one afternoon he flushed the biggest, fattest jack I'd ever seen and it didn't want to run. Fritz knew it. He took after it.

Instead of running straightaway, as usual, this jack just dodged around the hillside. Several times Fritz almost caught it and I was hoping he would. Finally the jack circled down the slope and came right toward me. Fritz closed in and was just about to make his grab, but the jack stopped short and Fritz went right over it. Then it came straight for me. That time Fritz caught it, not fifteen feet from me. He hardly seemed to touch it. He snapped once and it keeled over and lay there gasping, its eyes closed.

I ran to it. Fritz wasn't worrying it, the way he did any rabbit I shot when he was along. He just nosed it and stood there, panting. The rabbit twitched and drew up its legs and gasped, and suddenly it had babies. Four baby rabbits were born, right there while I watched. They popped out, one after another, wet little things like mice and not much bigger. Then the old mother went limp and dead. Fritz must have flushed her just as she was settling down to give birth.

I knelt and picked up one of the babies. It squirmed in my

hand. Its wet little ears were pink, with black tips. It nosed my hand for a place to suck.

Fritz sniffed the others and began to lick them. Two of them were dead. I picked up the other live one and the two of them weren't one good handful. They were even smaller than new-born kittens. But their eyes were open. The eyes were a filmy gray at first, then they turned clear and dark.

As they began to dry off in the sun they lifted their ears a little bit and their small black noses wriggled and their ribs throbbed with quick heartbeats.

I made a grass nest in my hat and took them home. Mother said they wouldn't live, but she found a cardboard box and I made a nest for them in it. I offered them a saucer of milk, but they couldn't drink, so I dipped my little finger in the milk and they licked it off and tried to suck. I fed them that way and they lived three days. Father said that if we'd had an old cat with kittens she might have nursed the baby rabbits and kept them alive. He said he had a baby gray squirrel once that nursed at a cat and grew up to a big, tame squirrel.

"And a big nuisance, I'll bet," Mother said.

"It probably was," Father said, "but I didn't know it."

Mother said, "Wild things aren't supposed to be pets. They're better off wild."

"It takes a while to learn that," Father said. And he helped me bury my baby rabbits.

They might have had a hard time even if they'd been raised by their mother, because it was very dry. We hadn't a drop of rain all through May. The sod corn came up, and so did the beans, with the moisture that had been turned under with the sod. But the bluestem was slow and the water hole in the gully shrank to a mud hole with pink smartweed coming up around the edges. Father kept watching the grass, and I knew he was worried. But we weren't broke. Mother was still making butter, and she was selling it at the store instead of trading it.

When we went to see the doctor the third time he said my

ankle was almost healed. We could take off the bandages, he said, in another week. Then I could walk on it. Mother opened the purse where she kept the butter money and asked what we owed him, and the doctor looked at her and at me and said, "Nothing. Take the money and buy the boy a pair of shoes."

It seemed a ridiculous thing to say. I felt as bad as Mother looked, except that I wasn't mad and she was. I didn't need shoes. Louie had half-soled mine and sewed up the rips. Maybe Louie wasn't a very good cobbler, and maybe we didn't have any blacking to put over the yellow thread he used to sew them up, but they certainly were good enough shoes.

We got down on the street and I said I wasn't going to have any new shoes, and I didn't care what the doctor said. New shoes always pinched. We went to the wagon and Father was there, and when he asked what the doctor said, Mother said, "He made me feel like two cents!" She told him about the shoes. I said I wasn't going to have new shoes, and I didn't care what anybody said. Father laughed, a funny kind of laugh, and Mother said I would have new shoes next fall or she'd know the reason, and I knew I'd won. We went over to the store and spent the money the doctor wouldn't take for a sack of flour and a sack of salt and a pound of coffee and a piece of salt pork. And Father told the clerk to put in a nickel's worth of cheese and some crackers and a can of mustard sardines. We had lunch in the sand hills, and even Mother began to get over her mad at the doctor.

The last day I was on crutches Fritz and I were up where the old Indian point-maker had left the flint chips. I was sitting there in the sun, going through the chips for the hundredth time looking for points, when Fritz began to bark up the hillside. I'd never heard him bark like that before, excited and angry at the same time. After a minute I got up and started toward him. It sounded as though something was wrong.

I got halfway up the slope, hurrying and skipping on the

crutches, before I heard the buzz. That mad bumblebee buzz. I knew that sound. I shouted, "Fritz! Come back here, Fritz." But instead of coming he got more excited.

I almost ran. I had to get to him, had to get him away from there, or he was going to be bitten. He was dancing around, leaping in, jumping back. And I saw the snake striking at him. He was going to be bitten by that rattler, and he would bloat up like a sheep and turn black and die. "Fritz!" I ordered frantically. "Come here to me!"

He barked still louder and leaped in again. The snake struck and Fritz leaped back. The more I shouted, the more excited Fritz became.

I got within twenty feet of them, shouting, ordering, pleading. Fritz leaped in again, the snake struck, Fritz jerked his head aside and uttered a little yelp of pain. Then he was a fury, in, out, dodging, feinting, yelping, snapping. He leaped in, caught the snake for an instant, twisted his head and flung the snake spinning into the air. As it struck the ground he was at it again, snapping, flinging it into the air. One more flip and it was all over. Fritz snapped his teeth. The rattler's back was broken. It couldn't coil. It writhed, jaws snapping.

I pounded at it with a crutch, beat the head into a pulp. Then Father was there. He had heard the uproar and come running with the spade. He chopped off the head and buried it.

Fritz was panting, shaking his head as though he had been bee-stung, licking his lower lip. There was a tiny spot of blood on the left side of his lip. Father examined it and shook his head. "Too bad," he said, "too bad."

"Is he—going to die?" I asked.

Father looked at me, not wanting to say it. "I don't know," he said. "Maybe he will. But he seems to have got only one fang." Then he said, "Don't take it too hard, son. You've had a lot of fun with him." He put his arm around me, but that wasn't what I wanted and he knew it.

We went back to the house. I forgot to use the crutches

most of the way and the ankle didn't pain enough to matter. Fritz's lip was beginning to swell. When we got to the barn he went down to the mud hole and drank, and I called him and we went to the house.

When we told Mother what had happened she said, "I'll heat some milk, with some grease in it."

Father said, "This is a different kind of poison."

"It may help anyway," Mother said. "Try it."

Fritz drank a little of the milk and grease and retched, but he couldn't bring anything up. The poison was in his blood, not his stomach. His whole head had begun to swell. His left eye was swollen almost shut. He tried to lick my hand when I patted him, but his tongue was swollen too. He lay in the shade and I saw the quick beating of his heart against his ribs. He was restless. He went out past the barn and down to the mud hole again. He lay down in the mud and wallowed a hole deep enough so the mucky water almost covered him.

He stayed in the mud all afternoon. By dark his head was swollen as big as a milk pail. Before I went to bed I wanted to take a lantern and go look at him, but Father said, "Not tonight, son. We'll take care of him in the morning." I knew he was trying to say, without saying it, that tomorrow we would bury Fritz.

I was up at dawn and thought I was dressing quietly. But Father pushed the curtain aside and said, "Wait for me, son." So he dressed too and we went together to look.

Fritz was still in the mud hole. His head didn't look quite so badly swollen. I called to him and he opened his good eye and lifted his head just enough to show he was still alive.

That afternoon he crawled out of the mud hole and went to the tank at the pump for a drink of clean water. Then he went back and lay in the mud again. And the second morning he came out of the mud hole when I called him. He shook himself and drank more clean water and Father said, "Maybe he's going to pull through."

He was in and out of the mud all that day, and that evening he drank a quart of fresh milk. By the next day his head was almost back to normal. He lay around, stiff and uncertain on his legs for a week, eating nothing but drinking lots of milk. Then he was his old self. The only thing he had to show for his bite was a little hard knot in his lip, half the size of a pea. He killed dozens of rattlers, over the years, and I don't know whether he ever was bitten again. If so, he had an immunity, because he never was sick again after a snake fight.

By the time Fritz was well it was time to start cutting the blue-stem hay. Because of the drought it was short, and we'd waited and waited for it to shoot up; but it began to head when it wasn't much above my knees and if we didn't cut it then it would be woody and no good for hay. We had a stack and a half left from last year, but we had to put up more. Next winter we would have Bessie's calf, which would be a short yearling, and two more calves, besides the cows and horses, and next winter might be a hard one. Of course, we would have the rye too, if it didn't fire too bad. It was already beginning to fire at the roots and head out. And we probably would have some corn fodder too, if the drought wasn't too bad. But we needed hay.

So we cut the two draws we'd cut the year before; but the two of them made only two small stacks. And it was short hay, hard to stack. Father and I got on the horses and went looking for more draws to cut. But the sheep had cleaned out all the good hay places near home. We kept looking, and at last, down in the sand hills beyond the big sheep camp, we found plenty of sand grass. It was a thin stand, but tall. Father said it would mean lots of mowing and raking, but he thought it would be worth the work. We had another week before we had to cut the rye, so we went down in the sand hills and mowed and raked for two days.

We went down to bring home our hay on one of those hot, early June days. It seemed twice as hot in the sand hills. I drove the wagon while Father pitched the hay on, and I loaded it. We had about a third of a load and were about half-way down a long, thin windrow when the team began to act nervous. Shorty especially wanted to shy off from the windrow. Then I heard the mad-bumblebee buzz. The team jumped and Father swung his pitchfork. He killed a rattler about four feet long.

I quieted the horses and we started on down the windrow. Dick began acting up, but I snubbed the lines and took my pitchfork and began to put the hay where it belonged on the load. Father gathered another forkful and tossed it up. Just as the hay left his fork he yelled, "Look out!"

I saw the snake wriggling in midair. Instinctively I thrust out my fork. It hit the fork between the tines, slithered off and fell to the ground. I saw Father hit it one blow with his fork, then I had to jump for the lines. The horses were really cutting up. They lunged and almost threw me off the wagon. When I looked again, Father had killed the snake and was standing there, gray as sheep's wool. He got out his blue bandanna and wiped his face. Then he picked up another forkful of hay and tossed it to one side, watching it. He went up the windrow fifteen feet or so, tossing the hay aside. Then he found another rattler. He killed it and climbed into the wagon and began pitching the hay off. He didn't find any snakes till the last forkful. He killed that one, right there in the wagon, and tossed it out and took the lines from me.

"What are we going to do?" I asked.

"Go home." He was still gray as wool. "The rattlers have crawled into those windrows for shade, and there are dozens of them in these sand hills. I wouldn't handle that hay for anything in the world. Or let you handle it."

We let all that sand grass hay lie right where it was. Two days later we cut the rye. It was short and the heads weren't very big, but the kernels were fat and hard. It was so ripe it shattered a little, but we hauled it down to the stack yard.

Mother let us have a bed sheet and we tossed a few forkfuls of rye onto it and flailed it out with a broomstick. When we had beaten the grain out we tossed the straw aside and winnowed the grain by pouring it from one pail to another and letting the breeze blow the dust and chaff away. It was hot, dusty work and the chaff and broken beards got inside your shirt and itched like mad. We flailed out about six bushels and stowed it away in gunny sacks, and Father said, "We'll thresh the rest next fall, when it's not so hot. Confound those beards, anyway!"

Mother said we wouldn't have to buy any flour next winter if the coffee grinder held out, because we all liked rye bread. Father said he had a better idea than that. When we flailed the rest of it out he would haul it to Brush and have it ground on shares at the mill.

But he never got to that. The next Saturday when we went to Gary for the mail he got a letter and read it and exclaimed, "Sarah!" He handed it to her and she glanced at it and hurried out to the wagon. We followed her and when we got to the wagon and Mother was crying I thought somebody was dead back in Nebraska. Then Mother exclaimed, "Oh, Will!" and began to laugh and cry at the same time.

Father said, "I knew something like this would come along." He tried to roll a cigarette but his fingers were trembling so much he spilled all the tobacco out of the paper.

Mother said, "You're going to take it, aren't you?"

Father said, "Of course I am!"

"Hadn't you better send Ed a post card?"

"It wouldn't get there till Monday. We'll drive in Monday morning and I'll tell him then." Father untied the team and we started home, and finally I found out what it was all about. The editor in Brush had written that there was a job up in the mountains for Father if he wanted it. A bank had taken over a weekly newspaper and wanted someone to run until they found a buyer. It might be a job for only a few months, but it was a job. And the bank would pay Father's transportation if he would come at once.

"I'll go Monday," Father said, "and you two can come later."

"We aren't going," Mother said.

"Why, of course you are!"

Mother shook her head. "Who would look after the cows? And the horses, and the chickens?"

Father was silent for a long minute. "We could sell the stock," he said.

"Sell out and quit?" Mother asked.

Father didn't answer. I thought: We can't sell old Dick and Shorty! We can't move to some closed-in town where you can't see anything or do anything! Where there aren't any jack rabbits, or prairie dogs, or meadow larks, or anything!

And I cried, "No!"

Both of them looked at me. Mother smiled and Father laughed. Then Mother said, "We're not going. We'll stay here and take care of things. There's not much to do this summer. . . . Oh, Will, it couldn't have come at a better time!"

And Father said, "I'll be back before the snow comes."

I felt a big relief. We weren't going. Father was going, but he would be back this fall. He was saying, "All we need is a little cash. Just enough to get us over the hump this summer. Get some food in the house for next winter, and some coal. And maybe even buy another cow or two. That's all we need. And this is the chance to get it."

That night Mother washed his shirts and sewed his buttons, and on Monday morning we took him to Brush and he got on the train to Denver and the mountains.

10

At first I couldn't quite realize that Father was gone. Every time I turned around I expected to find him there.

I would get up early, the way I always did, and dress very quietly and go outdoors and look at the morning. After I'd swapped a whistle or two with a meadow lark and washed my face down at the pump I would go to the barn and start the chores. I would put corn in the feed boxes and talk to the horses and speculate on how soon Daisy was going to have her calf. Then, without knowing it, I would wait for Father to come and brush Bessie and start milking. Just for a moment or two, I'd wait. Then I'd catch myself and get the brush from the box with the curry comb and go to work. I would put the brush away and get the pail and stool and press my head into Bessie's flank, the way Father did, and talk the way he did: "So, Bessie, so. Keep that foot out of the pail. And give me the milk. Let it down, Bessie."

Mother was always up and had breakfast ready by the time the milking was done, but I would always be surprised to see only two places set at the table. She would pour the coffee and put the pancakes on my plate and say, "Well, I wonder how your father is doing this morning."

After breakfast I would pump water for the stock and bring in a fresh pail for the kitchen. Then I would start to clean out the barn, listening for Father to say, "If we put down fresh bedding now we won't have to do it later." And pretty soon I would say it myself and go ahead and put down the bedding.

By then Mother would have fed the chickens and started her housework. I would wait there in the barnyard, expecting Father to say what had to be done that day, hoe the corn or the beans, tighten a loose wire or fix a gate at the stack yard, grease the wagon, mend a broken halter. Then I'd know I had to decide, and I'd take the hoe and tell Mother I was going to hill up the beans. And I would go up to the field and start on the beans, which weren't doing very well with only a couple of light showers since April.

I would hoe a while, then rest, thinking maybe I could go over to the big prairie dog town that afternoon. I'd ask Father pretty soon, I'd think. Then I would remember and know I shouldn't go before I finished the beans. My shoulders would begin to ache, but I would keep at it, knowing Mother would let me go if I asked her but also knowing I should finish the job I'd started.

Mother would call me to dinner, and again I'd be surprised at only two places at the table. And after dinner I'd go back to the beans, or the corn, or whatever it was. And if I got through by midafternoon I'd know I shouldn't go wandering then because it would soon be chore time and I should go get the cows. So I would tighten the slack wire at the stack yard and rivet a broken harness strap and then got get the cows and start the evening chores.

After supper Mother would be mending or darning or writing a letter to Father and I would start to read a story in *Adventure* or *Bluebook* and fall asleep over it. And waken with a start, thinking I heard Father and Mother talking. Mother would say, "You'd better go to bed son, instead of sleeping in your chair," and I would look around the room for Father and know he wasn't there and kiss Mother good night. And the next morning I wouldn't be quite as surprised when Father didn't come to the barn.

Then Father's first letter came and I accepted the fact, in-

side, that he wasn't there. He said he'd had a good trip, that
a man from the bank met him and put him up at the hotel
and that he'd found a room with nice folks and was doing
all right. The shop, he said, wasn't much of a place. A few
shirttailfuls of type, an old Gordon job press, and a rickety
flatbed that he had to overhaul before he could get out the
paper. But there was plenty of job work and enough legal
notices to make the paper pay. He hoped everything would
be all right with us. And he enclosed a money order. Mother
cashed the money order and put the bills away in her purse.
There wasn't anything we needed to buy. She had enough
butter to swap for coffee and baking powder and a chunk of
salt pork.

After that we had a letter every week, with a money order
which Mother cashed and stowed away. As she said, money's
kind of like water—you don't miss it till the well runs dry.
And we were eating every day. Not much variety, maybe, but
as she said, it was enough to satisfy. If you ate too much you
got fatty degeneration of the heart. We had a few eggs now
and then, and plenty of cornmeal mush. And sometimes, for a
treat, she parched corn for me to carry in my pocket and
munch on. "A growing boy," she said, "needs something to
munch on between meals."

I had a pocketful of parched corn the afternoon she said
I'd hoed corn long enough and deserved a trip over to the big
dog town. "Just watch out for snakes," she said, "and get
home in time to bring in the cows."

The big prairie dog town was almost two miles south of the
house. It was on a high flat, and there were hundreds of burrows, each one like a fat doughnut of earth. The town was the
busiest place you could imagine, with hundreds of prairie dogs,
dozens of burrowing owls, an occasional rattlesnake, and now
and then a badger or two, or a coyote, or a jack rabbit.

Fritz and I walked over there, taking our time, stopping to
watch an ant hill and catching grasshoppers and chasing a

big bull snake that was out looking for ground squirrels. There wasn't any hurry, and the walk over there was almost half the fun, especially when there were a few big, high clouds. There were two clouds this day, and they were spaced just right so I could run in their shadows a way and imagine it was cool. Then they passed the sun and I stood and watched the big blue shadows go sliding across the flats.

We got to the dog town and Fritz went over to one side and tried to dig out one burrow. I lay down on my belly and munched parched corn and watched the prairie dogs. The young ones, which had been born in early May, were out playing, squealing and chasing like real puppies. Burrowing owls were bobbing about, screeching at each other, now and then fighting with a terrific fuss and flying of feathers. Old prairie dogs were squabbling over the grass. Now and then a hawk would fly over, and a dog would give the alarm cry and everybody would race to the burrows and dive in, only to come peeping up a minute later, yip that the coast was clear, and come spilling out again.

It was a wonderful afternoon, even though I didn't see a badger or a coyote. And we put up three jacks on the way home and I found a fine lance point, like an arrowhead but as long as my hand. I cut west when I got near the draw and took the cows home and started the chores, thinking how lucky I was that we hadn't decided to sell out and move to town. Even to a town up in the mountains. And the next day I went at the corn again and gave it a real hoeing.

The hoeing probably helped keep the corn going. It was so dry, though, that the corn was looking pretty puny. The beans were doing some better, because they had some shade from the corn. Almost every day a few clouds came over, big puffy cumulus, but they stayed high and left nothing but their shadow as they passed. No question about it, we were having a dry summer.

Louie came over one evening to talk about the drought.

"Sure getting bad," he said as he sat on the step, hat in hand. "Don't know how much longer the grass will last if we don't get rain. Sheep's about picked the school section clean."

"Don't expect to bring them over on our land," Mother warned.

"Oh, I won't," Louie said. He thought for a while, then said, "Commissary man was up yesterday and he says all the herders is having trouble. Dutch George, one of the herders, got in a row over north. Let his flock get on Lazy Four range and the cowmen stampeded his flock and tipped his wagon over."

"Why did they do that?" I asked.

Louie shrugged. "They think they own the grass."

"It's their range, isn't it?"

Louie shrugged again. "Nobody owns the grass. Grass just grows." He sighed and stood up to leave. He thrust his hand into his pocket and drew out something and handed it to me. It was a bird point, a tiny arrowhead, pure white and not over an inch long. I exclaimed and Louie grinned. "Found it to-day. You got one like it?" I hadn't. "Keep it," he said. "It's a nice one."

The next afternoon Jake Farley came over. He wanted to know what we heard from Father, and he talked about the drought and the corn, and finally, after his usual preamble, he came to the point of his visit. "Will," he said to Mother, "said last year that maybe the boy could work out this year."

"What do you mean?" Mother asked.

"Well," Jake said, "there's an easy job for him if you'll let him take it. Pays fifty cents a day. Just leading a horse, hoisting dirt out of a well. I'm digging the well, so I'd kind of look after him."

"You're digging a well?" Mother said. "Why? You've got a well."

"I'm digging one for John Kraus."

"John Kraus, over north of us?"

"That's right. We need a boy to lead the horse."

"I don't like that man."

"Well, ma'am, it take all kinds to make a world, I say. His money's as good as anybody else's at the store. I could stop past mornings and bring him home nights."

Mother hesitated.

"Please!" I begged. "Please! I'll do the chores before I go and when I get home. Fifty cents a day!"

She still hesitated. "I don't know whether your father would like it." Then to Jake she said, "One thing I'll say for you, you don't use bad language. At least I never heard you to."

Jake rubbed his chin, embarrassed. "No'm, I don't. I tried to learn to cuss when I was younger, but the words never came out right, somehow. I never could get them straight. Folks laughed so much I give it up and let them cuss that could. . . . Shall I stop by in the morning for him, about seven o'clock?"

Mother still hesitated, but at last she said, "I guess he can try it a day or so. Then we'll see."

I did the best job on the chores that evening I had ever done, and I was up before the sun the next morning. I got everything done, even an extra pail of water for Mother and an extra pail of cow chips, before breakfast. Then I washed up and slicked my hair and put on a clean shirt and was almost too excited to eat. Mother said, "Now you do what you're told to do, over there. Any job worth doing is worth doing well. You can't go off watching birds or prairie dogs or poking in an ant hill. Remember that. And you needn't tell John Kraus I don't like him. I expect he knows that already. You just do your work and behave yourself."

Then Jake arrived and I got in the wagon with him and was off to my first job, my first job with pay.

A big, rough-haired dog roared at us as soon as we drove into John Kraus' yard. He was a mean-looking dog, so thin every rib showed. One ear was cropped, the other long, and one eye drooped half shut and had a scar over it. Jake drove on up to the house and shouted, "Call off your dog if you want us to go to work." To me he said, "Don't trust that dog any farther than you can throw him by the tail."

John Kraus came to the door and yelled, "Shut up, you dog!" The dog, hackles bristling, skulked around the wagon. John Kraus yelled, "Come here! Come here, I say!" and came out with a club in his hand. The dog's tail dropped between his legs and he crawled in the dust. As John Kraus walked toward him, brandishing the club, the dog sprang up and ran into a hole beneath the house. John Kraus grinned. "He knows who's boss. . . . Well, you bring the boy. Now we get some work done."

We unhitched Jake's team and put them in the barn. John Kraus went with us, carrying the club like a walking stick. Two scrawny cats scurried away as we went inside and a big black horse in one of the stalls snorted and jerked back on its halter rope, eyes rolling. Jake stalled his team and John Kraus harnessed the big black. It lunged once and there was a thump as he hit it with the club, and at another lunge he kicked it in the belly.

Jake said, "Let me harness that horse," but John Kraus paid no attention. He jerked the belly band tight, buckled the hames, and started to bridle it. Jake said, "You don't need a bridle. A halter's enough." John Kaus fought the bit into the horse's mouth, jerked the throat latch so tight it cut off half the horse's wind, and buckled it. "He don't like the bridle," he said, "so I show him. I teach him." He led the horse outside, wheezing and gulping.

While John Kraus went for a rope Jake loosened the throat latch and the horse breathed freely. I tried to pat its nose, but it threw up its head in fear and jerked back. Jake worked his hand up the horse's neck and said, "Easy, boy, easy." It quivered and snorted, tense, frightened.

Jake had the well already started, a hole three feet across

and six fet deep. Across the top was a rack of two-inch tim-
bers from which a big pulley hung. John Kraus fed the rope
through the pulley, fastened one end to a half barrel with a
sling, and hitched the other end to a singletree. Jake hitched
the black horse to the singletree, then took a spade and
dropped into the hole and began to dig.

When Jake had loosened a layer of dirt John Kraus eased
the half barrel to him, Jake loaded it, and I led the horse far
enough to hoist it up where John Kraus could swing it to one
side and dump it. Then I backed the horse and eased the big
bucket down for another load. If I led the horse too far the
big bucket would crash into the rack, tear it apart, and the
whole thing would crash into the well on top of Jake. If I
didn't hoist it far enough John Kraus couldn't swing it clear
and dump it. It looked easy, but for the first hour I was as
jumpy as the horse.

Then the horse began to quiet down, and so did I. John
Kraus still yelled orders I didn't understand, but by walking
backward and watching the bucket I kept things going all
right.

They went all right till just before dinner time, when a big
fly got on the horse's flank and he couldn't whip it off with his
tail. John Kraus ordered me to hoist away. The horse was trying to reach the fly with his mouth. I jerked at the lead rein
but he wouldn't move. John Kraus yelled at me.

I slapped at the fly, the horse jumped, lunged, and the big
bucket came sailing up. I swung on the lead rein and stopped
the horse just as the bucket hit the top of the frame with a
creak and a clatter. The rack swayed but didn't give way.

John Kraus cursed as I had never heard anyone curse. He
grabbed the club and started toward me. Jake, at the bottom
of the well, shouted, "What's going on up there?"

John Kraus turned back and reached for the bucket as I
carefully backed the horse. He swung the bucket aside, dumped
it, eased it over the hole again, and I backed the horse and
slowly lowered the bucket.

As soon as the bucket was down John Kraus came toward us, muttering, "Damn fool horse, damn fool horse!" He un-hitched the tugs from the singletree, grabbed the lead rein from me, and jerked at the horse's head. The horse reared and John Kraus clubbed it over the head. It lunged, almost broke the lead rein, and he clubbed it again.

Frantic, I cried, "Stop that! Stop it!"

John Kraus turned to me and for a moment I thought he was going to club me. Then he demanded, "Who you think you are?" and laughed. He handed me the lead rein and hitched the tugs again. He went back to the well and told Jake to come up on the next load. "Time we eat," he said.

That time I was very careful. Jake stepped off the bucket at the top and dumped it. I unhitched the horse and led him to the barn. When I asked John Kraus where the corn was for the horse he said, "He don't get corn today. I teach him to behave," and we went to the house.

The house was spotless. John Kraus was a worker, as de-manding of himself as of anyone else. And the food was good, a meat stew well cooked. But I wasn't hungry. I ate a few forkfuls and couldn't swallow any more. John Kraus said, "Boys got to eat. Clean up your plate." I forced a little more down, then gave up.

I have wondered since if John Kraus was as evil a man as he seemed to me then, or if I was a naïve boy to whom bru-tality was shocking. The answer lies in John Kraus' sadism. I had seen brutality, in bloody, merciless fist fights behind the livery stable in Nebraska, in a wild-tempered farmer who killed a vicious horse that attacked him, in a jealous wife who branded her husband with a hot flatiron while he slept, in a moronic boy who hatcheted two fingers from another boy who teased him. But those were acts of passion and violence, not sadism.

Man is not by nature a gentle creature. The veneer is thin. But cold-blooded brutality devised to cause pain and blood-shed as an end in itself is a perversion of even our impulsive violence. We are reluctant to admit even a racial kinship with the sadist, perhaps because he represents a primitive bestiality we would like to disown. Yet all through history sadism has been condoned in the name of dogma, evil tolerated on the perverse assumption that it led to ultimate good. Which only demonstrates the devious quality of human reasoning.

John Kraus was evil. Yet he was no more a product of that time and place than were Jake Farley or Louie, the sheep herder. He was by no means typical. Most farmers and most of the homesteaders were relatively kind to their animals, if for no other reason than that an abused cow is a poor milker and an abused horse becomes useless in time. It was the rare plainsman who gave his horse less than the best of care. Horses cost money, and horses were the plainsman's means of transportation in a vast land. A man left afoot was in trouble. He took care of his horses. But John Kraus was no plainsman.

The afternoon seemed endless, but there was no more trouble. I made sure there were no flies on the horse when the bucket was ready to hoist. And Kraus was almost jovial.

We worked till sundown. On the way home I felt more tired than I had ever been in my life. Not physically tired but somehow tired inside. Jake noticed it and said, "It'll be easier tomorrow. What happened this morning that started all the cussing?"

"He got mad at the horse." I couldn't tell him what really happened.

"Don't pay any attention to him. He can be meaner than Old Scratch. He didn't touch you, did he?"

"No."

"If he does, I'll climb right out of that hole and go to work on him with a spade." Jake sighed. He was tired too. "You have to take a lot to earn a dollar, these days," he said, almost to himself.

When I did the chores I patted old Dick specially, to make up for something, I suppose. And when Mother asked me at supper how it had gone that day I said, "All right." But I didn't read that night. I went to bed almost as soon as it was dark.

The next day went more easily. John Kraus was in a good mood. The well went down fast; by the end of the day we were down almost twenty feet and Jake said that if we didn't hit shale or rock we might get water at forty feet or so.

And the third day went all right. I was getting used to John Kraus by then, and I was thinking about how my wages were adding up. If the job lasted next week I would maybe have enough to buy a shotgun. A second-hand one, but a good one. I kept thinking about the gun but paying attention to the job, too.

Then, just as we were getting ready to quit for the day, there was an uproar in the barnyard. One of the cats killed a chicken. John Kraus grabbed his club and ran toward the barn. There was another uproar, a spasm of caterwauling, the dog howled in pain, and the chickens began to squawk again.

Jake, down in the well, shouted to me, asking what was going on. When I told him he said, "Hoist away. I'm coming up." So I hoisted him and he emptied the bucket and together we hurried to the barnyard.

Things had begun to quiet down, though the chickens were still squawking. Then I saw John Kraus back of the barn. He flung something from him. It was a cat. He came to us, grinning and shaking his hand. His hand was bleeding. "I killed the damn cat!" he said. "Gott fer damn cats, don't kill mice, just kill chickens! I teach 'em!"

That night at supper Mother asked, "What happened today? You look awful tired. You must have been working pretty hard."

"He killed a cat," I said. I had to tell someone, but I couldn't tell her he choked it to death.

"What for?" she asked.

"It killed a chicken."

"What does he keep cats for? Why doesn't he keep his chickens penned up?"

"I don't know."

"How near done are you with the well?"

"We hit shale today."

"How much longer will he need you?"

"I don't know."

"If it's too hard you don't have to stay. You know that. I don't know if your father would have let you work for that man in the first place."

The next morning when Jake and I drove into the yard at John Kraus' place the dog was howling. Faint howls, from inside the barn. When we took Jake's team into the barn we found the dog, hanging from a rafter by a rope tied to his tail, his forelegs barely touching the floor. Jake tried to release him, but the dog was frantic, snapping and snarling. He almost got Jake's hand.

We went to the house and Jake said, "Go let that dog loose."

John Kraus said, "He howls all night, let him howl all day. I teach him!"

"Let him loose," Jake repeated.

John Kraus scowled. "I pay you to work, not talk. I give the orders around here."

Jake turned toward the barn.

"Where you going?" John Kraus demanded.

"Home," Jake said, "I'm not going to listen to that dog howl all day."

John Kraus grabbed Jake by the arm. Jake turned and said, "Let go of me!" Jake wasn't over five feet six and didn't weigh a hundred and fifty pounds, and John Kraus was a six-footer and brawny. But there was something about Jake Farley that just wouldn't scare. Jake wasn't afraid of anybody or anything.

John Kraus let go of him, hesitated a moment, then went to the barn. There were new howls of pain this time; then

the dog scuttled from the barn and crawled into the hole under the house. There were snorts and the sound of hoofs
against the barn and John Kraus was shouting curses at the
horse. Jake had faced him down, and John Kraus was taking
it out on his animals.

The horse was jumpy that morning. I had got him almost
quieted down the past two days, but that morning he shied
at every move I made. And John Kraus was shouting orders
at me. I couldn't hoist one load to his liking, not one. The
fact that Jake was in shale and the digging was slow didn't
help, either. Finally, at about eleven o'clock, John Kraus
emptied a bucket and shouted at me, "Back it up! Stop loaf-
ing on the job! Back it up!"

I tried to hurry the horse. It shied away. The bucket creaked
against the frame. John Kraus cursed and ran and grabbed
the lead rein from me. He jerked the horse's bridle and kicked
it in the belly. The horse reared, struck at him with a forefoot.
John Kraus began to club it over the head. It backed away,
still lunging. Finally the rope slacked, the bucket at the bottom. John Kraus unhitched the tugs, clubbed the horse so
hard he broke the club, then jerked a tug loose and began
beating it with a trace chain.

I couldn't take any more of it. I turned and ran. I was at
the barn before I heard John Kraus shouting at me. I didn't
stop. I dodged around the barn and kept on running, just to
get away from there.

I must have run half a mile before I slowed down and
looked back. No one was chasing me. Then I began to curse,
all the foul, profane words I could think of, calling John Kraus
every vile name I could remember. And somehow it purged
me. I got all the foulness and meanness and cruelty and hurt
out of me, everything that had been eating into me there at
John Kraus'.

I was halfway home. Now I turned west, off across the flats.
I didn't know where I was going, but it didn't matter. I was

just going, getting away. And at last I found that I was following a pair of old grass-grown ruts. They led southwest. After
I had followed them a way I remembered that it was the old
trail, an old road Jack Clothier had said was an emigrant trail
in the old days. It used to lead from Fort Morgan, he said,
down to Deer Trail, sixty miles south. I'd seen it and wondered about it several times, but I'd never followed it.

As I walked along it that day something about it was sooth-
ing and quieting. It was so remote from John Kraus, so completely alien to everything about him. You don't have to know
history to sense the continuity, to know deep inside that the
generations rise and pass and that you are you because there
were others before you. And that pain and hurt pass, too.

I knew none of these things, consciously, but as I walked
that old trail I was going with others who had been there before I was born. I was with my grandfather, going from Indiana
to Nebraska, and my great-grandfather going from Pennsylvania to Ohio and Indiana. And with other grandfathers than
my own, crossing the plains to the mountains and even to the
Pacific. If I followed that trail far enough I, too, would see
the mountains.

I don't know how far I followed the trail. A mile and a half,
maybe two miles. Long enough to become an emigrant boy
following an emigrant wagon across the endless plains. And
then, in a place where wind and rain had washed the ruts into
a gully, I saw a piece of a cup, a gray cup. I tried to pick it
up. It wouldn't come and I dug at it with my knife. It wasn't
a cup. It was a mug, a brownish gray pottery stein with two
blue stripes around it and a handle with a broken pewter
hinge that once held a lid. A child's mug that once held a
pint of milk.

I sat on the grass and brushed away the dirt of the years.
The place where the lip had been exposed to catch my eye
was sun-faded. It had been there a long time. Holding it in

my hand I was the boy who had lost it and at the same time I was the boy who found it.

I stood up and looked for the mountains. I knew they weren't there; I couldn't even see them from the top of the haystack. And I began to accept the years and the hurt and the pain as a part of life, a part of the me, whoever I was or would be.

What happened, I suppose, was that I accepted the existence of evil and still knew that evil was not all or even a major part of life. I recognized the fact of the dream, the continuity of the search, which was above and beyond evil. I am sure it was not a conscious process, but I know it happened. We all come to that moment when an incident, essentially minor, arms us to cut through confusions of thought or emotion. Finding that stein beside the old trail gave me a sense of the reality of the search others had made for the substance of their dreams, and it made that search in itself worth the ache, the pain, the hurt and the evil. The mountains I could not see no doubt were in some way related to my father. And, if not then certainly soon after, I understood something of his own dreams and his own search. And those dreams, one way or another, would one day become mine, and I too would take up the search.

I sat there, the brownish gray stein in my hand, and I thought some of these things and felt some of them deep inside. And I knew I had to go home.

Mother saw me coming. She met me in the yard and asked, "What are you doing here? I thought you were working. Did you get fired?"

"I quit," I said.

"What happened?"

I couldn't tell her everything. Besides, it was no longer important to tell it. "He killed the cat," I said, "and he hung the dog by the tail, and he beat the horse."

Mother's lips tightened in that angry look of hers. "I'll bet you haven't eaten. Come on in and I'll get you something."

That evening Jake Farley stopped at the house. He talked to Mother a few minutes, then came out to the barn where I was doing the chores. He handed me two silver dollars and a quarter. "Here's your pay," he said. "Your ma said to give it to you."

It was the first time I'd thought of the money. There was a flash of the pang: I hadn't earned enough to buy a shotgun. I asked, "What did he say?"

Jake gave me a wry smile. "No matter. I quit too." He said it without emotion. He put a hand on Daisy's hip. "Looks like she's due any time. Ever help a cow with a calf?"

"No."

"You may have to help her, though she's a good big cow and ought to have it easy. Just don't try to take the calf too fast. . . . Well, I got to get home. Don't spend all your money in one place." He grinned. "Good night."

Daisy was down in her stall, having her calf, when I got to the barn the next morning. I helped her with it, frightened and awed, and by the time Mother called me for breakfast it was all over. The calf was on its feet and sucking. I was glad I'd seen the old jack rabbit have her young, because I knew just what was going to happen. But I was amazed that the calf was so big.

I went to the pump and washed up before I went to the house. All I said to Mother was, "Daisy had her calf. It's another heifer."

11

July brought only one light shower, not even enough to wet the ground. When I dug a hole in the rye stubble I found it bone dry a foot down. It wasn't that bad in the corn, for the sod held a little moisture, but the leaves stayed curled against the heat even though the ears did begin to fill out. We picked a few roasting ears from the corn before the kernels toughened into dough, and they tasted as good as any sweet corn we ever had in Nebraska. Mother said maybe that was only because we'd forgotten what sweet corn tasted like, but we enjoyed them. The garden she planted didn't survive June. If it had, the grasshoppers would have eaten it. We weren't overrun with grasshoppers, but some of them were three inches long. They ate quite a few of the pinto beans, but those that were left set pods and, with the shade of the corn kept growing. Jack rabbits were everywhere, dozens of them.

The pasture close to the house was grazed short by mid-summer, so we let the stock range onto the flats to the west. They ran loose in the daytime, but they never wandered more than a mile or two from home, and I brought them in every night. They were all thin, the cows, the calves, and the horses. Bessie's calf was getting to be a good-sized heifer, spotted yellow and white. Daisy's calf, the little one I had helped deliver, was brindle like her mother. With Bessie due to calve again in the winter, we would have five head by spring. Within another year we would have to build an addition on the barn.

Father wrote that the bank hoped to sell the paper and he might be out of a job within another month. That, he said, would be all right with him. Even if they didn't sell it, he wasn't going to stay longer than Thanksgiving. With what he had earned by then, he said, we should be pretty well off for the winter. We wouldn't have to go through another winter like the last one. Meanwhile, he was doing a little fishing. Trout fishing, back in the mountains. Last week he caught four nice ones and the folks at the restaurant cooked them for him. Wonderful eating.

Mother wrote back and said, "You'd better eat your fill of fish while you're there. I've no doubt they're good if you like fish, which you know I don't. Not even catfish, though I always cooked them for you back in Nebraska. That's one thing I don't miss here on the homestead, fish. The jack rabbits are so thick around here that we could eat rabbit most of the winter. If You-Know-Who gets the shotgun he wants. I told him he'd have to wait till you got home. We threshed out another five bushels of rye."

The rye in the stack had begun to shatter, with the heat and the drought. We had let it get too ripe before we cut it, and every time I forked it from the stack onto the threshing-sheet about half the grain shattered onto the ground. It wasn't all lost, of course, because the chickens pratically lived in the stack yard and we didn't have to feed them.

But we weren't having much luck with the chickens. Several of them died from what Mother thought was eating too many grasshoppers. And then a skunk got into the chicken house one night. The chickens made an uproar and Fritz began to bark and I went out with the lantern. The skunk had dug a hole under the chicken house door. He came out the same way he went in, and Fritz caught him. Both Fritz and I were skunked, but we killed the beast. I had to bury my clothes and Fritz wasn't allowed near the house for a week. The skunk had killed four hens.

I said that if I had a shotgun I could have killed the skunk before it squirted us, maybe even before it got in the chicken house. Mother said, "Don't talk shotgun to me! Wait till your father gets home. Meanwhile, go wash again. With soap. See if you can't get some of that smell off of you."

A few afternoons later I asked Mother if I might go over to the big prairie dog town. She still said I smelled of skunk, and she said, "Yes, go along. Get out in the sun and see if it doesn't sweeten you up a little. Just watch out for snakes, and bring the cows and horses when you come home."

So Fritz and I started for the big dog town.

It was a hot day. The sun was brassy, the way it had been for weeks, brassy and sizzling. There were dust devils, little whirlwinds that danced across the flats picking up dust and dry grass. There were simmering heat waves that made the horizon dance, and there were mirages. If half those mirages had been real lakes nobody would have had to wish for rain.

When we got to the dog town it looked as though half the hawks and coyotes and badgers in the country were living on the prairie dogs. I saw half a dozen hawks, and three coyotes skulked away as we came in sight. With the drought, the prairie dogs had eaten all the grass close to their holes. They had to go out to the edge of town to feed. They didn't know enough to dig new holes out at the edge, so there they were, away from their holes and squabbling among themselves. All their enemies were getting fat on them. There were even several new badger dens.

Fritz went off to the far edge of town, half a mile away, and I lay down on my belly in the sun. The longer I watched, the more I thought how stupid the prairie dogs were. The young ones were two-thirds grown, and if they had any spunk and gumption, as Mother said, they would move out and start a new town somewhere else. Or just go off by themselves. They didn't have to stay there, where grass was so scare, any more then we had to stay in Nebraska.

I watched a hawk swoop down and catch one of those young prairie dogs, not a hundred feet from me. The others screamed in terror and dived for their burrows, and the hawk flew away with the pup in its talons. And in no time at all, the others were out again, just as though nothing had happened.

One group began squabbling over a little patch of grass. They snapped and snarled like cats with their tails together. Then off to the other side a frightened yelp went up and the alarm cry was sounded. There was a rush to the burrows.

I turned to look. Not fifty yards from me was a badger in the midst of a group of pups. The pups were so scared they ran in circles. The badger had caught one pup. He lunged and caught another. The first one squirmed from under the badger's paw and tried so crawl away. One snap and the badger put an end to that.

Then it was so quiet all over that end of the dog town that you could have heard an owl flying. Not a dog was in sight.

I got to my knees and yelled at the badger. He crouched on his hunkers and hissed, his ears flat against his head. He was a big one, as long as Fritz, grizzly gray with a white stripe down his nose and white patches on his cheeks. He hunched there, glaring, lifting one front paw, then the other. Those paws were armed with claws as long as my fingers, but I knew he wouldn't attack me if I didn't charge him.

He glared at me and hissed several times, then picked up the two young prairie dogs and started away. He kept looking back over his shoulder, but he went much faster than one would expect, on those short legs. He seemed almost to flow over the ground to one of the new badger holes. There he turned and looked at me and hissed again before he went in.

Fritz had heard me yell. He came racing towar me. I was glad the badger was gone before Fritz got there. Fritz would have challenged him, and badgers are vicious fighters.

We went over and looked in the badger den. Fritz's hackles went up and he wanted to dig. I hauled him away. It was past midafternoon, time to start after the horses and the cows.

I knew where they were grazing that day, on the flats west of the house, a mile or so from home. I wished I'd brought a nubbin of corn and a piece of rope. Then I could catch Dick and ride him home, Indian fashion. But I hadn't. I took a look at the sun and the lay of the land and started across the flats.

In just about two miles, as I had expected, I saw brindle Daisy and her calf. Not far from her was the spotted heifer, Bessie's calf from last Winter. Bessie was nowhere in sight. Neither were the horses. But I was pretty sure they wouldn't be very far away.

I took my time. Daisy and the calves were on a little rise. Just before I got to them I heard a low moaning moo from somewhere beyond them, in the next hollow. It didn't sound right. I hurried to the top of the rise where I could see over.

There was Bessie, down on the ground, trying to get up. She would moo that moaning sound and heave herself and get one hind leg under her and almost get her rump up, and then just sort of collapse and lie there.

I ran toward her, and then I saw the horses just a little way on down that hollow. Old Dick was flat on the ground, all sprawled out. Shorty was lying near him, on his belly with his feet under him but with his head so low his nose was in the grass.

I ran past Bessie and down to the horses. Old Dick wasn't making a move. I shouted at him, and still he didn't move. Shorty lifted his nose and turned his head and groaned and his nose sagged into the grass again. They were sick. All three of them were sick. Very sick. Bessie was still moaning, trying to get to her feet. Then I watched old Dick's ribs. They weren't moving. He wasn't breathing. Old Dick was dead.

I couldn't believe it. I knelt beside his head and talked to him and forced open one eyelid. The eye was rolled back. It was dull, lifeless. His mouth was open a little, the lips loose and sagging away from his big teeth.

I was too awed to cry, awed and stunned. I looked around and saw several clumps of green shoots like coarse grass. Then I knew. It was camas, death camas.

I went back to Shorty and ordered him to get up. He looked at me with dull eyes. I pushed at him, pummeled him, finally kicked him. He was bloated. He groaned and lifted his head and got his front feet under him. But his head seemed too heavy to hold up. He heaved and tried to get his hind legs under him and fell back. I shouted at him and he tried again. This time he made it and stood there, quivering and wavering, his head low. I slapped him on the rump and he took a few steps, then stopped. He heaved and coughed and retched, making an awful, hollow sound. Nothing came up. I urged him and he started up the little rise, stumbling at every step.

I turned to Bessie. She was weaker now, not trying to get up. I slapped her on the rump and she got her hind quarters up and one front leg, but the other leg buckled under her and she fell with a loud *whoosh*, all the breath knocked out of her. She couldn't try again.

I was desperate. Old Dick was dead, but I had to get the others home. I had to!

I urged Bessie to try again, but it was no use. She was too weak. She couldn't make it. I knew it. Bessie was going to die, too.

Shorty was standing just a little way off, head down, his sides heaving. I drove him on up the slope. He got almost to where Daisy and the calves were grazing. Then he stumbled and went to his knees and got to his feet again. I shouted, "Go on, Shorty, go on! You've got to get home! Please, Shorty, go on!" And he stumbled slowly ahead.

I herded Daisy and the calves toward home, and I kept Shorty moving for maybe a quarter of a mile. But he stumbled more and more, and he kept stopping. It was too much for him. I knew Shorty wasn't going to make it. He would try, but he wouldn't make it. And when he stumbled and went down again and couldn't even lift his head, I knew it was no use. I hurried after Daisy and the calves.

It was impossible. It just wasn't true. It was a bad dream. And yet, here I was, with one cow and the spotted calf and the brindle calf. And Fritz. Heading for home with all the livestock we had left. This morning we had two cows and two calves and a team of horses. And now we had one cow and two calves and no horses at all.

We went down over the last ridge, the house and barn and haystacks just ahead. Until then I didn't even know I had been running, and making Daisy and the calves run. My mouth was hot and dry. My heart pounded. My legs ached.

We hurried down the last slope and Daisy and the calves went to the well for water. Mother came out of the house. She sensed something wrong. "What happened?" she asked, her voice tense. "Where's Bessie? Where are the horses?"

"Up on the flat," I gasped. "They're—they're dead."

"Dead?" Mother couldn't take it in. "Why, what—" She couldn't finish the question. She was pale as a sheet.

"Camas," I said. "They found some death camas."

Mother stood there, stricken. Daisy and the calves turned toward the barn. I closed the barn door. Mother still stood there beside the well. I went back to her and told her what had happened.

"Then Bessie and Shorty weren't dead when you left them?" she asked.

"Not quite. I thought I ought to bring Daisy and the calves home. And tell you."

She nodded. She drew a deep breath. "Oh, son," she said, "both horses, and old Bessie. Why—why, I can't believe it!" She bit her lip and fought the tears. Then her shoulders stiffened and her lips stopped trembling and she said, "Come on. Let's go see."

We went back up onto the flats. We came to Shorty. He was sprawled just as he had fallen when I left him. The bloat bulged his ribs but there wasn't even a quiver of breath. Then we found Bessie, dead too. And we went on and looked at Dick, and I pointed to the camas. Then we went home.

Neither of us felt like eating supper that night. When I went in after I milked Daisy, Mother's eyes were red and I knew she had been crying. But she had fried mush ready, and salt pork and gravy. We ate a little and gave the rest to Fritz. I helped with the dishes, and Mother said, "Maybe we'd have been better off to sell the stock and go up there with your father. But I don't know. Something might have happened there, too." She slowly shook her head. "I don't know why things happen. I thought we had everything going all right." She was talking to herself. "I don't know. I just don't know."

The dishes done, she sat down at the table, her head in her hands. Her shoulders began to shake and I knew she was crying. Then she reached for a handkerchief and dried her eyes and blew her nose. "Tears don't get you anywhere," she announced, and she got her purse. She counted the money she had put away as Father sent it home. She put it back in the purse and said, "Tomorrow morning I want you to go over and ask Jake Farley to take me to Gary. I'm going in to Brush with Con Hallahan."

"All right," I said. "I'll take old Dick and—" I stopped. I wouldn't take old Dick. Not tomorrow or ever again.

"You'll walk," Mother said. She thought a minute. "No, if we wait till morning we can't catch Con. We'd better go see Jake tonight."

"I'll go," I said. "I'm not afraid to go tonight."

"We'll both go. Get the lantern lit."

So we walked over to Jake Farley's, with only the lantern and the starlight to see by. It was only two miles, but it seemed like ten. It was a beautiful night, and what had happened that afternoon didn't seem real at all, out there under the stars.

Then we got to Jake's dooryard and his dog began to bark. Jake came to the door in his overalls and undershirt, and I shouted who we were. He went back and put on a shirt, then asked us in.

Mother told him what had happened. Jake couldn't believe it. "They're both dead? Both horses are dead? And the yellow cow?"

"Yes."

Jake just sat there, as stunned as we had been.

"Jake," Mother said, "I want you to take me to Gary in the morning in time to catch Con Hallahan."

"Yes'm," Jake said, "I'll take you. I'll take you all the way in to Brush."

"I just want you to take me to Gary. That's all I want. And I'll pay you for your trouble."

"You won't pay me nothing!" Jake said. "Losing both your horses that way! I should say not!"

Mother stood up. "Then I'll expect you first thing in the morning. I'll be ready." We went to the door.

Jake still sat there, shaking his head.

"You won't forget, now, will you?" Mother asked.

"No. No, I won't forget." Jake came to the door after us. "You two be ready. And I'll look after the stock while you're gone."

"I'm going alone," Mother said. "And I'm just going to Brush. I'll be back tomorrow night."

The walk home was endless. I was so tired I began to stumble and I thought I was going to fall, as Shorty did, and just lie there. But I kept going, right along with Mother, who seemed to have found some new energy of determination.

We got home and Mother said, "Go along to bed, son. I have to write a letter to your father."

I got ready for bed and glanced out at her before I crawled between the covers. She was sitting at the table, paper in front of her, pen in one hand, knuckles of the other hand at her teeth. Just staring, staring past the lamp and away off somewhere.

I went to sleep, and I wakened once maybe an hour later. The lamp was still burning. I shifted in bed and she heard me. She said, "You'd better get your sleep. I won't be much longer."

Jake Farley arrived early the next day and took her to Gary. I herded Daisy and the two calves on the flats just across the draw from the barn, making sure they didn't go over west.

Mother arrived home after dark that night, driving a speckled gray horse hitched to a second-hand buggy. She had looked at all the horses for sale in town, had driven a bargain, and we at least had transportation.

12

Father wrote that he knew we did all for Dick and Shorty that anyone could have done. Losing them, he said, was much worse than losing Bessie, because it left us stranded. Mother should go right out and buy another team.

Mother wrote back, of course, that she had bought Mack and the buggy. And in his next letter Father said he supposed we could get along with the one horse till he got home, but we had to have a team to farm with. When he got back, he said, he would buy a team. We could use three horses, if Mack was as good as Mother said he was.

But having only the one horse did raise problems. Particularly when we had any hauling to do. You couldn't hitch one horse to a wagon.

Early in September I started to cut the corn, the way we had the year before. The ears weren't very big, but they would make grain for the stock. So I cut two big bundles and tied them together and hitched Mack to them and dragged them down to the stack yard. That was the only way I could get them there. The blades were so brittle, from the drought, that they all knocked off. Mother took one look at those sorry-looking bundles of stalks and said there was no use trying to bring them in. We would husk out the ears in the field and then turn Daisy and the calves in and let them eat what they could find.

So we let the corn go and pulled the beans. They, too, had

dried up but they had a good many pods. We pulled them and took the threshing sheet to the field and flailed them out. The beans were small and a good many were shriveled, but we saved them all. It was a kind of game, seeing how little we could let go to waste.

We harvested almost two bushels of beans. Then I began husking the corn. I put the ears in gunny sacks and hauled the sacks down to the barn in the buggy. It wasn't the most convenient way to do things, but it was the only way we had.

Mack didn't think much of our ways, at first. Mack was just an old cow pony someone had broken to harness, a grizzled gray pony with a grumpy nature. He disliked the harness. Maybe he thought it was an insult to his dignity. He took it all right till I tried to put the crupper under his tail. Then he kicked, usually just a token kick but hard enough to knock you down if he hit you squarely. I learned to expect the kick and dodge it. And he could tell the driving bridle from the riding bridle, no matter how I tried to hide it. If I went to him with the driving bridle behind my back he would clamp his teeth and shake his head, practically saying, "No! I won't!" But if it was the riding bridle he opened his mouth for the bit and held his head down for me to buckle the throat latch.

Mack liked to be ridden. In harness he shuffled along, listless, but when I rode him he strutted. On cool mornings he bucked a little; but if he threw me, as he usually did in the beginning, he turned and waited for me to get back on, looking as though he wanted to say, "Aren't you ever going to learn to ride?" When I went to do the morning chores I had to feed him first or he nipped me every time I passed. After I fed him he nuzzled me, almost fondly.

Mack was salty and cantankerous as an old ranch hand. If he had worn a hat it would have been a battered black Stetson jerked down over one jaundiced eye. I liked Mack. I missed Dick and Shorty, but I liked Mack.

The second week in September Jack Clothier came over to see us. We hadn't seen him all summer. He said, "I'm glad to see you're still here. Some of the homesteaders over north couldn't take it. They packed up and pulled out."

I told him about Father, how he'd gone up in the mountains to work, and he nodded approvingly. Then I told him about Dick and Shorty and Bessie.

"No!" he said. "That, on top of the drought!" He shook his head then asked, "Are you sure it was camas?"

I described the plants I had seen.

"Sounds like camas. I hope you dug it up."

I hadn't. I hadn't wanted to go back up there.

"Get a spade," he ordered, "and come on."

I bridled Mack and we headed for the flats. He watched Mack as we rode along and he said, "That's an old cutting horse you've got there." A cutting horse was a cow pony used to separate steers in a herd, a horse quick on his feet. "Getting old," he went on, "but he's still all right. He's got a lot of savvy. And from the look in his eye, I'll bet if you threw a saddle on him some frosty morning he'd give you a time. Some of those old horses do that, just to keep a rider from getting careless."

I told him Mack bucked, even bareback.

He grinned. "I see you're still riding him. It's a funny thing, the way a wise old bronc will fight a man in the saddle but if you put a kid on him, bareback, he'll gentle right down. He's not mean. He's just showing that he's not going to be imposed on."

The nearer we got to the place, the more I wished I hadn't come. I hadn't been up there since the day I found old Dick dead. I didn't want to see him that way again. But when we came to the little hollow there was only a pile of bones. The coyotes had been there, and for once I was glad there were coyotes. That pile of bones wasn't Dick, and the other two piles of bones weren't Shorty and Bessie. They were just bleaching bones.

The camas had practically disappeared, with fall. But when I pointed out where it had been Jack found traces of it and began to dig up the bulbs. He dug up a hatful before he quit. He chopped them up with the spade and left them in the sun to dry up and die. "Watch for them in the spring," he said, "and dig up any more you find."

As we were riding back to the house he said, "Well, I guess I won't be seeing you folks any more."

"What happened?" I asked.

"I'm pulling out. Going up in Wyoming, up in the Wind River country."

I couldn't say a thing. We didn't see him often, but Jack Clothier seemed like one of the best friends we had. That's the way I thought of him, anyway.

"A few more years," he said, "and there won't be any more open range in here. The boss don't see it, but I do. There's going to be a little trouble, probably, and I shouldn't be surprised if it comes next spring. Somebody's going to try to drive Gerrity out, and I don't want any part of it. I went through my range wars. I don't want any more of them. I'm getting out. A friend of mine went up in the Wind River country three years ago and he's got a nice little layout. I'm going to do the same thing, get me a one-man place up there and settle down."

"When are you going?" I asked.

"Next week. I've got some business to tend to in Cheyenne. Then I'll go on up." He thought for a moment, then said, "A man's got to settle down some time."

He glanced at me, then looked at Mack. I thought he was going to say something about my riding bridle. It was just a cheap bridle with a curb bit and flat leather reins. The bridle on his horse was a one-ear, a broad band without a brow band or a throat-latch, just a hole to go over one of the horse's ears. I thought a one-ear bridle was just about the finest thing there was, especially one with braided rawhide reins, like Jack Clothier's. Some day I was going to earn enough money to buy one.

We got to the barn and I unbridled Mack and ran him into the barn. Jack said, "Let's see that bridle of yours."

I handed it to him. He flipped one rein around his horse's neck and took off that beautiful one-ear bridle. He put my old bridle on his horse and handed the one-ear bridle to me.

I didn't know what to do. "Take it," he said. "I'm giving it to you. For keeps."

"Ohh!" I was completely awed.

He grinned. I held the beautiful bridle in my hands, feeling the rawhide reins with their soft leather tassels. "You've got a cow pony," he said. "Now you've got a cow-pony bridle."

"Thanks," I whispered. I couldn't say it out loud.

He put a hand on my shoulder and gripped it, hard. "You're a good kid," he said.

We walked over to the house. Mother came to the door and Jack Clothier said, "Well, we got the camas out. I'll be going along. Goodbye."

Mother said the usual casual goodbye, but he hesitated a moment.

"I'm going to Wyoming," he said. "Next week."

"Not for good," Mother said.

He nodded. "So I won't be seeing you again, I guess."

"Are you going alone?" Mother asked.

He blushed.

Mother laughed and said, "I thought not."

"Well, I'm going alone as far as Cheyenne," he said, grinning.

"And getting married there?"

"Um-hmm."

"I hope she's a nice girl, Jack."

"She's the nurse that took care of me when that horse fell on me. That was in Fort Morgan, but she comes from Cheyenne. She's got dark hair and dark eyes. Like you." He flushed and turned away and got on his horse. "It's been awful nice knowing you folks," he said. "All of you." He reached down and shook hands with me. "So long, fellow," he said, and turned and loped away.

We watched him, both of us, down the draw and out of

sight. Then I remembered the bridle and told Mother. "He shouldn't have done it," she said. "But it was nice of him." She looked down the draw and said, "I just hope she's good enough for him."

The last Saturday in September we got a letter from Father saying the bank had sold the paper. The new man wanted Father to stay on another week and help him get the hang of things, but Father would be home next week. He would get to Brush on the noon train from Denver on Monday and come out to Gary with Con Hallahan. Would we meet him at Gary?

Mother looked at the date again and said, "That's day after tomorrow. That's this coming Monday!" And a little later she said, "We'll drive all the way to Brush. Con charges a quarter, and we can use that quarter just as well as he can."

So I put extra hay in for Daisy and the calves on Monday morning and locked them in the barn, and we drove to Brush. We left Mack and the buggy at the hitch rack by the post office and waited for the train. Mother was wearing a hat and her Christmas shirtwaist and her black skirt and coat. I felt stiff and strange in a pair of Father's cut-down pants, a cut-down shirt of his, and my new shoes. They were black work shoes and we bought them at Gary just before the horses ate the camas. It was the first time I'd worn them and they felt stiff and awkward because we'd bought them big enough to fit my growing feet next spring.

I'd almost forgotten how a train looked and sounded. I guess Mother had too, because we backed right up against the depot when the locomotive roared in. It was so big, and it came so fast! There was a shower of tiny cinders and the steam billowed and the brakes screeched. The station agent rattled the express truck over the brick platform, and the conductor swung down and dropped his metal step box with a hollow clatter.

People came down the steps of the cars, people all dressed up, women in skirts that barely cleared the ground, men in black suits with tight pants and most of the men wearing derby hats.

Then I saw Father, in the clothes he had on when he left, the old brown suit and the narrow-brimmed soft brown hat. The only difference was that his face looked pale. All his tan had faded.

He saw us, gasped in surprise, waved, almost missed a step. Then he swung his suitcase down and ran across the platform. He caught Mother in his arms, kissed her, exclaimed, "I didn't expect you here!" and hugged me. "Good Lord," he said to me, "how you've grown!" He looked at Mother again. "You're all dressed up! Jiminy, you're pretty!"

Mother said, "Hush! . . . The buggy's right across the street, by the post office."

Before he put his suitcase in the back of the buggy Father said, "Say, it's noon. Time to eat. We'd better get something before we start home."

Mother shook her head. "I've got sandwiches."
Father started to say something, didn't. He put his suitcase in, then helped Mother in. I untied Mack. Father got in the driver's place and I got in the other side. He backed around, crossed the tracks, and we started for home.

After the first greetings there didn't seem to be anything to say. At least nobody knew where to begin. It was almost like having a stranger there in the buggy with us, a stranger we knew and yet didn't know.

Father said, "Mack you call him, huh? He seems like a good little horse."

"He's sound," Mother said. "He's ten or eleven years old, but he's sound. And it's a pretty good buggy, too."

"He's a good saddle horse," I said. "He bucks sometimes, but I can stay on."

"Good for you!" Father turned to Mother and nodded at me. "I can't get over the way he's grown. He's almost as tall as you are!"

171

Mother said yes, and the talk ended for a while. Mack, who had started out at a fast trot, slowed down to the singlefoot he could keep up all day, a kind of easy fox trot that covered a lot of ground.

We came to the first range of sand hills. "My," Father said, "the country looks dry. And flat."

"It is dry," Mother said. "We had an awful dry summer."

"It seems impossible," Father said, "that just day before yesterday I was up in the hills on a trout stream. There's snow in the mountains, quite a lot of it in places. The water was ice cold. So cold it hurt your teeth when you drank it. . . . Confound this collar! It's too tight, or something."

"Take it off if you want to," Mother said. "But put it on before we stop at Gary for the mail. I don't like to see a man in a suit all dressed up and without a collar."

Father took off the stiff linen collar, and at the same time he seemed to take off the strangeness. He relaxed, and so did we. Mother got out the bread-and-butter sandwiches and we ate and talked about the homestead, and Louie the herder, and the corn, and the beans, and Jack Clothier. Finally we talked about Dick and Shorty and Bessie, and the death camas.

Father put on his collar again before we stopped at Gary. Then we went on, and Mother told him about my working for John Kraus. She told the story, as much as she knew of it, and I didn't add anything. Finally she said, "I guess I shouldn't have let him work there in the first place. Not for that man!"

Father said it was all right, that he'd probably have done the same thing if he'd been home. Then he exclaimed, "Say, I *am* home! Do you realize that? I'm home! I can hardly realize it myself. Just over that next rise and we'll start dropping down to Ketchem Holler." He sighed. "I've been so homesick sometimes that I almost walked out on the job."

"You might have said so in your letters," Mother said.

"What good would that have done? It would just have made

both of us feel worse. Anyway, I'm here." And he squeezed her hand.

Then we were in Ketchem Holler, and soon after that we saw Louie's windmill and turned up the trail to our house. Fritz heard us coming and ran to greet us, barking. When Father got out of the buggy Fritz backed away, not knowing him; then he sniffed at Father's pant legs and barked, a delighted yelp, and jumped at him, licking his hands. You'd think Father owned him, the way he acted.

It was almost chore time. We changed clothes and Father went out to the barn with me. He hadn't seen Brindle, Daisy's calf. I told him how I'd helped it to be born, and he said, "Your Mother didn't say anything about that. She just wrote that Daisy had her calf. Well, you're getting to be almost a man, aren't you? You had to be, this summer. . . . Here, let me have that pail. I haven't forgotten how to milk."

Father did the milking and I got in the hay; and the drought, the poor corn crop, the wrinkled little beans, the skimpy haystacks, even the death of the horses and the cow, didn't matter the way they had yesterday. If Father had come home discouraged, or if he had indicated by one word or one look that he felt we hadn't done things right, the world would have been a very sad place. If he had said that everything had gone against us and it was no use going on this way any longer I would have felt miserable because I would have known that we were through with the homestead.

Instead of that, he looked around the barn and he slapped old Mack on the rump and he looked in the corn bin and said, "You got a little corn, didn't you? Next year we'll get a real crop."

He went outside and looked down the draw and he said, "One thing, the short hay crop won't matter much. We won't need so much hay this winter." And he looked at me with a grin.

We went to the house, and Mother felt the same way I did out at the barn. For weeks she had gone along, carrying a load on her shoulders, and now Father had come home and taken the load and it didn't seem nearly as heavy, just because of the way he carried it. Supper wasn't much of a meal, when you came down to what we had to eat; but it wasn't a matter of what we ate or how much, it was the way we all felt. We were together again, and we knew that whatever came we could handle it. We'd had some rough times, but what happened now was going to be better.

When we had eaten, Father said Mother and I had things pretty well in hand. The next thing to do was to find another horse to match up with Mack. Mother wasn't so sure. "Can't we get along with one horse for a while?" she asked.

"How are we going to get any hauling done?"

"What hauling have we got to do?"

"We have to get some groceries in."

"We can haul groceries in the buggy."

"And coal."

"Yes, we ought to have some coal. But we can haul it, a few hundred pounds at a time, in the buggy."

"And we'll have to haul cow chips and sheep chips."

"Oh, Will," Mother exclaimed, "I just don't want to spend our last cent again!"

"What are we going to do next spring," Father asked, "when we have to start plowing? I heard once of a fellow with only one horse who hitched his wife up to make a team." He grinned. "But she was a big Percheron type."

"Just you try that with me!" Mother said, laughing.

Father had got out his wallet. He opened it and took out fifty dollars. Mother stared at it. "Will Borland," she said, "have you been playing cards?"

Father laughed. "I never won that much at cards in my life. Anyway, I promised when I married you that I'd never play another hand of poker." He fingered the bills. "I saved about half of this, a little at a time, last summer. And the bank gave me an extra week's pay when they let me go."

"Oh, Will!"

"So we can get another horse."

"Yes. But not right away. Not for a week or so, please. Let's feel rich, just for a little while!"

He handed the money to her. "Let's see," he said. "For that money we can get you a whole new outfit, shoes to hat. We can all take a trip to Denver and stay at a hotel. We can buy new rugs for the floor and one of those new kitchen cabinets for you. We can't buy a piano, but we could get a reed organ. Now there's an idea. Let's get an organ and put it right over there. You play and I'll sing—"

"Stop it, Will. You know perfectly well what we're going to do with this money."

"What?"

"Save it till we get around to buying another horse." She tried to hand it back to him.

"Money? Don't need it." He turned his pocket inside out to show that he had a quarter and a dime. Then he said seriously, "Keep it. Put it away till we go to town."

So instead of going right out to buy a horse Father and I got the rest of the corn in. Then Jake Farley came over and said he was going to lay in some sheep chips and if we wanted to help he'd haul some for us, seeing we were a little short of horses.

Father and I went down to Louie's sheep camp with him and in a couple of days we got enough sheep chips to fill our fuel shed and stack one end of the barn with them, since we were a little short of cows, too.

We would have put even more sheep chips in the barn, but Father wasn't feeling well. Just ten days after he got back from the mountains he woke up with a headache, and the next day he was sick at the stomach. He hadn't any appetite. Mother said, "Maybe it's my cooking. Maybe it's too rich for your blood, you've been eating out so long."

But she couldn't make much of a joke of it. And when he was still sick the next day she was worried. She felt of his head and said, "You've got a fever." She killed a hen and made noodles, and he tried to eat some of that. It was his favorite dish, but he just couldn't eat.

That night Mother said, "I don't like this at all. You can't keep anything on your stomach and you're running a fever. If it was inflammation of the bowels you'd be too sick even to sit up by now, and so sore in the stomach you couldn't stand to have me touch you. But it's something, and if you're not better by morning we're going to Brush to see the doctor."

Father said, "That's the last thing I want to do, ride all the way to Brush."

"Maybe," Mother said, "you'd rather be hauled. In a box."

Father forced a smile, but he groaned when he tried to move.

The next morning Mother helped him dress and I hitched Mack to the buggy and said I'd look after things till they got back. Mother said, "If we're not back tonight, you know how to strain the milk into the crocks for the cream to rise. Lock the door and don't forget to gather the eggs. We won't be gone more than overnight."

She and I helped Father get into the buggy and Mother took the reins and they started for town.

13

Except for an occasional cold and an attack of rheumatism a few years before in Nebraska, Father had never been sick. While I finished the morning chores and turned Daisy and the calves out to graze I kept wondering if he had pneumonia. Mother was always warning about pneumonia. If you got a cold she kept feeling of your head to see if you had a fever, and if you got what she called a deep cough she got out the mustard and made a plaster. She put it on your chest and put you to bed, and it burned like fury and you sweated till your nightshirt was soaked. You burned and sweated, but the next day you felt better. Weak as a cat, but better.

But Father hadn't had a cold. He hadn't been sniffling or coughing. He said he just felt sick all over. His head ached and his back ached and his legs hurt and he couldn't keep anything on his stomach. I decided he didn't have pneumonia, and since pneumonia was the worst thing anybody could have I knew he was going to be all right. The doctor would give him some medicine to take and they would come right home.

After the chores, there wasn't much that had to be done. I wished I had a shotgun so I could go hunting. There was the .25-20 rifle, but I knew I shouldn't take that. It wasn't a good rabbit gun. Besides, there were only a dozen shells for it and I shouldn't waste them.

For the hundredth time I wished I had a bow. If I had a bow I could make arrows and hunt as the Indians did. I could make arrows, feather them with chicken feathers, and put the best stone points from my collection on them. But there wasn't any wood for making a bow. The only wood for miles around was the willow brush over on Badger Creek, and willow was too soft and brittle for a bow. You need hickory or Osage orange, and the only place I knew to get that kind of wood was back in Nebraska.

I thought again of making a slingshot; but you need a tough wooden crotch and strong rubber bands. You could shoot pebbles with a slingshot. Bigger boys, back in Nebraska, killed sparrows and pigeons and now and then a squirrel with slingshots. But I hadn't anything to make a slingshot from, either. Weapons like that needed materials you found only in a wooded country. You couldn't even make a good snare on the plains; you needed a sapling to jerk the snare when a rabbit tripped it. You needed a gun to be a hunter, so there wasn't much use to think of going hunting. I couldn't even go over and borrow Jake Farley's .22. He had traded it in on a shotgun, and I knew I couldn't borrow his shotgun. Besides, I didn't have any shotgun shells.

And, finally, I shouldn't go hunting. I should be busy around the place, as Father would have been.

I took Mother's dishpan and went to the barn and sorted a pile of ears from the corn bin and began shelling corn by hand. I sorted corn and shelled it most of the morning, so that Mother could grind corn meal. And I saved the cobs because she liked to have them for kindling.

There didn't seem to be any need to cook anything for dinner. I fished a piece of cold chicken from the bowl of chicken and noodles and had chicken and bread and butter. Then I took the hammer and a pocketful of staples and inspected the fence around the cornfield and the rye stubble, and afterward I tightened the wires on the fence around the stack yard. Then I put hay in the manger and gathered the eggs and got Daisy in, and the calves. By the time I had done the milk-

ing and strained the milk into the crocks it was almost sundown.

I kept waiting for the folks to get home. It got to be seven
o'clock and it was dark. I had the lamp lit so they could see it
from down in the Holler and know everything was all right.
And finally, at seven-thirty, I built a fire in the stove and fried
two eggs and made two sandwiches. Then I washed my dishes
and got a fresh pail of water and tried to read for a while. By
nine o'clock I was too sleepy to stay up any longer, so I locked
the door and left the lamp burning and lay down on my bed
with my clothes on. Fritz came and lay on the floor beside me,
and I went to sleep with one arm hanging over the edge of the
bed, touching him.

I woke up about eleven o'clock, panicky. I had had a bad
dream. In the dream my right arm had been cut off. I sat up,
terrified, and my arm was completely numb. It had gone to
sleep hanging over the edge of the bed. As soon as I sat up it
began to tingle. It had pins and needles in it. I rubbed it with
my other hand till it came to life again. The folks still hadn't
got home. I took off my shoes and pulled a cover up over me
and went back to sleep, feeling very lonely.

Morning, and they still weren't there. But it didn't matter
so much in daylight. You don't get half as lonesome when the
sun is shining, or even if it's cloudy but daylight, as you do at
night. I went out and did the milking, as always, and got the
early chores done, then came in and made coffee and ate breakfast, thinking that the folks wouldn't be home much before
noon.

I was right. It was a quarter of twelve before I saw Mack
and the buggy turn in at our trail. I went down to meet them.
But when I was close enough to see, Mother was alone.

Mother stopped the buggy and I got in beside her. The first
question I asked was, "Where's Father?"

She tried to smile, but it was an awfully tired smile. "I left
him in Brush," she said. "He's pretty sick. He'll probably be

there a couple of weeks. How are you? How did you make out? Were you worried when I didn't get back last night?"

"No," I said. Then I said, "Well, a little. But I knew you would be home today."

I let Mother out at the house and took the buggy to the barn and unhitched Mack and put him away. He kept nipping me until I put a few ears of corn in his feed box. When I went to the house Mother had changed her clothes and was heating the chicken and noodles for dinner.

We sat down at the table, but Mother didn't seem to have much appetite. She picked at a piece of chicken and finally said, "Your father has typhoid fever."

That meant nothing to me.

"I had typhoid when I was a girl," she said. "I almost died. They had to keep me wrapped in ice and wet sheets. Afterward I lost all my hair."

That was hard to believe. Mother had heavy hair so long it reached below her knees when she combed it. I couldn't imagine Mother without any hair. But it wouldn't matter so much with Father. He was partly bald anyway.

Mother talked about cases of typhoid fever she had known in Nebraska. It seemed that most of them died. I didn't know whether she meant Father was going to die too, but I couldn't bring myself to ask that question. She said the doctor said he was a very sick man, but that the crisis wouldn't come for another week and that she might as well come home meanwhile. You caught typhoid, the doctor had said, from water or milk. Judging by the time when he took sick, and the fact that Mother and I weren't sick, Father probably got it before he came home from the mountains, maybe from the stream water he drank while he was fishing.

Finally Mother said, "You know what this means, don't you? Your father being sick and in the hospital."

"What?"

"It means we'll have to get along with Mack this winter.

And we'll have to make out the best we can with what we have. There will be doctor bills, and the hospital. Oh, I'm so glad we didn't go right out and spend that money for another horse!"

She sat staring out the window for a moment, then slowly shook her head. "I don't know," she said, talking mostly to herself, "I don't know why things happen the way they do. Unless it's like Job, in the Bible, God seeing how much a person can bear. . . . Oh, I shouldn't talk that way! You are all right, aren't you? Here, let me feel your head."

She was satisfied that I hadn't any fever. "And," she said, "the way you eat, there's nothing wrong with your stomach. I guess you're not going to be sick." She got up to clear the table. "We'll just have to do the best we can. That's all anybody can ask. We'll make out with what we've got, and that's all there is to it."

So we settled down to a week of waiting, meanwhile doing the chores and whatever things we could to get ready for another winter of skimping. I put corn through the coffee grinder and sifted out the coarse part and Mother stowed the meal. She hadn't much grease to make soap, so we dug half a bushel of soapweed roots. Mother tried them and said they might do for washing clothes, but she doubted that soapweed root would get all the dirt out. Hopefully, I dug a buggyload of sagebrush roots and hauled them home to see if they made a good fire. They were hard to burn and they made such a smell that Mother said she'd rather pick up cow chips. So we gathered cow chips and stowed them in the half-empty barn.

And all the time I kept thinking about Father. Remembering the way he looked, and the way he talked, and the stories he told. About the time he was riding a skittish pony and it shied at the railroad tracks and threw him off. He broke one wrist when he fell, but he grabbed for the reins with the other hand. The pony stepped on the other wrist and broke it too, and one of his sisters—he was just a boy, then—had to feed him at the table for two weeks. Or the time he and his brother Walt were swimming in the mill pond and Walt dived and hit his head on a rock and didn't come up. Father dived in and hauled him out, and when Walt had coughed up all the water in his lungs he had a fight with Father because Father had hauled him out by the hair. The stories about swimming, and fishing, and skating. About the way he and his brothers begged a chicken from their mother and took it down among the horse weeds by the creek and plastered it with mud and roasted it in the campfire. After a while they cracked the baked mud off, and the feathers came off too and they had a fine roast chicken. Except they had forgotten to take out the innards.

And the later stories. How, after he learned the printer's trade, he worked for a man in Iowa who owned a furniture store as well as the newspaper and was also an undertaker. Father slept in a back room where the man stored his coffins. The story about how his father died of kidney trouble when Father was nineteen. For weeks before he died, Grandfather Borland had been working at some secret project, tapping something on the anvil and hiding it when one of the boys came into the shop. After he was dead, when they went through the desk in his blacksmith shop looking for a record of the money people owed him, they found a dozen tiny horseshoes. Perfect little horseshoes, calked and burnished, just about as big around as a silver dollar. Father's brothers said Grandfather Borland must have been crazy, but Father said he wasn't crazy at all.

There were so many stories, and I couldn't remember them all. There must have been many stories he never got around to telling me. I hoped he would get well soon, so I could hear the rest of them.

The week passed, and Mother said she was going to town the next day. I wanted to go along, but she said, "Not this time. Maybe he'll be well enough to come home, and it's pretty crowded with three in the buggy, especially if he's not feeling very good. But I won't stay overnight. I'll come home, even if it's late."

All that day, while she was gone, I kept planning what we would do tomorrow, with Father there. He wouldn't be feeling very well, so I would go ahead doing all the chores. He could rest. And I planned all the things I wanted to ask him, all the stories I wanted him to tell me again.

But Father didn't come home. Mother didn't get there till almost eight o'clock and she looked grim and tired and red-eyed. "Your father," she said, "is an awful sick man. His fever has gone up a hundred and five and they can't break it." She sat there in the lamplight, just staring for a moment. "I don't know what's going to happen. I'm to phone the doctor from Gary day after tomorrow." She stood up. "You'd better go to bed, son, and get your sleep."

Later, in the night, I wakened and heard her crying.

We drove to Gary two days later and Mother telephoned the doctor. When she had finished at the phone she said, "He said he's still the same. They can't break the fever. I'm to call him again day after tomorrow."

Two more days and we went to Gary again. That time when she called the doctor she listened a moment and began to cry. She said, "All right, Doctor, we'll come right on in."

I didn't have to ask any questions. I untied Mack at the hitch rack and we started right to Brush. "He's worse," Mother said. "The doctor says his bowels are punctured and he's getting weaker. He wants us there."

A little later Mother said, "If we'd thought, we could have stopped and asked Jake to milk Daisy tonight. But I didn't think we'd have to go on such short notice. Well, Daisy will just have to go unmilked tonight. That's all there is to it."

I pushed Mack along at a steady trot, but it was almost five o'clock when we got to town. We drove over to the doctor's house. There wasn't a real hospital in Brush. The doctor had fixed up rooms with hospital beds in the lower floor of his house and had a nurse and his wife, who had been a nurse before he married her, to take care of patients there.

The doctor's wife, in a white uniform, let us in. "Mrs. Borland," she said, whispering. "And this is the boy. I'm so glad you got here. Doctor's been expecting you."

"How is he?" Mother asked.

The doctor's wife forced a kind of sympathetic smile. "He's a very sick man."

She led us to a room at the end of the hallway. It smelled of strange drugs, the first hospital smell I had known. Something about the doctor's wife and the whole place made me aware of sickness and death as I had never before been aware. I tried to walk on tiptoe and I felt the tears pushing up inside.

The door of the room was part way open. Inside I saw the doctor beside the bed. In the bed was a stranger who looked a little like Father. His face was all bones and a tallowy white color. His mouth was partly open. He was breathing in little quick gasps. His eyes were closed. His hands lay on the sheet, his stubby fingers looking too big for the thin bones of his arms.

The doctor saw us and beckoned us inside. As we edged over to the bed I felt the tears on my cheeks. The doctor said, "They're here," speaking to Father.

Father opened his eyes. They were as big as saucers. He looked at us but he didn't see us. He ran his yellowish tongue over his dry lips and whispered, "Sarah. Sarah, why don't you come? I want to talk to you, Sarah!" He sighed, and for a long moment there wasn't any breathing at all. Then the quick respirations began again. His eyes closed and he seemed to sleep.

"He was rational just a little while ago," the doctor said. "Now he's in delirium again."

Mother took Father's hand, but it was no use. His hand was listless.

We left the room. The doctor followed us. He took us to a small waiting room at the front of the house. "I'm sorry, Mrs. Borland," he said. "I thought he might know you. You'd better wait here. He may have another rational period, and I'll call you."

"Doctor," Mother said, "tell me the truth. Is he dying?"

The doctor fingered the lodge emblem on his watch chain. "It's touch and go," he said. "We're doing all we can." He drew a deep breath. "I'm afraid he's pretty near at the end of his strength. That's why I told you to come."

For a moment there was a look of panic in Mother's face; then her jaw tightened and her eyes flashed. She looked the way she had that night after Dick and Shorty got the death camas. "Doctor," she said, "I didn't come in here to watch him die!"

The doctor cleared his throat. He looked at his fingers. "We're doing all we can," he said, and he turned and left us.

We sat down and waited. We waited an hour, and Mother got up and went to the front window and looked out. Her back was stiff as a poker. I could see the muscles along her jaw working in little knots. She came back and sat down, not even seeming to know I was there.

We waited another hour. Supper time came and went, and we weren't even aware of it.

It was almost eight o'clock when the doctor's wife came and motioned to us. As we followed her, Mother asked, "What happened?"

"He wants to see you."

I didn't know who wanted to see us, Father or the doctor. We went to Father's room. The doctor and the other nurse were there. Father lay just as before, but this time he really saw us. From the moment we entered the room he followed us with his eyes.

We went to the bedside and Father whispered, "Sarah! Son!" He tried to lift his hand. It fell back on the sheet and tears came to his eyes.

Mother said, "Will, you're going to get well. I had typhoid like this, and I got well. Do you understand?" There was iron in her voice.

There was a faint movement of his head. He was trying to nod yes. His hand moved again and Mother took it between hers. He looked at me and I took his other hand. It was so hot and weak that I let it go, then took it again, and he squeezed my fingers, very hard. He whispered, "I'm so tired," and his eyes drifted shut. He forced them open again and looked at Mother.

"Will," she said, "you're going to get well. You've got to!"

His eyes closed, but I saw his nostrils quiver the way they always did when he fought the tears of emotion.

We went back to the waiting room. A few minutes later the doctor came in and said, "At least, he recognized you. All through his delirium he's been talking about you."

"Has he passed the crisis?" Mother asked.

The doctor hesitated. "I'd say he's at the crisis now. This afternoon and tonight. If he hasn't lost too much blood, from the hemorrhages, and if his heart holds out—well, he may make it. Three hours ago he didn't have much chance." He started to go, then turned back at the doorway. "You'd better stay right here tonight. Here in the waiting room."

When the doctor had gone Mother said I'd better take Mack over to the livery stable for the night. When I got back the doctor's wife had brought a blanket apiece for us. Mother told me to lie down on the couch; she said she wouldn't sleep a wink anyway, so she would sit up in a chair.

I lay awake a long time, almost afraid to go to sleep. I didn't quite know why; I'd already had the shock of thinking Father was going to die, and the relief of knowing he didn't die when I thought he was going to. I kept thinking about the was he looked when we saw him the first time. I kept feeling that tight squeeze of his fingers. And I was aware of the strangeness of the hospital, the strange smells, the rustle of a uniform in the hallway, the quiet. I thought about the homestead. I listened for the sound of the sheep, and the bells. I thought about that night out there, the first night on our own land, when we walked out in the darkness to get the horses, and came back and Father pointed out the stars. And then I slept.

Once I wakened and saw Mother sitting there, staring at nothing, that never-say-die look on her face. Another time I wakened and she saw me move and said, "It's all right, son. Go back to sleep." And finally I wakened and saw that it was daylight outside. Mother was asleep. She heard me sit up and wakened with a start.

A few minutes later the nurse came to the door and Mother asked, "How is he?"

"Sleeping," the nurse said in a whisper. She helped Mother fold the blankets, and a few minutes later she came back with two cups of coffee. "Doctor's wife," she said, "said you ought to have something."

The coffee was hot and strong and wonderful, but it made me remember that we hadn't had any supper. Then I heard the doctor's voice in the hallway. He came in and said, "Well, he weathered the night. And his fever's down half a degree."

"Then the crisis is past," Mother said.

"Let's say it's passing. His heart is still doing pretty well. Now we'll see if he's too weak to hold his gain. If his heart can keep on—" He hesitated.

"Yes?"

The doctor sighed. "All I can say is that it isn't quite hopeless this morning."

"When will the next crisis come?"

"We'll have to watch his heart as the fever subsides. The next crisis probably will come in a couple of days."

"Should we stay?"

"That's up to you."

"I can stay if you want me to." She glanced at me. "He can go home and do the chores, and I can stay."

"Why don't we wait until ten o'clock and see if he holds his own. If he does, and if the fever continues to recede, I'd say you could go home. And phone me tomorrow."

"Yes?"

"And plan to come back the next day."

Father was still sleeping at ten o'clock. His fever had gone down another half a degree and his heart was doing pretty well, the doctor said. We went home.

When we drove to Gary the next morning and phoned the doctor he said that Father was still holding his own. "That is all we can expect at this point. You're coming in tomorrow?"

On the way home from Gary we stopped at Jake Farley's and he said he would milk Daisy and see that she and the calves were watered the next evening. And the next morning we drove to Brush again.

Father was delirious that afternoon and early evening, but about midnight he had a few clear minutes and recognized Mother and talked to her. The next morning he was asleep. The doctor said the fever was down to just over a hundred and the hemorrhages had slowed up. "His heart keeps laboring along," he said. "I don't know how, but it keeps going. And now we have a pretty good thread of hope."

For the next week we drove to Gary every day and telephoned. The reports were just a little better each day. "I don't know how he does it," the doctor said. "He has some shred of strength there, something, that keeps him going. His heart is getting a little stronger, just a trace, day by day. Why don't you come in tomorrow? He has more and more lucid periods. I think it may help if you come and see him."

Apparently it did help, though Father was too weak to say more than a few words. But when Mother said to him, "You are much better now. You are going to get well," he managed to nod, a real nod. "Don't worry about us," Mother said. "We're making out all right. All I want is for you to get well enough to come home." He smiled, the first real smile. And we knew he was going to pull through.

14

Father was in the hospital six weeks. Mother drove in and got him the Monday before Thanksgiving, and the doctor said as he was leaving, "I'll tell you now that I never expected to see you walk out of here. Come back and see me in a couple of weeks."

When he got out of the buggy at home I could hardly believe it was Father. He never had been a big man, only about five feet seven and slender, but now he was so thin a good wind would have blown him away. In his thin face, his eyes and his teeth looked twice their natural size. I had to push Fritz away or he would have knocked Father over in the eagerness of his greeting. Father hugged me and just stood there, one hand on my shoulder, and looked around. It was as though he'd wondered if he'd ever see the house and the barn and the draw and the flats again, and there they were.

I put Mack away. When I went to the house Mother was making a pot of coffee. Father was sitting at the table, still in his overcoat. Mother handed me a pail and said, "Get some sheep chips and start a fire in the heater. It's chilly in here."

Father started to get up. "I'll get them."

"You," Mother said, "stay right where you are."

"But I feel so useless!"

"You aren't here to do chores," Mother said. "You're here to rest and get your strength back."

I got the chips and started the fire. It began to warm up,

Mother poured the coffee, and I took Father's overcoat and hung it up. He kept watching us, and finally he said, "I can't quite believe it. It's been so long that I was away."

"It's been six weeks," Mother said.

"And now it's almost the end of November. Winter is coming on."

"Don't start worrying about winter," Mother said. "We came through last winter all right."

"I wanted this winter to be better. I wanted to have plenty of coal, and—"

"We've got sheep chips. And there's more where those came from."

"And things to eat."

"We've never starved yet."

"Do you know how thin you are, Sarah?"

"You should see yourself."

He glanced down at his skin-and-bones arms, the big pleat in the waistband of his trousers. He had lost more than twenty pounds.

"I don't want to be in debt." He said it quietly, but from down deep inside.

"I don't either. But the doctor said he would wait."

"Not forever. And you must be down to your last dollar."

"Does it matter now? Oh, Will, stop worrying! I did enough worrying for both of us. But now you're home. We'll pay up, somehow." She went to the stove for the coffeepot. "More?"

Father shook his head. "It doesn't taste right. Oh, it's not your coffee. It tasted the same way in the hospital. I guess something happened to my taste."

Mother smiled. "Then I guess we can save on coffee." She glanced at the clock. "It's almost milking time, son."

Father said, "I'll do it," and started to get up.

Mother gave him one look. He eased back into his chair. I put on my coat and went to the barn.

That's the way it was going to go, and we knew it. Father

wanted to do everything, and he hadn't the strength. He complained that we were babying him, and he would sit for half
an hour at a time, just staring out the window. But his strength
began to come back. Thanksgiving morning he pumped a
whole pail of water and had to stop for breath only once. But
I had to carry it to the house for him.

Mother and I thought things were going very well. When
we sat down to dinner on Thanksgiving Day Mother said,
"Oh, it's good to be here, all three of us!" Then she laughed.
"But I don't know whether we ought to eat or not."

"Why not?" Father asked.

"It's chicken and noodles again. Don't you remember what
happened the last time I killed a hen and made noodles for
you?"

But Father didn't think it was funny. He took the bowl and
helped himself. He picked up his fork, then laid it down again.
He said, "I don't know whether we're lucky to be out here or
not, but I know I'm glad to be alive." His voice choked up. He
waited a moment, then said, "Maybe I don't know the right
way to say it, but I'd like to say how thankful I am."

He bowed his head, and so did Mother and I, and I said to
myself, "Thank you, God."

We never said grace. It just wasn't our way. Mother once
said, "If you're not thankful to have something to eat, saying
you are out loud doesn't change things one bit. I think my
thanks every time I sit down at the table." We all did, except
once in a while, as on that Thanksgiving Day. We didn't often
talk about God or religion, though back in Nebraska we always went to church and Sunday school. And mother taught
me my prayers. But we weren't the praying-in-public kind of
people. My most fervent prayers were said in the morning,
when I first went outdoors and saw the world, all clean and
bright and brand new and full of wonder. Or sometimes at
night, when the stars were all out or the moon was there. And
I didn't bow my head to say them; I looked up at the sky or

out across the plains. Religion wasn't the way you talked; it was the way you lived, and mostly it was the Golden Rule and the Ten Commandments.

Father rested and ate, and we made things easy for him, but when it snowed the day after Thanksgiving he began to worry again. It wasn't much of a snow, only a couple of inches, and it made the whole country bright and shimmery. After the dry summer we were glad to have it. But Father said he hated to see the snow come so early. He went out and looked at the haystacks and the corn in the bin. Mother asked what was the matter, and he said, "We haven't much laid by for the winter."

"You," she said, "are worse than your brother Walt. Unless Ida put up two hundred quarts of fruit and vegetables, and unless he had twenty bushels of potatoes and ten hams in the cellar, he was sure he was going to starve to death. We could have got fat on what Walt had to throw out every spring."

Father smiled, but it was a wan smile.

"Stop worrying," Mother ordered. "With only one horse and one cow and the two calves, we've got enough."

But Father said, "You aren't fooling me one bit. When I wasn't here you didn't eat the way we're eating now."

"I'm trying to put some flesh on your bones. You heard the doctor say you had to build yourself up."

"What are we going to eat later? Do you expect to live on credit at the Gary store?"

"No," Mother said. "We'll eat cornmeal mush, if we have to. Or parched corn. Or something. We'll eat what we've got. And be glad to have it."

Father ate, and he gained strength day by day. The deep gauntness began to leave his face. His arms began to get some of their old strength. He was strong enough to walk up to the cornfield and back. He tried to milk Daisy but had to give up when he was half through. His hands and wrists just didn't have the strength. But a few days later he tried again, and milked right down to the stripping.

Except for what it meant to him, it didn't matter whether

he was strong enough to do the chores or not. It was enough just to have him there, up and around and alive. You don't appreciate things like that until you've faced the possibility of never having them again. So we all looked after him, even Fritz, who didn't try to jump on him. Even Mack, the old cow pony.

The first Saturday he was home, Father and I went to the barn to hitch up and go to Gary for the mail. Father said he would harness Mack. He tossed the harness on and buckled the belly band before I remembered about the crupper. Even if Father remembered that Mack kicked when you put the crupper under his tail, he probably couldn't get out of the way.

"Wait a minute!" I said.

Father was holding the crupper, reaching for Mack's tail. "What's the matter?" he asked.

"He kicks when—"

Father lifted Mack's tail. Mack jerked up his hoof to kick. Then he looked around, saw Father, and put his hoof down. Father buckled the crupper and asked, "Who kicks what?" Then he remembered. He slapped Mack on the rump and exclaimed, "You old devil, are you babying me too?" He stepped back and said, "You can bridle him."

It took me five minutes to get the bit in Mack's mouth. He hadn't changed at all, but he must have known that Father must be treated rather special.

It was the middle of the next week when old Pat Thompson came to see us. Pat was the horse ranchman from over on Badger Creek, the old-timer who had come from Texas long ago, had been a buffalo hunter and finally settled down on the Badger, an eccentric hermit who rode about the plains like a ghost out of the past. He had never been at our place before.

Father and I were at the barn, doing the morning chores. I was forking out the manure and Father was spreading fresh bedding. And this strange horseman came down off the flats to the south. His big bay horse watched the barn with ears pointing, but the rider slouched in the saddle, a hunch-shouldered man turtled into a short brown coat and wearing a low-crowned flat-brimmed hat tilted low over his eyes. He was wearing smooth leather chaps.

He rode into the barnyard and I saw that he was an old man. A very old man. He must have been at least seventy. His face was leathery beneath a white stubble and he wore a long gray mustache that drooped at the ends. His eyes were half covered by eyelids that sagged at the corners so you saw only a little triangle of eyeball.

He drew up and said, "Howdy," and eased himself sideways in his saddle.

Father said, "Hello."

The old man glanced inside the barn, looked at the haystacks, gave the fenced field up the slope one quick glance, and said, "So you're still here." His voice was a soft drawl.

"Yes," Father said. "What can I do for you?"

The old man didn't answer. He dropped his looped reins over the saddle horn, reached inside his coat for tobacco and papers, and rolled a cigarette. He flicked a match with his thumbnail and lit it. Then he said, "You'll starve out. They all do."

That didn't need an answer.

He nodded toward the school section and Louie's windmill. "So will Gerrity," he said. "He's lost a pot of money this year. This is cattle country. Cattle and horses. Grass. If God Almighty had meant it to be plowed, He'd of plowed it to begin with. Nor," he added, "did the Almighty mean it to be stunk up by sheep."

Father said, "You seem to know. Won't you get off and have a cup of coffee?"

The old man said, "I ought to know. I've seen enough of 'em come and go. . . . I had my coffee. . . . I first come up this way in the seventies, with a herd from down on the Brazos."

"That," Father said, "was quite a while back."

The old man stared at him a moment. His eyes were an almost milky blue, eyes that had looked a long way and a long time. "Before I was his age"—he nodded toward me—"I was riding herd. Before I was as old as you, I'd fathered four kids and fought a war." He shifted in his saddle as though easing a painful leg. "Where you from?"

"Nebraska. My name's Borland."

"I'm Pat Thompson." He stared at Father again and asked, "What the hell did you come out here for?"

Father flushed. "I came out here to stay," he said.

The old man's mouth gave a flicker of a smile. "You'll go back. Like the rest of them. Go back and live on your wife's folks." He spat in disgust. "You'll dry out, or you'll blizzard out, or you'll just quit."

"No," Father said.

The old man looked beyond the barn, up the hill and into some remote distance. "I seen the buffalo go," he said, "and the Indians. Grass is growing over the Indian graves, and it'll grow over mine, and it'll grow over yours, if you stay. That's all this country is, grass." He focused his eyes on us for a long moment, then lifted the reins, squared himself in the saddle, and turned his horse. He rode back up the slope to the south at a slow half-lope, riding as though he had been in the saddle ever since the first saddle was invented by the Romans.

We watched him out of sight. Then Father got another forkful of bedding. He put it in the barn and stood in the doorway a long time, staring out at the plains. Then he went to the house and talked to Mother for a while. When he came back I heard Mother singing, and I knew that Father had made up his mind to something.

It's a strange and wonderful thing, what a few words can do to a man's spirit. Father had been pretty well discouraged. He'd been about ready to call off the whole homestead venture, pull out, move to town, and start all over again. He had his conscience to fight, of course, because he wasn't one to leave a job half finished. But he had a sense of responsibility, too. He thought it was too much for Mother to take, with all the setbacks we'd had. Then old Pat came over, his mind set on discouraging us. All the ranchmen were the same way. John Gerrity had tried it while we were digging the well. If we hadn't found water that afternoon, Father might have kept thinking about Gerrity's words and begun to defeat himself right there at the start. Instead, we struck water and Gerrity's words didn't mean a thing. Pat Thompson, too, came at the wrong time.

When Pat Thompson talked about grass growing over Father's grave he didn't know how close Father had come to that grave, or how recently. He wasn't scaring Father one bit. And when he said, "You'll go back, like the rest of them. Go back and live on your wife's folks," he was calling Father a quitter. You can call a cowardly man a coward and make him afraid and ashamed, but if you call a brave man a coward and a quitter you usually get him fighting mad.

Long afterward I mentioned Pat Thompson's visit to Father and recalled what he had said. Father said, "I remember that, vaguely. I can't remember a word he said, but I know he made me mad as a wet hen. If he said what you say he did, it sounds harmless enough now. It even makes sense. I probably got mad because I was thinking about leaving the homestead, for your Mother's sake. Wasn't that just a little while before Christmas?"

I said yes. He said, "Maybe I wanted to quit, and it made me mad to have him call me a quitter. The odd thing is that you don't have to be a coward to quit, sometimes. The outsider never knows all the reasons." He smiled. "Anyway, we didn't quit that winter. Maybe we can thank Old Pat Thompson."

The day he had to go in to see the doctor again was a brittle winter morning. Mother said she wasn't going, that Father and

I could go in alone. So we wrapped ourselves in horse blankets and put the lantern at our feet and started long before daylight.

Dawn came about halfway to Gary, one of those winter days when you can almost see into the beyond. It was getting close to the winter solstice, and when the sun finally came up it was away off to the south; but the horizon seemed twice as far away as usual. The world, on the plains, spreads out like forever at any time of year, but it is even bigger in winter. There aren't any heat waves or mirages to dazzle the skyline and catch the eye. It's just a clean line, away off there, with the deep blue of the sky above and the tan-brown of the earth beneath, and very little in sight anywhere. Old men who have lived there a long time, like Pat Thompson, have some of that distance in their eyes, like sailors who have known the ocean's distances for years.

It was that way all the way to Gary that morning, and it was a little that way the rest of the trip to Brush, except that the houses and barns and fences on the farms changed it and made you see and think about short distances.

Then we came to the hard road and drove up the long aisle of cottonwoods. It looked twice as cold with all the naked trees as it had out on the flats without any trees at all. We crossed the tracks and went up Main Street and turned across to the doctor's house.

The doctor took Father into his office and I waited in the wating room, thinking how different it seemed in daylight and when Father wasn't down the hall in a white bed, so sick he didn't even know me when I stood beside him. Then he and the doctor came back, and the doctor was saying, "You're doing fine. By the first of the year you should really be on your feet again." He turned to me. "You and your mother have been taking good care of him. Keep it up."

Father said, "I'll clean up the bill just as soon as I can."

"When you can," the doctor said. "Everybody seems to have bills, even us doctors." He took Father's hand. "Good luck."

It was almost noon. Mother had said we should get something hot to eat on a cold day like this, at least a bowl of hot soup. We drove back down Main Street to the café. While I was tying Mack at the hitch rack the editor came out of his office, just across the street, and shouted to Father, "Come on over here! I want to see you."

We crossed the street to the newspaper office and went inside where it was warm. I sniffed at the ink and paper smell, and I saw Father do the same thing. The editor said, "Good to see you back on your feet. How are you?"

Father told him what the doctor had said, that he was doing fine.

"Do you want to go to work?" the editor asked.

Father said, "Yes."

"How soon can you start?"

"How about the first of the year?"

"I need you right now," the editor said. "My man's out. And all this Christmas rush on my hands."

Father drew a deep, long breath. "Tomorrow?" he asked.

"Tomorrow will be fine. I wish you could start right now."

"I've got to go home," Father said, "and get my clothes. And tell my wife." His voice was shaky. "I may not be much good for a week or so. You know that, don't you? I doubt that I could lift a form yet. But maybe I can be of some help."

"You can set type. You can feed the jobber. You'll come in tomorrow, then?"

"Yes. For how long?"

"As long as you want to stay. I'm sick and tired of a booze fighter who buys a bottle every time I get a rush of work."

"It'll be the middle of the morning," Father said, "before I can get in. It's quite a drive."

"And look," the editor said, "I'll fix up a cot for you in the back room, if you want it. Then you won't have to put out money for a hotel room."

Father nodded. I knew he was afraid to try to answer. I saw his nostrils quivering, his teeth clenched on his lip.

We went back across the street to the restaurant and had hot soup and crackers. Father's fingers were trembling at first so much that he could hardly hold the spoon.

Mother had done the milking and the chores, so we sat down to supper as soon as we got home and put Mack away. Father told her that the doctor said he was doing fine, that everything was all right. And then he said, "I've got a job."

"No!"

"Ed wants me. He saw me on the street and offered me a job."

"Oh, Will, isn't that wonderful!"

"I told him you'd take me in, first thing tomorrow."

"Not tomorrow! Why, you can't—"

"I told him I would start tomorrow. He needs me right away."

"But you've only been out of the hospital—"

"I am starting work tomorrow," Father said firmly. "It's all settled."

Mother was silent a moment. Then she asked, "Just what did the doctor say? He didn't say you could go to work yet, did he?"

"He said I could go to work when I felt like it. Sarah, I told you just the other day, after Pat Thompson had been here, that I was going to get a job. That's the only way we can stay, if I get a job and pay off the debt."

"Just two more weeks," Mother pleaded. "Wait till the first of the year."

"Ed needs me now. Tomorrow. I have to go."

Mother cleared away the dishes. Then she got her needle and thread and began sewing on buttons and turning up frayed shirt cuffs.

15

There was little talk at breakfast. Father said, "I'll get out for a weekend now and then. Ed will let me off at noon Saturday once in a while and I can come out with Con."

"Not too often," Mother said.

"Now and then."

"Not in bad weather. You might not be able to get back."

"I'll let you know ahead of time. I'll have a letter waiting at Gary, and if I'm coming you can wait for Con."

Neither of them was saying what they wanted to say. Father didn't want to go and leave us, and Mother didn't want him to go, especially so soon. But we had a debt and it had to be paid. There were no two ways about it; you paid your debts. If you didn't owe money, you could go on short rations and make out somehow, but when you owed a debt you got to work and paid it back. It was more than a financial obligation; it was a moral obligation. The man who died with debts unpaid had failed his family, for they had to pay them after he was gone. You paid your bills, you squared yourself with the world and, if you were thrifty, you put enough aside to pay for your final illness and burial. It was more than a custom; it was a way of life.

So Father was going to work two weeks after he left the hospital. He couldn't yet carry a full pail of water from the well to the house, but there were doctor's bills to be paid. That was why Mother hadn't argued too long or too hard last night. You can't argue against your own deep convictions.

We ate breakfast and I harnessed Mack and hitched him to the buggy and they started to Brush an hour before sunup.

It was a raw December day and I thought before they left that I felt a threat of snow in the air. By midmorning I was sure of it, but it held off till afternoon. Then it began to come, a fine, slow snow with only a little wind. There was almost an inch of it on the ground when Mother got home soon after four.

I put Mack away and did the evening chores and carried an extra pail of sheep chips to the house. The snow was coming harder and it was getting colder, but it was just a snow, not a blizzard. The wind hadn't risen, and you don't have a blizzard without wind.

At supper Mother said, "Well, your father has a nice, warm place to sleep. And he promised he would eat regular meals at the restaurant. If he takes care of himself I guess he'll be all right." She looked at me, appraising. "I don't think he could take the cold out here this winter, the way we can. He complained about the cold today, driving to town. And," she added, "he never did care for beans."

I helped with the dishes, and Mother said, "I do wish he could have waited a little longer. Till the first of the year at least. But I guess everything works out for the best. We'll make out. And by next summer we'll be out of debt."

That was the important thing. I knew it as well as she did. Last winter we had just held on, waiting for spring. This winter we would hold on, waiting to get out of debt.

The snow kept coming, fine and fluffy, till the next noon, five or six inches of it. Then the sky cleared and the cold clamped down. For a couple of days we kept both stoves going, the cookstove and the heater. Then Mother said, "If we keep on this way we'll be out of fuel before winter's half over. I think we can get along with one fire. We'll keep the cookstove going and we'll let the fire in the heater go out."

After that we had a fire in the heater only when Father was

at home. We piled the covers on the beds at night and Mother always had flatirons heating to put at our feet, and we didn't even try to hold fire overnight. I started the fire again when I got up in the morning, and the bean kettle simmered all day long. Beans take a long time to cook, especially at that altitude where water doesn't boil as hot as it does in Nebraska.

The next Saturday the Christmas box from Nebraska was waiting for us at Gary. And there was a letter from Father. He said he was feeling fine. They had more work at the shop than they could handle, and he was working overtime. Ed had him doing all the color work, and most of the Christmas printing was color work. He would be home the following Saturday, and since Christmas came on Monday he would have two days at home and then go back with Con Hallahan on Tuesday morning.

On the way home from Gary I kept thinking about the box from Nebraska and about Christmas. It had come along so fast that I hadn't realized it was just over a week ahead. Finally I asked Mother what I should make for Father's present this year.

"Don't try to make a thing," she said. "Nor for me either. Your Father and I decided not to give any presents this year. We'll have the box from back home, and that'll be all. Next year, when we're out of debt, we'll have Christmas again."

I just sat there in the buggy, staring past Mack's ears at the road ahead. I felt numb all over. It wasn't the presents. It was—well, it was just Christmas. I felt almost as bad as I did the Christmas when I was six years old. Father took a new job that winter, in a town fifty miles from where we had been living, and he had to go ahead and start work the week before Christmas. For some reason, Mother and I couldn't go till the day after Christmas, and Father couldn't get home. So Mother, thinking it was the best thing to do, told me there wasn't any Santa Claus. The blow of that Christmas, even though I had more presents than usual, hurt and ached for months and even years. It still hurt a little. And the old ache came back when she told me there wasn't going to be any Christmas this year.

The more I thought about it, the deeper the hurt grew. I was too big for tears; anyway, the hurt was too unreasonable to be eased by crying. But the disappointment was an ache that started in my throat and reached all the way down to my toes.

Mother said, "Don't you know, son, that you are giving us the best Christmas present anyone could ask?"

I couldn't answer.

"Without you," she said, "I couldn't stay out here on the homestead. And your father couldn't go to town and pay off the doctor bill. We'd have to give up the homestead." Then she said, "I'm sure there's something nice in the box from back home."

But the dull ache in me kept right on aching. I wasn't doing the chores just to make Mother and Father happy. I was doing those things because they had to be done. When I milked Daisy I didn't think: This is my Christmas present to Father. When I pitched a forkful of manure onto the steaming pile beside the barn door I didn't think: This is my present to Mother, so she can stay here on the homestead. I did those things because they had to be done and I was there to do them.

But you don't grow up all at once. And even after you're grown up you have hurts and disappointments that ache and hurt; and you can't always get rid of them by telling someone else. You learn to live with them, and eventually you grow some kind of scar tissue over them.

I ached for several days. Then I began to accept it. Next year we would have Christmas. This year we would have the box from Nebraska. With another childish fairy tale for me. All right, I told myself, so there wouldn't be any Christmas this year. And I half wished it would snow and blizzard so much that Father couldn't get home. Then we could forget Christmas till next year. But that was a selfish wish, and I knew it, and it didn't make any sense at all. Father wanted to come home for Christmas, and I wanted him to, and so did Mother. That was going to be Christmas this year, just having Father at home and well.

And something began to straighten out inside of me. Christmas wasn't presents. It wasn't even talking about Christmas and singing Christmas songs. It was something that happened deep down in you, some happiness you had or those around you had. And the inner ache began to fade.

We went in late, the Saturday afternoon we were to meet Father for Christmas. Mother said that if we went late we wouldn't have to wait so long, but I knew that she meant that we wouldn't see or hear so much about Christmas at the store and maybe feel bad about it.

When we got there we walked in and it looked and smelled and sounded just as it had the year before. But I felt like a person watching someone else's party, standing off to one side. The Christmas that everybody was talking about wasn't our Christmas. The cranberries and candy and oranges and nuts were pretty, but they weren't Christmas. Not our Christmas. The only reason we were there was to meet Father, not to have any part of that Christmas they were talking about.

We had just got warmed up when Con arrived, whooping and hollering, and people surged out to meet him. Con leaped down and carried the mail pouches inside and the men began unloading the boxes. Father climbed down and hurried to Mother and kissed her and went back and got his suitcase and a package and put them in the back of the buggy. We all got in and arranged the blankets, with the lantern at our feet, and we started home.

Mother asked about the job. She said Father looked worn out.

"Sure I'm tired," he said. "Been working overtime every night this week. But now I've got two whole days to rest up. I'm not going to do a lick of work all the time I'm home." He laughed. "Why should I, with a big fellow like this around? How are you, son?"

It was just the way I hoped it would be. We weren't having Christmas, but we were having two days with Father at home. I hoped they wouldn't sing Christmas songs, the way they did last year.

But they did. Just as soon as they had asked and answered all the questions, as soon as we got out in the sand hills and the dark settled around us with all the stars, Father started singing. Mother joined him. And pretty soon I was singing too. We sang all the way to Ketchem Holler.

When we got home I started a fire in the heater before I did the chores. And after supper Father talked about the printing office. He told about the three-color jobs he had done, and how Ed said he was the best color man he'd ever had working for him. "I taught Ed a few things about underlay," he said. "And I showed him how to put a mask on the grippers so you could do three-color work with only two colors. He'd never heard about it."

Mother said, "I guess he appreciates a good man when he sees one. Have you any idea how long the job's going to last?"

"I sounded him out the other day," Father said. "I said I'd like to take a week off in the spring and get a corn crop in. He said he thought we could arrange that. So I judge he expects to keep me on."

They were still talking when I went to bed.

It was snowing when I got up the next morning and built the fires. Not hard. We hadn't had a real blizzard yet that winter, and this didn't look like one. But at breakfast Mother started worrying, afraid we would be snowed in and Father couldn't get back to town. It kept up all morning. Then, in midafternoon, the snow stopped and the sky cleared. Before we went to bed that night Father went outdoors and came back and said, "A fine day tomorrow."

"How do you know?" Mother asked.

"Stars are shining. Anyway, it can't snow on Christmas!"

It was the first mention of Christmas.

Mother said, "I've known it to. Remember last year?"

Father laughed. "That was last year. This year is different. This year is going to be better."

I went to bed telling myself the same thing. This year was going to be better. And next winter we would have Christmas again. Then it hit me. This was Christmas Eve.

All that wall I had built up began to crumble. It was Christmas Eve and there wasn't going to be any Christmas. Tomorrow would just be Monday. I gritted my teeth and bit my lip and pulled the covers over my head. I scrooched down and put my feet on the hot flatiron wrapped in a towel and I fought the tears.

I thought of Gary and the people talking and laughing, full of Christmas. I thought of all the Christmas things. I had heard without listening and I had seen without looking, and it was almost too much to fight down. Then I heard the sound of Father's voice and slowly the hurt began to relax away. Tomorrow was only Monday, but Father was home. That was our Christmas this year, Father being home.

The next morning we ate breakfast without anybody saying "Merry Christmas." Father looked out the window and said, "It is a nice day, just like I said it was going to be."

I said it was pretty cold out. Mother said it wasn't as cold as yesterday. The ice on the water pail wasn't as thick, she said. She cleared away the dishes and she said, "Well, we might as well open the box from Nebraska, I guess. Go get it, son."

I brought the box and Father opened it. There was a necktie for him, this time a blue one. And a pair of blue socks. There was a knitted scarf for Mother and a pair of matching mittens. There was a pair of embroidered pillow cases. There was a stocking cap for me, a red one, and mittens to go with it. And the book. This year it was *The Sleeping Beauty*. And a peck of black walnuts, half a peck of hazel nuts, two glasses of grape jelly and two glasses of currant jelly. None of them was spilled or broken.

Mother looked at the gifts. "They're nice," she said, "every one of them. A lot of work went into them." She picked up one of the pillow cases. "This looks like Eva's work."

She took her things and put them away in her dresser. Father put his in his suitcase and came back and put a long brown-paper package on the table. It was the package he had with his suitcase when he arrived.

Mother asked, "What's that?"

"Just something I picked up." Father couldn't hide his grin.

"Will, you didn't!"

"Open it," he said to me.

I started to tear the brown wrapping paper. Mother said, "Will, you promised."

"It's not a Christmas present," Father said. "It's something I meant to get when I got back from the mountains."

I tore the paper enough to reveal a gun barrel. I ripped the rest of it. There was the stock. A shotgun, a .12-gauge shotgun. And a box of shells for it.

I stood there speechless.

"Know how to put it together?" Father asked. He showed me. I stood there holding it, and he said, "It's not for Christmas. It's for—well, for last summer. And for taking care of things while—while I was sick." He turned to Mother. "Ed paid me a little extra for the overtime, and—and he can use it this winter to—well, to help out at the table. It's—it's just a second-hand gun."

I don't know what Mother said, or what she looked, but it was all right. I couldn't take my eyes or my thoughts off the gun. Then Father said, "Let's go out and try it."

We went out to the stack yard. Father penciled a mark on a fence post and I fired the first shot. It kicked because I didn't have it snug to my shoulder, but I put a dozen pellets around the mark. Then Father tried it and said, "It's a good gun." He handed it back to me, and I fired one more shot with the butt up tight to my shoulder and it hardly kicked at all.

Father said, "Keep it clean. Drop a string through it and tie a rag on the string and pull it through the barrel. Clean it every time you get home after you've been hunting. Never crawl through a fence with a shell in it and never have it loaded in the house."

I said, "Thank you. I wanted a shotgun more than anything else in the world, but—"

"You earned it, I guess. I suppose you'll want to go hunting."

"Can I?"

"Wait till after dinner and I don't think your mother will mind."

I gave him the gun to take into the house and went to work on the chores. If I didn't do the best job of choring ever done it wasn't because I didn't try. I did everything that had to be done and quite a lot of things that had waited weeks for doing. I was still at it when Mother called me to the table at eleven-thirty. She had dinner ready early just for me.

I cleaned my plate before either she or Father was half through, and Mother said, "All right. You're excused. Your father says you want to go hunting. Put on your overshoes and mackinaw and run along. At least, you do know how to handle a gun. Which way are you going?'

"I think I'll go over west."

"Just so we know. Be careful."

It was a glistening cold day, cold enough that the snow hadn't melted. It lay soft and almost powdery, about five inches deep. I climbed the ridge back of the house and started west.

It's strange, when you're not out after rabbits you see dozens of them, and when you are after them you can go five miles and not see one. That day, of course, they were lying close because of the cold. I was clear over beyond where Dick and Shorty found the camas before I saw the first jack. He was a big white-tail, and he jumped out of a clump of bunch grass twenty yards ahead of me. He ran like mad, quartering away from me, but I got a shot at him. I didn't lead him enough. The shot kicked up snow just behind him. Then he really ran.

I reloaded and took after him, hoping he would settle in and give me a chance for another shot. But he wasn't settling. I trailed him two miles and saw him twice, both times far out of range.

I was at least three miles from home when I saw a thread of smoke over the next rise half a mile away. It must be from the Bromley place, I thought. The Bromleys were the Chicago people who came out with the strange farm implements. Mr. Bromley was the man about whom people had joked, quoting his ridiculous questions and no doubt making up as many as he really asked. We still hadn't met them, because they had been using the road over west and doing their trading in Fort Morgan, which was eleven miles west of Brush.

I saw the thread of smoke and I remembered the funny stories. Then my rabbit jumped, just out of range, and I knew he was getting tired of running. Next time he might let me get close enough for a shot. I hurried on. Then, just as I topped the rise, another big white-tail lunged out of the snow right in front of me. I was lucky. I led him just right and he went end over end. I'd got my first rabbit with the new gun.

I was running down the slope to pick up my rabbit when I heard a man shouting. I looked up and there was the Bromley house just below me, a little white-painted house, and a tall stooped man was standing in the doorway shouting, "Hello! Hello! Come on in! Merry Christmas!"

I picked up my rabbit, proud as a young Indian who had killed his first fat buffalo cow, and went down to the house.

Mr. Bromley had on a store-bought suit and a white shirt. I

left my rabbit in the snow outside the door and went inside. The house was as big as ours, but it looked smaller because the bedroom was partitioned off, not just curtained, and there was a rug on the floor and lace curtains at the windows. It was full of savory cooking smells. Mrs. Bromley, a tall slender woman with gray in her hair, had on a city dress. Both of them were old folks; they must have been in their forties. She greeted me and took my mackinaw and she urged me to sit down.

I sat on the edge of a chair beside a bookcase and a few minutes later Mrs. Bromley brought a cup of hot cocoa and a plate of cookies. Then they both sat down and began to ask questions.

I drank cocoa and ate cookies and told them who I was, and that Father was a printer, and that we came from Nebraska. And I told them about my new gun and the rabbit.

"You are rather young, aren't you," Mrs. Bromley asked, "to be out hunting alone. Aren't you afraid you will get lost?"

I smiled. I never got lost.

Mr. Bromley said, "You are talking to a young plainsman, Alice, not to a city boy. A direct descendant of Daniel Boone and Kit Carson." He smiled.

I don't know what she answered, but she didn't laugh. I wasn't paying much attention, because I had seen the books in that bookcase beside me. There must have been thirty or forty books. One group of them were all alike except their titles. They were large red books with figures of Indians and frontiersmen outlined on their covers.

Mrs. Bromley was talking to me, asking, "Do you read?" and I remembered my manners.

"Yes, ma'am," I said. "I read everything. I've read hundreds of stories in magazines Jack Clothier gave me. He's a cowboy from over at the Lazy Four, but he's gone to Wyoming now."

"Have you ever read Cooper?" she asked. "James Fenimore Cooper."

"No, ma'am." I wasn't sure whether that was the name of a book, a magazine, or an author.

"Or Scott? Or Dickens?"

"No, ma'am."

"I think you might like them," she said. She took one of the large red volumes from the shelf and handed it to me. I opened it and began to read *The Last of the Mohicans*.

I don't know how long I read. At eleven a boy can immerse himself completely in Cooper newly discovered. Mr. and Mrs. Bromley, their house, the plains themselves, were completely forgotten. But at last I heard Mrs. Bromley saying, "Here's another cup of cocoa to warm you on your way. You must start home before dark or your mother will worry. And you might get lost."

I put down the book and drank the cocoa, still in the woods with Hawkeye and Uncas. Then I put on my mackinaw, and Mrs. Bromley gave me a little package of cookies for my pocket. And she asked, "Would you like to take a book with you?"

I didn't have to answer. She saw my face. She took the book I had been reading, wrapped it carefully, and said, "Put it inside your coat and keep it dry. When you've finished it, bring it back and get another."

I picked up my shotgun, remembered to say my thanks, and started for home over the hills where the purple shadows of early dusk already lay deep across the snow.

I was halfway home before I emerged from the story of Uncas and a land I had never seen or heard of, before I really saw the Colorado plains and felt the numbing cold of that Christmas evening. Then I remembered that I had left my rabbit beside the Bromley doorway. The first rabbit I had shot with my new gun.

The quick of a boy's being is close to the surface. I began to cry, excusing the tears because my hands were cold and I was bitterly disappointed. I wanted so desperately to be a man and a provider. Father had given me the gun so we could have meat for the table.

The thoughts of boyhood are at once so simple and so complex, and the feelings can be so deep, so immediate. He hasn't

211

yet calloused himself with adulthood. The world is at once close about him and remote as the stars; it is friendly, and intimate, and hopelessly baffling. He hasn't yet made his compromises with it.

I had just discovered a world of horizons beyond horizons, a world I couldn't see even from the top of the haystack on a clear day. I had found something that would shape my whole life. It was too late now to go back for the rabbit, and as I trudged on I began to sense my discovery, a discovery even bigger than the plains. The tears stopped and I hurried on home, hugging both the gun and the book.

16

Father went back to Brush the morning after the Christmas that wasn't going to be Christmas but that turned out to be the best Christmas I could remember. And on the Saturday before New Year's Day we had our first blizzard of the winter.

I thought it was going to be a beautiful storm, and it started out that way. But after about five inches of snow the wind got the better of the snow and all we got was a blow. It cleaned off the hilltops and piled four-foot drifts all over the place. By skirting the drifts I was able to ride Mack over to the Bromleys' and return *The Last of the Mohicans* and get *The Pioneers*. The trails were too drifted to get out in the buggy and I wanted go to Gary on horseback, but Mother said there was no need of it. She said next weekend we'd get there, and by then she would have enough butter to trade for a pound of coffee and some salt pork. So I went out on foot and shot a couple of jack rabbits.

I wanted winter to be exciting. I wanted some real storms. Summer storms were fun, and they gave you a shivery feeling sometimes, when the great, towering clouds boiled like foam in a kettle and lightning flashed in all directions and the thunder made the hills bounce. But there weren't many summer storms like that. And with the exception of the Christmas storm, when Dick brought me home from the big sheep camp, last winter hadn't amounted to much. I wanted a real rip-tearing blizzard.

I got it.

The Saturday when we were all set to try to get to Gary in the buggy it began to snow in midmorning. It was just a slow, quiet snowfall with hardly any wind, but Mother said we'd better not start out in it. I thought she was being too cautious, but by the middle of the afternoon I knew she was right. The wind came up and it really began to blizzard.

Dark came early, and I started the chores. The wind was still gusty when I began the milking, but by the time I was through it was roaring. I headed for the house with the milk, and the minute I got out of the shelter of the barn the wind almost knocked me down. The pail was only half full of milk, but that wind blew almost a third of it right out of the pail. I made it to the house and said, "We've got a *real* storm this time!"

Mother said, "I'm afraid so. We'd better bring in some extra sheep chips for the night."

I said I'd bring them in when I finished the chores, but she said, "We'll get them right now," and she started to put on her coat and overshoes.

"You'd better stay here," I said. "That wind is whooping."

She laughed. She wasn't afraid of wind or weather. She tied a scarf over her head and took a fuel pail and we started for the barn. We barely got around the corner of the house when the wind hit her. It blew her skirts against her legs and knocked her feet right out from under her. When I ran to help her, both our pails blew away. I helped her to her feet and the wind blew us down the slope to the well. She grabbed the pump and shouted, "Go get the pails! Don't let them blow away!"

I had to chase those pails halfway up the slope on the far side of the draw. When I started back the air was so full of snow the light in the window at the house was only a faint, distant glow. This was really a blizzard.

I got back to the pump and told Mother she'd better go back to the house; I'd bring in the chips. She said she came out after a pail of chips and she was going to get them. And, she did, though the wind blew her down twice more before she got to the barn. I helped her back to the house, then finished the barn chores. By then it was drifting so much that I had to wade waist deep in snow to get to the door, and I stopped and got a shovel to take in the house. If this kept up we might have to dig out by morning.

While we ate supper the wind sifted snow in around every window and made such eddies in the air that the flame in the lamp flickered and smoked. We hung old quilts over the windows to break the gusts of fine snow and we stuffed a towel under the door. Mother put the hot flatirons in our beds and I tried to read for a while, sitting with my feet in the oven. But the fire died, sucked right up the chimney, and I went to bed. The wind was shaking the house so much that the dishes rattled on their shelves.

It snowed and blew all night. When I wakened the next morning there was a little drift of snow on the edge of my bed, and when I stepped down I went into a drift a foot deep on the floor. There was a drift under every window in the house. We ate breakfast before I tried to get to the barn. When I opened the house door I found a solid wall of snow. The drift there was six feet deep.

We knew it was still blowing. We could hear it. But we didn't know it was still snowing until I tunneled through that drift at the door and got into the open. It took me an hour to get clear, and it was still snowing. It was eleven o'clock when I reached the barn and got the door open there.

Everything was all right at the barn. The snow had banked it and the animal heat made it almost as warm as the house. I did the milking and rationed out the extra hay I had got in the day before and started back to the house. I had to dig out every path because they'd all drifted full again. Before I got to the house the milk was full of slush, half frozen though it had been warm when I left the barn.

The wind eased off somewhat that evening, but the snow

continued. The second day I had to dig out all over again. And that day I had to water the stock. They couldn't go any longer without it. Mother said she was going to help. She'd learned what the wind could do to her skirts, so she put on a pair of Father's overalls, belted them at the waist, tied them at the ankles, and put on overshoes, coat and scarf. She carried kettles of boiling water and thawed the pump while I got on Mack and broke trail from the barn to the well. When we had a trail opened through the shallower drifts, Daisy and the calves followed to the well, drank, and were very happy to get back in the barn. And that afternoon I had to find some way to get hay. The only way was to dig a path to the stacks, carve off a big slice of one stack with the hay knife, and carry it into the barn.

Before I got the hay into the barn I began to wonder if I really wanted a blizzard. My arms ached, my ears stung, I was sweating like a horse and when I stopped to catch my breath the sweat seemed to turn to icicles in my armpits. But I got the hay in, and I did the evening chores, and I shoveled my way back to the house, where the big bowl of steaming pinto beans was worth all the sweating. The Mexican wants his beans hot with chili peppers. The New Englander wants his sweet with molasses and salt pork. We had ours simmered for hours with no seasoning but salt and swimming in their own brown juice. To us they were bread and butter and meat and potatoes, as they were to many an isolated homesteader. On a cold, blizzardy night they were more than sustenance; they were warmth and comfort and a promise for tomorrow.

That was our pattern for four days, wind and snow and shoveling, and pumping and milking and carrying sheep chips. Soft snow turned to ice crystals which, wind-driven, bit cheek and knuckle and made you a sentient part of the storm. It became a kind of game to see how much cold you could take, how much wind you could face, how much snow you could shovel. And, as the storm progressed, it even added comfort to the house. Until the snow banked the house to the eaves the stove cast so small a circle of warmth that I could stand with my hip pockets practically on the stove lids and still see my breath. Then we were drifted in and I could go clear across the room before my breath was visible.

The snow probably stopped on the third day, though we couldn't tell. There were flashes of sunlight, but the air was still full of snow, undoubtedly blown from the hilltops. It seemed impossible that the snow could continue to drift, but it did. It seemed that the drifts had been built as high as they could stand and all the ridges had been swept bare. But they weren't. The wind continued to reshape the world.

But at last the wind eased away and the plains lay white and silent. And new—white, gleaming, pristine new.

Long later I was to hear people talk of pioneer strengths and virtues. Hearing such words I think of the homesteader alone in a blizzard world, as alone as the last man on a Himalayan mountaintop. He mustered strength when strength was demanded, but even more important was the dogged determination to survive. If pioneers died young—and many of them did—it may have been because they didn't know how or when to quit, and because they faced stern demands with often meager resources. I doubt that it was a matter of heroics, though heroism is a difficult word to define. Man persists because it seems important to persist, to go on living.

But during that winter we had no time, and no reason, for such speculation. It was important to us to go on living, and the odds weren't too high. We even had a sustaining necessity. When a cow or calf was bawling for water, there was only one thing to do—get water to them. If it meant shoveling a path for the hundredth time or thawing the pump for the fourth time that day, the pump had to be thawed and the path shoveled. When the mangers were empty they had to be filled, and one could think later how easy it would have been to pitch the hay down from a mow if there had been a mow.

At the moment, the thing to do was shovel and wallow a way to the haystacks and get the hay into the mangers. And when those essential tasks were done the body itself made its demands, for food and rest. So one ate beans and felt a warm and satisfying comfort, and one slept, despite cold or ache; and the next day one went back to the demanding rounds.

Then the storm frayed out into a deepening calm and a stupendous white cold silence, and the outer demands relaxed enough for one to see this new world and absorb its wonder.

After such a storm, the world of the plains is a strange and magnificent place. It is as though all the earth-shaping forces have been at work on a vastly quickened scale of time. Hills, valleys, hollows and hummocks have all been reshaped to a new pattern. The wind has had its way, at last, the wind that is forever trying to level the hills and fill the valleys. It has been able to work its will with an obediently plastic, though transient, material.

Our wind had been somewhat thwarted, by a fence post, a haystack, even by a tall weed stem. It had swirled and eddied, and we could see all the swirls and eddies frozen in the snow. Change was everywhere, but there was one constant, the soft curve. You saw it in the eddy around a fence post, the swirl around a haystack, the shape of a hill, the flow of a valley, and in a thousand variations of the amazing curl of a snowdrift.

The wind had all but obliterated the house, the barn, the fences, the haystacks. They were still there, but they had been merged into the drifted landscape, their own shapes lost and distorted. There was virtually no trace of human tenancy except the smoke from our chimney. Paths were drifted over. Fences were buried under the drifts. Haystacks were only larger drifts, as were both the house and the barn. And we, the human survivors, had been driven back, in a way, into a cave; the house was little more than a cavern in a hillside of snow. There we had survived as a kind of human outpost in a world suddenly engulfed in a new ice age. An ice age, though, that would retreat and vanish in a matter of weeks rather than centuries and eons.

The initial vacancy of that world was beyond belief. It was a vast white void, without a wing in the sky or a moving paw upon the snow. In time, of course, in another day or two, the prairie quail huddled in bunch grass caves beneath the drifts would work their way out. Field mice, tunneling under the snow from one seed storehouse to another, would come to the surface and explore. Jack rabbits would break through the drifts that sheltered them beside the soapweed clumps. Prairie dogs would open their snow-sealed burrows and yip at the white and hungry world. And coyotes would come from their dens and make lean shadows on the starlit snow and send their hungry yelps echoing among the white hills. But now they were as snowbound as we were.

More so, for we could get out at least a little way. To the barn, to the stacks, to the well, to the chicken house. But we could no more have gone to Gary than we could have gone to London. Even the higher ridges, where the wind had swept relentlessly, lay under almost six inches of fine packed snow. And the first few hours of thin sunlight softened the snow's surface just enough for the night's deep cold to seal everything under an icy crust. A man in desperation might have walked to town, given luck enough not to fall and break a leg, but it would have taken several days. A man on horseback might have tried it, skirting the horse-high drifts; but within an hour he would have been as good as afoot, for the icy crust would slash and cruelly wound a horse's legs.

We had to stay where we were.

The morning the storm first eased Mother said, "That's the last of the coffee. When you go to the barn, bring me in a panful of rye." She parched the rye, ground it in the coffee mill, and brewed what her mother used to call "hard-times coffee." It had the color of coffee, it was hot, and mingled with its taste of scorch and cereal there was a flavor that did resemble coffee. Best of all, it was as good without sugar as with, for we had no more sugar. But we still had beans, and we still had rye and corn to grind. We had milk, though Daisy was beginning to dry up, and we had an occasional egg. We had salt and we had a little lard. And I had a shotgun and fifteen shells for it.

A few days after the storm stopped, when the rabbits had worked their way out of the soapweed drifts, I went hunting. But the same ice crust that bore me up, and made treacherous footing for anything afoot that lacked claws or hairy pads, made a racecourse for the jack rabbits. They could see me coming a mile away, and they loped over the crusts like shadows. I couldn't get within a hundred yards of a rabbit, much less get a shot at one.

For ten days the snow lay crusted. Then we wakened one morning to the bawling of cattle. I went outside and saw a thin and wavering band of a dozen steers working their way slowly toward the house from Ketchem Holler. They would walk a little way through the crusted drifts, then stop and bawl, and the snow behind them was dark with the blood from their ice-gashed legs. They would bawl and stand, hock-deep in the snow, and come on a little way, and stop again. Then those behind would crowd those in the lead and they would lunge into those knife-sharp drifts again.

As they came closer to the house Fritz and I worked our way over the drifts toward them, I shouting, Fritz barking, trying to turn them back. But by then they must have smelled the hay. They milled there in the snow, in a drift almost belly-deep, and bawled. They were rib-thin and red-eyed and several of them were so weak they wavered as they stood. But they kept pushing ahead, closer and closer to the house, the barn and the stacks. If they got to the stack yards, starving as they were, no fence could hold them. The leaders might wince and turn back at the barbed wire, but those behind would crowd them into the wire and through it, and that would be the end of the hay. One taste of it and they would go mad; they would stay till they'd finished the last of it.

I ran back to the house for the buggy whip. Mother was up and ready to help. She took the whip and I got a pitch fork. We went back and lashed and jabbed and clubbed the steers till they milled a big hollow in the snow and we almost fell into the hollow with them. But they wouldn't turn and go back the way they came. One or two would turn and start away, but the others would lunge at the drifts and crowd us back a little, and the retreat would end.

We fought them for half an hour, a losing fight. Then Mother ran to the house and came back with the .25-20 rifle. She stood on a drift and aimed at a big red steer. The steer stood staring at her, a perfect target. Then she lowered the rifle and asked, "Where do you shoot a steer to kill it, the head or the heart?"

"The head," I said. "I'll do it." I reached for the rifle.

"No!"

Again she aimed. Again I held my breath, waiting for the shot. It didn't come. Again she lowered the rifle. She closed her eyes and shook her head and whispered, "I can't. I can't!"

"Here!" I reached for the rifle again.

"No!" And she turned and fired a shot, at last. Over the heads of the steers.

The steers snorted, turned, and lunged away. Mother fired another shot. Those nearest us crowded the others into the path they had made up from the hollow. Fritz was at their heels, yelping and snapping. I was shouting. One more shot and they were trotting down that bloody path, away from the house and the hay. I ran along the drifts, shouting encouragement to Fritz. Together we kept them going all the way down into Ketchem Holler. There they turned north, down the big valley, no longer even bawling. They were still going, still crowding through those ice-edged drifts, when we turned back to the house.

Before the week was out a thaw set in. The crust softened and the jack rabbits, which had skipped so lightly over the frozen drifts, began to bog in. Within half a mile of the house

I shot or clubbed ten big fat white-tails. As we ate rabbit that night Mother said, "Any of those steers would have been too thin to eat, even if I could have brought myself to kill one. And if we'd been really starving, I guess we could have killed the big calf. At least, it was our own, if we had killed it."

That night we stayed up till ten o'clock, stripping meat from the rabbit carcasses, grinding it in the little food chopper, and making rabbit hamburger which Mother shaped into cakes and put down in a crock of lard. The next day I got eight more rabbits, and we had enough hamburger to last us for a month.

The thaw thinned the snow between the drifts enough for me to ride over to the Bromleys' and get the last two volumes of Cooper. But it was the middle of February before we could get to Gary. There were several letters from Father. The week of the blizzard he had known it was useless to try to get word to us. The week after that he tried to rent a team, or even a saddle horse, at the livery stable, but the liveryman wouldn't let his horses out to anyone who wanted to go "down in the South Country." Finally he reached the Gary store by phone and learned that it would be weeks before the roads were open, but that as far as Tom McDowell knew everybody was all right. That was small comfort, but there was no more word to be had. All he could do, he said, was wait and hope.

There was a money order in each letter. Mother endorsed them all and mailed them to the doctor in town. And she added a postscript to the letter she had written, saying this was the first time we'd been able to get to Gary, that we had his letters, that everything was all right, and that he shouldn't even try to get home till the weather cleared a little.

The next week we had another blizzard, just a minor one that lasted only two days and a night. And in February we had two more storms. We didn't get to Gary again till the first week in March. By then Daisy had gone dry and we had no butter to trade, but it didn't matter. We still had almost half a bushel of beans. And winter was almost over.

17

March, particularly on the plains, never has much to recommend it. Winter is essentially a clean, white, wind-bitten time of trial. Spring is relief and a renewal of green and reassuring life with its own hope and promise. But March is neither winter nor spring. The winds of March have the bite but lack the cleanliness of winter. The March sun is strengthening, but even after the equinox it lacks the benevolence of spring. The ground is still stiff with frost, the vestiges of the snowdrifts are dirty, the ice in the ponds is alternately slushed and brittle. Even the jack rabbits look forlorn. And the earliest meadow larks, which sometimes arrive in March, sit with fluffed feathers and sing half-hearted songs of regret that they left southern Texas so soon. The wonder is that they don't turn around and go south again, but they never do. They stay and wait, as we waited, for April and spring.

Father came home for a weekend. It was only the second time he had been able to get home since Christmas. As we drove home from Gary he said, "It looks like a wet year. Water standing everywhere. Once it warms up, things should begin to boom."

Mother said, "Yes, once it warms up."

"We'll have to get a crop in."

"Yes. But it'll be another month or six weeks yet."

"I've asked Ed if I could take the second week in May off."

"That'll be when? It's hard to keep track of dates."

"That'll be the week of the twelfth. The twelfth is a Sunday."

"Then you'll be home for your birthday."

"Yes."

Father's birthday was the thirteenth of May. Mine was the next day, the fourteenth.

That evening, at the homestead, we had rabbit hamburger for supper. Hamburger and corn bread and boiled beans. Father ate his hamburger cake without seeming to taste it, but as he finished eating he said, "I'd like to get a couple of shoats this spring. And have meat for next winter."

"It looks like a good corn year," Mother said. "We ought to have something to feed them, at least."

"What was this meat we just ate?" Father asked.

"Rabbit.'"

Father nodded. "We'll get the corn in," he said, "when I take that week off. I'll buy another horse and—"

"We're going to plant corn with a hoe," Mother said.

"It'll take forever! With another horse—"

"We'll get another horse," Mother said, "when we're out of debt. And the shoats too. Corn's been planted with a hoe before."

Father frowned. "About that bill. I was talking to the doctor the other day. He told me about your sending those money orders to him. What did you do that for?"

"To get the bill paid."

"I meant for you to have enough to eat!"

"We did."

"You're thin as rails, both of you!"

Mother smiled. "Then I guess we won't die of fatty degeneration of the heart."

"What have you been living on? Mush and rabbits?"

"And beans," Mother said. "Oh, Will, don't you realize that for weeks we couldn't get to the store? Even if I'd wanted to spend that money, how could I? By the time I got the first money order we'd lived through the worst of it. How much do we still owe?"

"About a hundred dollars."

"It must be more than that."

"It isn't."

"Then you got a raise."

"No." Father rolled a cigarette and carefully brushed the few spilled flakes of tobacco back into the white cloth bag. "If you must know, I saved a little. On meals. I've eaten some of my meals at the office, in my room. Crackers and cheese goes quite a way. I paid the doctor what I saved."

"You promised," Mother said, "that you'd eat at the restaurant."

"I did, at least one meal a day."

Mother stared at the lamp and at last she said, "We can buy the horse in time for haying."

The next day was almost mild. The ground was soggy underfoot. Father and I walked up to the old cornfield with its ragged stalks. Last year's rye patch was green. It had been so ripe when we cut it last summer that enough shattered to reseed it. The seed lay there all through the drought, then sprouted with the late fall moisture and got enough start to carry through the winter. We had a volunteer crop, and it was doing very well. We would have a rye harvest that we hadn't expected.

Father looked at it and said, "Well, there's one crop we won't have to plant. All we'll have to do is cut it when it's ripe."

We walked on up the rise. There wasn't yet a sign of green in the buffalo grass, and last year's mat wasn't springy underfoot. Growth had been short last summer, with the drought, and now you could feel the knots of frost in the ground. We walked along the rise a little way, then turned back down the draw toward the house. Suddenly a covey of prairie quail burst from a ragged clump of bunch grass and went sailing down the draw. We stood and watched them and Father said, "A covey just like that flew up from just about here the first time I saw this place. It was in March, a day like this. I came out with a land locator from Brush."

We went on down the draw toward the house. "Remember the way it was the first time we came out here, son?" Father asked. "Remember the buffalo wallow, and the wiggle-tails in the water?"

I remembered.

"I'll never forget that day. That whole week. This country was the prettiest place in the world." Father sighed. Then he said, "That first night here on the place, when we worked till dark, and I asked if you wanted to go back to Jake's house. Because of the coyotes. And you said, 'Let's stay.' You were scared, but you said, 'Let's stay.'"

We walked in silence a little way, and he said, half to himself, "You've stayed ever since."

On the way to Gary the next morning we took the lower trail, the one that went halfway down Ketchem Holler before it climbed onto the flats. It had been a warm night, the first really mild night of the year, and all the smells of the plains were strong, the grass smell, and the water-hole smell, and even the sheep smell down along the valley. We came to the place where the trail turned up the slope and a new, rank smell of dead flesh came from just ahead. Mother said, "What do you suppose that is?" and Father drove on down the valley another hundred yards. Then we saw the carcasses of six red steers at the foot of a cut-bank where they must have bogged in the drifts during the big blizzard.

Mother held her nose and Father turned and drove back to the trail and up the hill. The air was clean and sweet again. Mother said, "All that beef, gone to waste!"

Father said, "It's certainly gone!"

Mother told him about the day the steers came through the drifts, trying to get to our hay, and how we turned them back.

"I'll bet those are some of that bunch," she said. And after a minute or two she told him how she tried to kill one and couldn't. "I still couldn't do it," she said, "even if I had it to do over. But I can still remember how I had my mouth all set for steak, that morning."

When we got to Gary, Father said he had an errand in the store. Mother drew the blanket up over her old dress and the old brown coat and said, "You two go on in, if you want to. I'll wait here in the buggy."

Father and I went in and he bought a chunk of bacon, a sack of flour, a few pounds of sugar, a can of corn and two cans of tomatoes. When he paid for it I saw that he had a dollar and forty cents left.

Con Hallahan was coming when we took the box of groceries out to the buggy. Mother asked, "What's that?"

"That," Father said as he put the box in the back of the buggy, "is a few dollars you can't send to the doctor. It's groceries, and it's a sin to let food spoil."

Con drew up in front of the store, Tom McDowell handed him a mail pouch, and Con shouted to Father, "You going with me?" Father kissed Mother and said, "I'll be out the eleventh of May," and climbed up beside Con. Con swung the broncs around, headed them for Brush, yelled a shrill, "Yee-owiee!" and they were gone.

We had tomatoes for supper that night, and I knew why the cowboys rode to Gary in the spring just to buy canned tomatoes. A cowboy would ride up, tie his horse at the rack, clump in, and come back with a big can with the red label. He would sit on the step, cut the top out with his pocket knife, and drink the juice. Then he would eat every scrap of the tomatoes, lifting them out on his knife blade. Those tomatoes were the most satisfying thing we'd had to eat in months. We sopped up the last drop with the biscuits Mother made.

It was late April before spring really came. It came first as a greenness in the hollows beside the shallow ponds of snow melt, but soon it began to spread like a faint green mist on all the hillsides and across the flats. After that the chilly days and the raw nights didn't seem quite so raw or chilly.

Timbered country has spring subtleties, rising sap and first buds, florets on trees and bushes, half-hidden flowers among the rocks and leaf mold. But the plains are a vast simplicity at any season, their moods and changes swift, evident, and decisive. On that boundless open grassland neither spring nor any other season can hide or creep up slowly. Spring comes in a vast green wave rolling northward, a wave as evident as were the buffalo millions that once swept northward with new grass, as evident as the winter-hungry Indians that once swept northward with the buffalo. Spring on the plains has little more subtlety than a thunderstorm.

Winter ends, March drags its cold, muddy feet but finally passes, and there is spring, a rebirth that assaults all your senses. The surge of life at the grass roots penetrates your soles, creeps up through your bones, your marrow, and right into your heart. You see it, you feel it, you smell it, you taste it in every breath you breathe. You partake of spring. You are a part of it, even as you were a part of winter. Spring is all around you and in you, primal, simple as the plains themselves. Spring is, and you know it.

I rode over to the Bromleys' to return *David Copperfield* and get *A Tale of Two Cities*. Mr. Bromley said, "Well, it looks like spring is really coming, at last. Is it always this late?"

I told him that spring had been early last year, and the year before.

"Back home in Illinois," he said, "the farmers are already out plowing. And the robins are back. Aren't there any robins out here?"

"Not out here," I said. "There are robins near Brush, but not out here. The horned larks are back, though. I saw a couple of them this morning."

"Horned larks?" Mrs. Bromley asked.

I described them.

"Oh," she said, "those little birds. Remember, Walter, I said they must be our equivalent of the English skylarks? They fly high in the air, singing as they fly. Last fall I sometimes heard them singing when they were so high I could scarcely see them."

"They're the ones," I said. "The big red ants are getting busy, too. And last night, just before dark, I saw two big flocks of geese go over."

"Seems late to me," Mr. Bromley said. "I still miss the robins."

On the way home I saw a badger cleaning out his den. He was down in the hole kicking dirt out with his hind feet almost as fast as a man could toss it out with a shovel. Then I saw a flock of meadow larks. Most of them were busy looking for beetles, but two of them were so full of song they just strutted around whistling at each other. And when I got to the head of our draw I saw the first of the lark buntings, which we called prairie bobolinks. Half a dozen of them flew up, singing on the wing, and I knew that before long I would be finding their nests in the grass, and light blue eggs in the nests.

A few days later I rode over to the big prairie dog town. Even there, where the prairie dogs had eaten the soil bare last summer, the grass was beginning to come back. The prairie dogs were out by the hundred, chipper and noisy as though they hadn't an enemy in the world. Over at the far side of the town an old badger was waddling along, watching me over one shoulder. The dogs over there were all out of sight, but a hundred yards from the badger other prairie dogs paid him no attention.

Two little owls were bobbing and screaming at each other; they saw me and forgot their own quarrel and screamed at me, but the minute I was past they began hopping at each other again.

Most of the old mother prairie dogs were fat with pup. The

pups would be born in another week or two, but would stay in the dens for a month. The thin old males were feeding greedily on the grass, truculent and quarrelsome among themselves.

I dismounted to watch an ant hill, and I saw two tumble-bugs pushing each other around in the grass. They butted and rolled and nipped and got to their feet and butted each other again, until one of them drove the other off. The victor pursued a little way, then came back and began rolling the ball of dung over which they probably had been fighting. They were strange creatures with the mark of antiquity on them, though I didn't know then that they were close cousins of the ancient Egyptian scarabs. All I knew was that these big, dark, timeless-looking beetles fashioned balls of cow manure three-quarters of an inch in diameter and rolled them from place to place, walking backward and rolling the balls with their hind legs. They laid eggs in the balls and the eggs hatched into grubs which ate their way out and eventually turned into beetles which laid their own eggs in other dung balls. It seemed to me that the way the birds did it, laying eggs in nests, eggs with shells on them and food inside, was much simpler.

I watched the tumblebug maneuver his ball to the edge of the bare space around the ant hill, and I watched the ants gather to repel the invader, who paid almost no attention to them. The tumblebug rolled his ball across the little clearing and into the grass beyond, the ants rubbed feelers in a conference as though telling each other that they had driven off a major threat to the colony, and everybody went back to work.

The sun was warm. Even the ground was beginning to lose its March chill. I lay there thinking about the beetles and the ants and the prairie dogs and the badgers and the owls and the meadow larks. They had been here a long time, all of them. They were here when the buffalo first came, and that was so long ago that the Indians couldn't remember that far back. Time was a strange thing. It was days and nights and months and years, and then it stretched out into something else. Into grass, maybe, or into clouds. Or into the earth itself. You lay watching a cloud overhead, and you closed your eyes and pretty soon the cloud moved over the sun. You felt the coolness and the darkness of the shadow. You lay and waited for the brightness and the sun's warmth again. You could count, slowly, and that was time. You counted slowly, and the cloud passed the sun. The shadow was gone.

Time was strange. A prairie dog pup was born in May, and by fall it was practically grown up. A meadow lark laid an egg in a nest in May, and before frost in the fall the baby bird hatched from that egg was as big as its mother and flew south with the other birds. But it took years for a boy to grow up.

We had been out there two years. When we first came I was so short I had to stand on a manger or a cut-bank to get on a horse. Now I could mount Mack from the ground, just put my hands on his withers and jump and throw my leg over his back.

I wondered how many ants had grown old and died while I was growing up enough to get on a horse from the ground. A year must be a long time to an ant. Or a beetle. Or a prairie dog. Even a day must be a long time. Maybe time was like distance. If an ant got twenty feet away from the ant hill he was a long way from home, much farther than I was right now from the house. And it probably would take a tumblebug all day to roll that ball of dung fifty feet, especially with all the obstacles it had to get over and around.

Some day, I told myself, I would find a tumblebug early in the morning and watch him all day and see just how far he did go. I would catch him and tie a thread around him, or mark him some way, so I could be sure to know which one he was if he had a fight with another beetle.

But not today. I caught Mack and whistled to Fritz, who was still trying to catch a prairie dog, and I rode west, to circle back toward our place.

I rode only a little way when a kit fox jumped not fifty yards ahead of me. He had been catching ground squirrels until I startled him. A kit fox was like a small coyote with a very bushy tail. He was really a fox, but not much bigger than a good-sized cat. There weren't many of them around, and most of them were here on these south flats. This one jumped and ran like a streak, its bushy tail floating behind, graceful as a bird. It ran maybe twenty yards; then, without slackening pace, it veered and ran off at an angle another twenty-five yards or so, then changed directions again. That's the way a kit fox always ran, zigzag. Dogs would seldom run kit foxes, and anyone who ever watched one knew why. It made you dizzy just watching that zigzagging. I yelled, and the kit veered again. One more turn and it vanished in a little hollow.

I rode over to the hollow, but I couldn't find the kit fox. It must have darted down the little wash and out onto the flats again where I wasn't watching. But as I rode down the hollow I came to a fresh cut-bank that had washed out in the spring melt. The grass had caved away, leaving a bank of fresh gravelly soil. Such a place was always worth searching for arrowheads. I got off and began poking through the gravel.

It was different from the gravel on our land, coarser and full of lumps of sandstone. The sandstone was grayish yellow. There was a thin ledge of it reaching back under the grass. I sifted a few handfuls through my fingers and stood up, about to leave. Then I scuffed at it with my toe and a smooth, rounded flat piece caught my eye. It wasn't a pebble. It was almost the size of a silver dollar, but smooth and rounded.

Even as I picked it up I sensed that here was something out of time so remote that my mind could not quite grasp the distance. It was a fossil clam, and the place I found it was fifteen hundred miles from the nearest ocean.

There it was, a clam turned to stone, a petrified clam with fluting around the edges of the twin shells, with bits of sandstone still clinging to it. Different from the fresh-water clams of the Missouri River, but still a shellfish, something from an ocean that once had been where I stood. And somehow, stand-

ing in the warm spring sunlight on the High Plains, I compre-
hended the matter of eons and ages. Without knowing geology,
I sensed geologic time. I touched the beat of the big rhythm,
the coming and going of oceans and the rise and fall of mountains. And, for a little while, I was one not only with the Indians who had been there before me, but with those who were
there before the Indians; not only with the grass which had
greened with a thousand springs, but with that which was there
before the grass.

There had been ranchmen before we came, and Indians before the ranchmen, and buffalo before the Indians. And long
before the buffalo there had been an ocean, and clams. Back,
back—how far back? And how far ahead? Time was indeed a
strange thing. The time of the ant, the time of the tumblebug,
the time of the prairie dog, the time of a boy. The time of a
fossil clam.

I got on my horse and rode slowly home in the late afternoon of that spring day, with a strange, hard, smooth fragment
of time in my pocket.

Mother said, "You've just got time to get the chores done
before supper."

18

There is an ebb and flow of settlers in any new land. They come, and they go. A dozen families had taken land east of Jake Farley's since we arrived, and as many more had settled east and south of there. But some had not stayed beyond last summer's drought; last fall there were several empty soddies and abandoned barns. Now, after the kind of winter that always winnows out the misfits, others were going.

Spring does that to shallow-rooted people, and roots go down slowly on the plains. Summer can be lived with comfortably. Fall brings a measure of harvest and contentment. Then comes winter with its demands, only to be followed by spring, when hills are green on both sides and the horizon is clear and inviting. Dreams of a new self or a new life shimmer in every sunrise, especially for those who have wintered on loneliness and discontent.

Some had given up after the first blizzard. Others had trailed away through the mud and ice of March. Now, each time we went to Gary, we heard about still others who had waited only for spring to get up and go.

There was the man who got on his horse one afternoon and told his wife he was going to bring in the cows. She watched him ride off across the flats. He came to their two milk cows, grazing half a mile from the house, and he rode around them and kept on going. She watched him to the top of the rise a mile away, and she waited and waited. He never came back. "I don't know what got into him," his wife said. "He didn't even say goodbye."

There was the man who, as soon as the last snow was gone and the roads were open, took his wife to Brush to get a load of groceries and a hundred pounds of chicken feed. He gave her the grocery money and let her off at the store, saying he would get the chicken feed and meet her there in half an hour. Meanwhile, the Denver train came in and left. When the man went back to the store to meet his wife, she wasn't there. He couldn't find a trace of her until he went to the depot and described her to the station agent. Yes, the agent said, he'd seen a woman like that. She bought a ticket and she got on the train. And the man walked out, dazed, and got in his wagon and drove home again.

One family over east lost a little girl, probably of pneumonia, during the big blizzard. But most of the homesteaders had weathered the winter safely, cured their own ills, faced their problems and solved them. As always and everywhere, you heard little about them; the stories that people repeat are filled with the drama of trouble. We heard the tales and Mother said, "I guess we're lucky. At least, we pulled through."

They went, and they came. Every time we went to Gary we saw a load or two of lumber coming out from Brush. Each load had a newcomer at the reins, often with his wife and children on the load beside him, and most of the loads were going south, out onto the plains. Most of the newcomers were farmers, but not all.

George Grant was no farmer. He wasn't looking for a farm. All he wanted was a beautiful hilltop.

George Grant got off the Denver train in Brush one day and walked over to the newspaper office. Father was the only one in the office at the time. George introduced himself and said, "I'm looking for a homestead." Father took one look at him and thought he'd better be looking for a lot in a graveyard. George was six feet two and weighed about a hundred and ten pounds. He had been in a tubercular hospital in Colorado Springs for two years and the doctors had told him there was no hope. They gave him one more year, at most, to live.

George was a veteran of the Spanish-American War, had a small pension and a thousand dollars or so of savings. He told Father, "I've looked at the white walls of that prison, that hospital room, as long as I can. I had to get out. I'm not going to die there."

So they talked land. George Grant didn't want land that anyone else might want. "I want waste land, land not good for anything. I don't want to deprive anyone of a farm. But I would like to find a hilltop where I could build a house and just sit and watch the clouds."

Father knew what George meant. He thought of the prettiest place on the plains except our homestead and he said, "I think I know the place. It's in the sand hills. Nobody can farm that land, because if they plow it up it'll just blow away. A few range cattle graze there, but not many. It's a pretty place."

George hired a livery man to take him out, liked it, and filed on the land. It was the hilltop where Father and I stopped to eat our lunch the first day we went out to the homestead. Then, as Emily Woods had done the year before, George had lumber hauled out and built his own house, just a one-room place with a shed at one end to stable the horse he needed to get to Gary for supplies.

George's place was five miles from Miss Woods' white house and picket fence. From his hilltop, George could see her place as a white speck far off to the southeast, and at night he could see the light from her windows. And she could see his light.

At first I resented George Grant. He was an intruder. He had no right to homestead that hill, which was ours by right of discovery and use for many lunchtime rests. But George was a friendly, unobtrusive person, and when Father told us his story I could accept him. I came to look for him each time we went to Gary, to expect his friendly wave.

It wasn't long before we began to see Miss Woods' black horse and her spick-and-span buggy at George's place. Other people saw it too, and there was a little gossip. But Miss

Woods was such a nice friendly person, and George Grant was so evidently a sick man, that the gossip didn't go far.

Gradually people came to accept them and, in a vague way, to understand. I never heard it put into words, but people knew there was a bond between George and Miss Woods that had its basis in their mutual maiming. Neither had to be sorry for the other, and in both of them was an acceptance of what life had done to them. Both of them were patient with life, and perhaps that explains it all. Each had arrived at a philosophy that sustained; each had an admiration for the other's courage that needed no words.

Their acquaintance grew, this one-legged, middle-aged woman and this middle-aged man with a brief respite from death. He rode over and helped her water the petunias. She drove to his house and put dimity curtains at the windows. They sat on his hilltop and watched the clouds, and they sat in her picketed dooryard and listened to the birds. There was an air about them that in younger folk would have been naïveté but that in them was serene self-confidence. So instead of gossip, there was a quiet admiration and a vague awe. Besides, that was the spring when the Jim Walkers came.

Nobody knew where the wild Walkers came from. Some said Texas, some said Oklahoma, but Jim Walker said nothing about his origins. They simply appeared, one miserable March day, in a covered wagon with a tattered canvas tilt. Jim and Netta, his wife, were in the wagon and the three youngsters were on horseback. They had five horses, all rough-coated and rib-thin. They drove through the settlement over east and folks thought they were gypsies. They kept going till they had passed Jake Farley's place and finally stopped in a gully two miles south of Jake's. There they dug a hole in a bank, roofed it with the wagon tilt, and settled in. To those who asked, Jim said he had homesteaded that land.

Jim Walker was a tall, thin, stubble-faced man, a talker. Netta was fat and smiling and silent; some said she was an

Indian, and she looked it, black-haired, dark-skinned and with high cheek bones. She even wore her hair in braids over her shoulders. But it was the youngsters who became best known. Willie, eight years old, was a wizened little gnome. Elmer was ten and frog-faced and red-haired. Gracie was twelve, tall and skinny; she looked like her father except that she had her mother's black hair. Gracie dressed like a boy, in shirt and overalls, and she wore her hair like her brothers, hacked off at the bottom of her ears.

Whether they were half Indian or not, the youngsters rode like Indians. There wasn't a saddle among them, or a bridle. They tied a light rope around a horse's lower jaw, tossed a strap with a loop at each end over the horse's back for stirrups, and were off. They seemed to live on horseback.

Jim may have been a less prosperous member of a shadowy group of back-country horse sharpers who lived by their wits in the West and Southwest at that time. They were usually disarmingly simple men who traveled with a boy and a half dozen sad-looking horses and called themselves horse traders. Now and then they did trade horses, but in their easy talk they always got around to horse racing. They'd rather watch two good horses run than eat.

Most communities had a fast horse or two. With a little persuasion the stranger could be talked into matching one of his horses with the local favorite. Just for fun, of course, but with a small side bet to sweeten it, five or ten dollars. It usually happened that the stranger had two horses you couldn't tell apart. He put the boy on one of them as a jockey and the boy lost the race by a length or so.

The stranger paid off the side bet and said he'd sure like to see those horses run again. So another race was arranged for the next day. This time there were plenty of bets. The stranger reluctantly covered them all. A man wasn't a sport if he wasn't willing to back his own horse, was he? And this time, of course, he switched horses. The boy won going away; the stranger collected his bets and got away fast.

But ours wasn't a horse-trading or a horse-racing community. And if the Walkers were horse sharpers they had other talents too. The youngsters roamed and pillaged the countryside.

A homesteader would be at the barn doing his chores, not a stranger in sight. Suddenly his dog would bark. The chickens would begin to squawk. The man would step out of the barn and see a strange boy in the yard. Ten-year-old Elmer—it usually was Elmer, but occasionally gnomish Willie—would have a fat hen by the neck and would be grabbing another. The homesteader would shout. There would be a rush of horses from behind the barn as the Walker kids charged across the yard. Elmer would toss one of the hens to Willie, thus freeing a hand. Gracie would reach down and swing Elmer up behind her, going full tilt. Elmer, still holding his hen, would hop from Gracie's horse to his own, which Gracie was leading, and away they would go, yelling derisively. Just like an Indian raiding party.

Or a homesteader would go to Gary for the Saturday mail and marketing. He would come home to find the house door open and the place ransacked. Blankets vanished, and overalls, and caps and jackets. One woman said they took two frying pans. Another said they made off with a flitch of bacon. Still another said they stole a clock.

They never raided us, perhaps because there were better pickings over east. But they put in full time elsewhere.

Finally one homesteader, who had been raided three times, went to the Walker dugout to have a showdown. Jim was sitting on the wagon tongue, paring his fingernails with his jack knife. Netta was washing clothes in a tub beside the water hole where they got water for cooking, drinking and washing. Jim grinned at the man as he rode up, and Jim started talking. The homesteader could hardly get a word in edgewise, but he finally said that if Jim's kids came raiding just once more they would catch a load of number four shot.

"Go ahead," Jim said. "Go right ahead. That's just what I'd do with them kids. I can't do a thing with them. Off helling around all day, running the bejesus out of the horses. They won't stay home and do a lick of work. Look at their poor mother, down there working her fingers to the bone for them. And them kids is off again. I hoped to build a house and get some plowing done, but can I get a lick of work out of them? Not on your tintype! Go ahead and give 'em a lesson, mister. But shoot 'em in the butt, not in the head. That's where all their brains is, right in the seat of their pants. Damn good-for-nothing kids! Eatin' me out of house and home, and their mother workin' her fingers to the bone—"

Jim was still talking when the homesteader left. And his wife was still washing clothes and laying them out on the grass to dry. The homesteader rode past the dugout and got a quick look inside. There wasn't a stick of furniture. Not a chair or a table or anything. Just a few piles of old blankets. Beside the door was a heap of cow chip ashes, and a Dutch oven and a big frying pan.

Things went on that way for about six weeks. Then the young Walkers stole a pig, a good-sized shoat. They took it right out of the pen while the homesteader was in the barn. He heard the squealing and ran out, armed with a pitch fork, just in time to see them ride away, Elmer holding the pig in his arms, the pig squealing to high heaven and the kids whooping in triumph.

That night the pig's owner made the rounds of his neighbors and organized a posse. Folks had had enough of the Walkers. Seven men went to the Walker dugout, three of them on horseback, the others in a couple of wagons. Jim heard them arrive and came out with a lantern and started to talk. Nobody listened. They crowded into the dugout and began dismantling the place.

There wasn't much to dismantle, but when they took the blanket pallets apart they found everything from a dollar watch to a sack of flour. Jim stood by, holding the lantern for them to see by and still talking. His wife watched for a few minutes, grinning, then began to pick up her things as the men threw them aside. She carried them out and stowed them in the Walker wagon.

Willie and Elmer scuttled out, but Gracie backed into a corner and called the posse every name she could lay her tongue to. The posse piled the stolen goods beside the door, everything from a handsaw to cans of corn and tomatoes, from a clock to a cotton flannel night gown. They tossed the Walker blankets out to Netta, and finally two men climbed up and stripped the canvas tilt from the roof and tossed that to her.

Jim kept right on talking. Gracie used up all her words and went out into the darkness. Willie and Elmer harnessed a team of the Walker horses and hitched them to the wagon. Everyone knew what to do; apparently they had done it before, over and over.

Finally everything was sorted out. Jim was saying how hard up they were, how hard his wife worked, and what a trial the kids were. One of the possemen tossed the bacon and a few cans of beans into the Walker wagon, another grabbed Jim by the seat of the pants and helped him after the groceries. Netta climbed in and took the reins. Out in the darkness Willie and Elmer were mounting their horses. The Walkers drove away into the night.

The posse loaded the stolen things into one of their wagons, to be sorted out the next day. Those who had come on horseback went to get their horses. The horses were there, but the saddles were gone. So they mounted bareback and took after the Walkers. They caught up with Jim and Netta in the wagon half a mile from the dugout, but none of the kids was anywhere around. They went through the wagon, endgate to endgate, but there wasn't a sign of the saddles.

They never did find the young Walkers, or the saddles. They spent half the night looking, and they went out again the next day. But by then they couldn't even find the wagon. The Walkers, every one of them, had vanished as mysteriously as they had come.

But theft was rare. Most of the settlers were honest, hard-working people. Not all were farmers. They never are in a new community, and they never were in any homestead area. Only a fraction of the homesteaders became permanent settlers. The homestead act put no restrictions on a homesteader once he had proved up on his land, got a deed to it. He could sell it or lease it to whom he pleased. Seldom did more than half the original homesteaders stay more than a few years after they proved up. They sold out to farmers who came after them, and they moved to town and started stores or worked for someone else. They settled the towns as well as the country.

Among the new homesteaders that spring were a coppersmith from Ohio, and a carpenter from Michigan, and a house painter from Kansas. A settler over east who had been a blacksmith in Iowa set up a forge in a shed beside his barn and had all the blacksmith work he could handle. Another settler who had once been a surveyor's helper bought a transit and spent his time between his farm chores working as a surveyor.

But most of the settlers, families from rural Iowa and Missouri and Indiana, were quiet, hard-working folk about whom no stories grew. They had come out there to get a start on their own, to possess land, to farm it the best they could, maybe to sell it later and move to better watered land near Brush, but first to prove up on a homestead and provide themselves with a financial stake. They, too, were glad to see spring come.

19

April passed. May was at hand, and another summer. And Father would soon be coming home for a week off when we were going to plant the corn.

May meant greens, cooked greens, and Mother and I were down at Louie's sheep camp picking them the day we saw the hawks. The sheep must have carried the weed seed in their wool from Gerrity's home ranch, because there were patches of lamb's-quarters and milkweed and dock down there every spring. As soon as the sheep arrived they ate them off, but until they came we had all we wanted.

We picked a dishpanful, there beside the windmill and the old pen sites. Before we went home I wanted to go see if the pincushion cactuses were about ready to bloom. Their blossoms were lovely many-rayed pink stars. So we walked up the hillside and found pincushions in bud but not yet open. As we started back Mother looked across at our land and the flats beyond, and she said, "Your father always said that this country out here was the prettiest land in the world, and at this time of the year I think maybe he was right. There were times last summer, though, that I wouldn't have given a nickel for all of it."

She stood and looked, at our draw coming down from the west and the house and the barn and the remnants of the haystacks and the bright green of the volunteer rye and brown of the old corn patch. "It's pretty now," she said.

I had been looking at our place, too, but something off to

the northwest caught my eye. I said, "Look at all the hawks over there." Circling in the sky high over the flats were six hawks. They were going round and round, so far away they were only dark specks against the deep blue. Mother frowned and said, "They must be over John Kraus' place."

As we watched, one of the distant hawks left the circle and drifted toward the ground. A moment later it climbed into the circle again and the flight went on, round and round. Mother said, "Probably a calf." She glanced up our draw, and so did I. Daisy was there, and Mack, and both our calves, grazing quietly.

"Whatever it is," Mother said, "it's none of our business."

We went back down the hill, got our pan of greens, and went home. I said I would get on Mack and ride up and have a look, see what the hawks were after, but Mother shook her head. "It's none of our business," she said again.

I had forgotten about the hawks the next morning. Then, just before noon, Jake Farley drove down to our place from the north, hurrying. He called to Mother and said, "John Kraus is dead!"

"John Kraus!" Mother exclaimed. "Dead!"

"Dead as a doornail." Jake was shaken. "Horses must have run him down and tromped him, right there at his gate. Looks like he was going somewhere and got out to open the gate and the horses run him down." Jake shivered. "I stopped past to tell you, so's you wouldn't go up that way, not knowing, and see him. I got to go get witnesses and notify the sheriff, or somebody."

"I never liked the man," Mother said, "but that's an awful way to go."

"I guess he didn't linger," Jake said, gathering his reins. "I just thought you ought to know." And he hurried away.

John Kraus had added another to Jake's store of strange tales, this one more lurid than any Jake could imagine. John Kraus had intended to go to Gary that morning, the morning before Jake found him. He had harnessed his horses, with the usual beatings and kickings, had hitched them to the wagon, and had driven down to his gate on the section line. There he got out to open the gate.

It was a simple wire gate, three strands of barbed wire fastened at one end to the fixed post and at the other to a pole. The gate was closed by setting one end of the pole in a wire loop and hooking another loop over the upper end. As he went to open the gate, the horses shied, fearing another beating. John Kraus cursed them, as usual, then lifted the wire loop and tossed the gate aside. He shouted to the horses to go on through the gate. It was the way he had gone through that gate a hundred times, letting the horses go through alone, shouting for them to stop, closing the gate, then getting back in the wagon and driving on. It saved a few steps for him.

But this morning the horses did not come at his call. He shouted again. Still they didn't come. Furious, John Kraus ran to them, grabbed their bridles, and began abusing them. And the horses, as if in sudden rebellious agreement, reared, wrenched free of John Kraus' grasping hands, and lunged ahead. The neck yoke caught him in the chest. He went down. One horse struck him in the face with a hoof, the other crushed one of his feet. He writhed in pain and lifted his head just in time for a horse's hind foot to strike him squarely on the skull. The wagon lurched over him.

The horses went through the open gate, made a big circle on the grass beyond, and turned back toward the barn. They went through the gate again, retracing their path, and tromped him a second time. Then they went back to the barnyard. And within an hour the hawks began to circle.

The team was still in the barnyard, still hitched to the wagon, when Jake found John Kraus' body beside the gate. And the story of what had happened was written as plain as print in the dust and on the grass. Anyone could read it.

Jake told us that John Kraus was dead and he hurried away

to get witnesses. Late that afternoon he came back, accompanied by several men on horseback. They crossed the hollow down by the sheep camp and cut over the hill. An hour later they went back, the same way, avoiding our house. Jake in his wagon was driving slowly, and the riders were herding John Kraus' horses and his old cow and calf.

We watched them out of sight and Mother said, "Well, we've lost a neighbor. At least, somebody who lived close by. I still wonder what that man was so mad at that he couldn't even live with himself." Then she said, "I'm glad I didn't let you ride over there yesterday afternoon."

Down deep inside, I was glad too. It was years before I could watch a hawk circling without thinking of John Kraus.

The following Saturday we went to Gary to meet Father. It was a cool day for early May, but the sun was bright and the meadow larks were singing. We had the top down on the buggy, so we could feel the sun and see the world. The plains were green, every hill. Shallow pools of water still stood on the flats, and there were ducks in many of them, mostly mallards and teal.

We passed the sand hills, and George Grant waved, as always. He was sitting on the front step of his house, whittling and watching the world spread out below his hill. Then we reached the hard road again and passed a wagon, a weather-beaten old wagon with a rough-haired team that looked as though they hadn't felt a curry comb all winter. A man and a woman with a baby in her arms were on the spring seat, just sitting and looking straight ahead. Behind them, sitting on two old kitchen chairs among bundles of bedding, were a girl of maybe eight and a boy no more than ten. Back of the children was a kitchen stove.

We caught up with them and waved as we passed. The youngsters waved back. Neither the man nor the woman seemed to see us.

Mother said, "It looks as though they're moving, and that little girl has barely got enough on to cover her skin and bones."

We got to the store and found the usual Saturday crowd. But as I looked around it seemed like a strange place, almost like a store I had never before been in. Mrs. McDowell was back of the counter, measuring off yard goods and folding elastic and cutting table oilcloth for the women customers. Tom McDowell not only had on a white shirt and a vest, but a necktie. He kept saying, "Yes, ma'am" and "No, ma'am," and ma'aming it all over the place, because the women were doing the trading. The men were outside, talking weather. And practically all the men were in bibbed overalls and plow shoes. There wasn't a high-heeled boot among them. They were all farmers, homesteaders.

The store even had a strange smell. There wasn't a saddle in the place, or a set of harness with that rich, oiled-leather odor. The coal oil barrel was gone; now there was a big tank out back. The cheese that used to stand out on the counter now was in a glass case with a cloth over it, and the crackers were in cardboard boxes. I couldn't even see the square cans of mustard sardines among the round cans of tomatoes and corn and peas and baked beans. The store had been changing steadily for two years. I'd never been aware of it till that afternoon.

I was still looking for the sardines when the man from the wagon we had passed came in. He was tall and thin and he wore poorly patched overalls and a faded blue jacket that hung loose on his shoulders. He went to the counter and waited for Tom McDowell. When Tom got to him the man emptied a worn leather pouch into his hand and counted out a few dollars' worth of change. "Want to settle my bill before I go," he said.

McDowell took the money. "You sold out?" he asked.

"Sold the cow," the man said, "and ate the hens. Couldn't

sell the claim." He sighed. "A man can take just so much. Between the weather and the woman—" He shook his head and fingered the few coins in his hand.

"Where are you going?" McDowell asked.

"Back east. That's what she wants. Better give me a couple pounds of oatmeal. And a nickel plug of chewing tobacco."

I followed him to the door and watched him get into the wagon and drive away, east along the back road. The woman didn't even look up, but the boy turned and stared out across the plains.

I was still thinking about the man and the little boy when a man out front shouted, "Here comes that crazy Irishman!"

Con Hallahan was driving a team of blacks. They glistened with sweat and were flecked with foam as he reined them up in front of the store, leaped down, and snubbed the reins around a front hub. Father came over to the buggy and kissed Mother. "Get in," she said. "I've already got the letter from the folks, so there won't be any more mail."

Father tossed his suitcase in the back and took the lines. We started home. Father seemed glad to be there, but something wasn't right. Mother told him about John Kraus. He said, "I heard about it. Too bad. There he was, a big husky man, apparently never sick a day in his life. And doing what he wanted to."

He asked the everyday questions, about the calves and the grass and the chickens and the jack rabbits. He commented on the alfalfa in the fields at the roadside, which was almost ready for a first cutting. Then he was silent until we got to the sand hills.

We came in sight of George Grant's house. Miss Woods' buggy was there, and as we got a little farther we saw her and George on the hill beyond the house, she swinging along on her crutches and he walking slowly beside her. They were both bareheaded and the wind was blowing their hair. George recognized us and waved.

Father said, "I'm glad George took that place. All he wanted was a hilltop of his own. He didn't want to die cooped up." And after a little pause he said, "It's good just to be alive. You don't appreciate that, I guess, till you've been sick. Then you are thankful to be able to get out where you can breathe and see the sky and feel the ground under your feet."

"Have you seen the doctor lately?" Mother asked.

"I saw him yesterday. Paid him the last cent I owed him. He looked me over and said I was doing fine."

"You're all right?"

"Perfectly all right."

"And we're out of debt?"

"We don't owe anybody a penny."

We passed the sand hills and came to the hard land again, the hard, high flats. Father looked out across them, and I wondered if he was thinking of that first day we came out here. When there wasn't a trail anywhere; when the only mark was the press of our own wheels in the grass. Now we were following a pair of ruts that were almost a road. Our own wheels had cut those ruts, two years of coming and going.

Father slapped Mack with the reins and said, "Get a hustle on, Mack. We're going home."

That evening, out at the barn doing the chores, Father said, "I'd expected to build a real barn, by now. One with a hay loft. It must have been quite a job getting hay in from the stacks in the blizzard."

"If we moved the stack yard fence," I said, "we could let the stock get their own hay in bad weather. We could put a gate here, and one over there."

"I suppose we could." He didn't seem interested.

"And if we put up a windmill," I said, "it would save a lot of pumping. And Mother could have her garden down below the well, where we could irrigate it when we don't get enough rain."

He smiled. "Any more ideas?"

"I wanted to dig a cave, but Mother said I'd better ask you. If we had a cave close to the house we'd have a cool place for milk and butter when Daisy comes fresh. We could keep potatoes there, too. We ought to plant some potatoes this year."

Father looked at me a moment, then turned away. "We'd better go in to supper," he said.

The next morning I wanted to start moving the stack yard fence, but Father said no, not on Sunday. He went out with me and looked at the fence and listened while I talked, but I knew he was thinking about something else. We walked up the hill and looked at the rye, which was almost knee-high. It would soon be heading out. He looked at it as though it was somebody else's rye field, then turned and walked down into the old cornfield. He crouched down and dug a handful of soil. He held it up and looked at it and crumbled it in his fingers. He reached down for another handful and said, without looking up, "You like it out here in Colorado, don't you?"

Of course I liked it. This was home.

"But you've had it pretty hard here on the homestead," he said. "You and your mother."

Suddenly I had a flash of the boy in the wagon at Gary, and of his father saying to Tom McDowell, "A man can take just so much. Between the weather and the woman—"

"It hasn't been hard at all!" I exclaimed. "It's been fun! You used to like it here. If you'd just come home and—"

He looked at me and I could have bitten my tongue off. His jaw tightened and his nostrils quivered. Without a word he got up and went down the hill toward the house.

I watched him all the way to the stack yard. Then I went around the rye and up onto the ridge, walking west, away from the house. I had almost said, "If you'd just come home and stay, everything would be wonderful." And I knew that wasn't fair at all. He hadn't been away because he wanted to be away. He went to the mountains to make money for us to live on last winter. When he came back he took sick and nearly died, and he went away again to work and get us out of debt.

I saw the look on his face again as he dug that handful of soil and held it as though it was something precious. I didn't know what to do. Some things you know and feel and can't say, and those were the things I wanted to tell him. I wanted to tell him how I felt about the plains, and—everything. I wondered if the boy in the wagon felt that way too, there at Gary. I wondered if Father wanted to say that a man can take just so much.

The sensitivity of youth is a splendid thing, but maturity begins when that sensitivity first reaches beyond self. The world of a boy is a special world created for him and his private exploration. He approaches manhood when he begins to find room in that world for others, when the wonder of that world begins to have meaning beyond itself and himself. Maturity consists of an understanding of reasons and necessities beyond one's own impulses and desires. But it never comes in a moment; it comes bit by bit, year by year.

As I walked along the ridge I looked out across the plains, the hills barely rippling in the sun, each hill so small in the distance. I began to feel a beat, a rhythm, like the beat of my heart but much, much bigger. A beat that had been going on for years and years, since the Indian first came, since the first buffalo, since there was an ocean here, and a clam. A beat like the coming of spring, that slow; like the swish of a meadow lark's wings, that fast. Like sunrise, like sunset, like the full moon.

It was the beat of the plains, the hills and the draws and the flats, and yesterday and today and tomorrow, and Father and Mother and me, and everybody who lived here on the plains. I knew and accepted that pulse. It was a part of me. I accepted it without thinking, as I accepted the plains. Someday I would know who I was, and I would accept that. I didn't have to know now.

I walked and walked, and suddenly a meadow lark hopped

almost from under my feet. It fluttered as with a broken wing, trying to lure me away. I had startled it from a nest.

The mother bird fluttered and uttered a distress cry, and for a moment I thought she was hurt. Then I looked around, carefully, and almost at my feet I saw the nest, in a grass clump. It had four eggs, white eggs speckled with purplish brown. I walked away slowly and the mother lark flew back on two perfectly good wings.

I turned and went back toward the house, stopping only to pick a few wild geraniums, little coral-red flowers that sprang from low gray-green plants that had a faint geranium odor.

I went to the house and Mother asked, "Where's your father?"

"He came back to the house."

"Go look in the barn. Tell him if he wants anything to eat he'd better come in. Dinner's ready."

Father was in the stack yard, sitting in the sun. He got up and threw away a cigarette and we went to the pump and washed our hands.

Practically nothing was said while we ate. Mother looked worried. Father's thoughts seemed to be far away, though he looked at her a couple of times and frowned. When we had finished, Mother said, "You'd just as well go on outdoors. It's a nice day. I've got a little headache and I may lie down."

We went back to the stack yard and sat down with our backs to the warm hay. Father picked up a rye straw and broke it into little pieces, and finally he said, "It's time you got some schooling. And one of these days I want you to learn a trade. I don't know where we'd be if I hadn't had a trade to fall back on."

I couldn't think of anything to say.

"That," Father went on, "is a man's first responsibility. To take care of himself. And his family. He's not much of a man if he can't do that."

It was all confusing. Out on the ridge before dinner I had

felt that I was a part of everything, the plains and the grass and the sky—everything. Now I was just a boy who had to get some schooling and learn a trade. It was all mixed up. He had asked if I didn't like it out here, and of course I did, because it was home. And now he talked about going to school, as though being out here didn't matter at all.

Fritz, lying beside me, lifted his head and pointed his ears down the draw. Jake Farley was coming, riding one of his big black work horses. Father waved to him and Jake tied his horse at the fence and came and crouched down on his heels beside us.

"Good to see you," he said to Father. "I heard you were going to be home."

"I took a week off," Father said.

Jake picked up a straw and chewed it. He talked about the winter, and the grass, and John Kraus. Finally he said, "I'm going to build a new house and I wondered if the boy could help me out."

"What's wrong with the house you've got?" Father asked.

Jake grinned and looked at the ground. "Well, like you said once, a woman don't like to live in a barn."

"Don't tell me," Father said, "that you're getting married!"

Jake flushed. "Yes." And he told how lonesome he'd been last winter, snowbound and cut off from everyone. One day he started a letter to the hired girl on the farm back in Iowa where he'd been the hired man. He added to it every day, and when the storms let up and he could get to Gary he mailed it. She answered him and he wrote and asked her to marry him. "I told her," Jake said, "that maybe she could do better, but again she might do worse. She felt the same way. So," he concluded, "she's coming out the first of July. After I get a crop in. And a soddy built. It would help a lot if the boy could lend me a hand."

Father said, "Maybe he can. We'll see."

"I'd sure be obliged." Jake got to his feet. "And there's one other thing. Would you and the missus stand up with us before the minister?"

"Where?"

"In Brush."

"Of course, Jake. Come on in and tell her about it."

Jake shook his head. Blushing, he edged toward his horse. "You tell her. I got to get home." He untied his horse and got on. "I'm sure obliged to you!" he said, and he rode away.

We went to the house. Mother wasn't lying down. She was sitting at the table, just staring out the window.

Father said, "Jake is going to get married."

"Jake Farley? No!" Mother exclaimed.

"In July. He wants us to go to the preacher with them."

"And you said we would?"

"Yes."

"Well, thank heavens! You've finally made up your mind."

"What do you mean?"

"You know as well as I do what I mean. About staying here."

"I haven't made up my mind about that," Father said slowly.

"You'll be thirty-four years old tomorrow," Mother said quietly. "You're old enough to make up your mind."

"Yes," Father said, "thirty-four years old. And what have we got to show for it? This shanty of a house. That miserable excuse for a barn. When we came out here two years ago we had better than two thousand dollars, and a good team, and two good cows. What have we got now? One old cow, two calves, and a broken-down old nag. And I've got exactly twenty-four dollars and forty-five cents in my pocket. That's what we've got to show for thirty-four years!"

"We've been worse off," Mother said. "We've been in debt. Why did we come out here, anyway?"

Father didn't answer.

"Because you liked this land," Mother said. "You wanted it, didn't you? This homestead was pretty important, then."

"Yes, but—"

"Well, we two-thirds own it right now. One more year and we can prove up. It'll be ours."

Father shook his head. "It's not worth having you two out here another winter like the last one. Living on beans and mush. Doing without clothes, without coal, without everything you ought to have. Including school."

"As for school," Mother said, "I heard yesterday they're going to build a sod schoolhouse right east of Jake's place for a term this fall. And as for the other things, what do they matter?"

"I'm not much of a man if I can't provide them."

"Has anybody asked for them? Just wait till we can afford them and you'll hear from me! Will, we never started anything we couldn't finish. You want to finish this job, don't you?"

"Of course I do, but I can't ask you—"

"Nobody asked me to do anything. We came out here to Colorado to stay, didn't we? We took this homestead intending to prove up."

"Yes. . . . You really want to stay, then?"

"After what we've gone through? I wouldn't think of quitting now! But I began to think you'd had enough. Being away from home so much, working overtime, living in that smelly little room back of the shop."

Father shook his head. "I had it easy. You're the ones who had it hard. Scrimping, and fighting blizzards, and—Sarah, I never wanted you to have to put up with things like this. Many a time I wanted to throw everything over and rent a place in town—"

"You couldn't!"

"I could have. The doctor would have waited a little longer."

Mother shook her head. Then she smiled. "We're out of debt now. Just a few more weeks in the shop and you can buy another horse. Then we can all be together. Out here."

"That's what you want to do?"

"Of course it is! I want to finish the job we started, prove up on the homestead!"

"So do I." Father drew a long, deep breath of relief. "And all the time I thought you were just putting up with things because I didn't provide something better."

"Well," Mother said, "I wasn't." She laughed. "I've got to think about getting supper for my menfolks. And see if I've got what I need to bake a birthday cake. And you two had better go get Daisy and the calves. There's no hurry. You'll have time to take a walk and look at the sunset. You may not have time tomorrow, because we're going to plant corn. With a hoe!"

Father and I walked up the draw, where the bluestem was almost knee-high. It would be good hay this year. We walked up to where Daisy and the calves were grazing, and beyond, up onto the ridge where the lush, curling buffalo grass was plush-soft underfoot.

We stood on the ridge and looked off across the flats, and they were like that land of Genesis again, reaching into forever. The sun was almost down on the horizon. Bullbats were sailing overhead with their *eeep-eeep* cries and quick, darting flight. The meadow larks were singing their evening songs. From somewhere far out on the flats came the soft *coo-cooeee* of the turtle doves.

Father looked and listened, and he was smiling a deep, inside smile. I wanted to tell him how the world out here was under the towering snowdrifts, and how spring came up through the soles of your feet and through the marrow of your bones, and how it was the night before Christmas that wasn't going to be Christmas, and how it was when the shotgun and the rabbit led me to the Bromleys and the books. I wanted to tell him about the old Indian point-maker and the flint chips, and about the gray mug beside the emigrant trail, and about the fossil clam.

I turned to try to tell him these things and I saw his face, and I knew I didn't have to tell him. He knew. Then I saw something more in his face, an inner certainty.

I was to know that quality better and better in him over the years, but I sensed it then. In summing up what there was to show for his thirty-four years he had omitted the one possession that mattered, the certainty, the belief. Take away everything else and that remained. He had been forced to a decision between the dream and the responsibility, not knowing until the decision was made that there is no choice, that the dream encompasses the responsibility or it is no dream at all. That was the distillation of the homestead years, as it was the distillation of the frontier through all the years. The pioneer started with the dream, and the unique achievement was his persistence in the dream even while he met his obligations to self, to family, and to society.

We stood there on the ridge and watched the sunset. The rim of the sun touched the horizon and shimmered all the hills across the west. Then Father said, "We'd better go back."

We went down the draw in the coolness and got Daisy and the calves and cantankerous old Mack and put them in the barn and did the evening chores. Daisy was fat with calf. There would be another calf before the month was out. This fall the spotted heifer, Bessie's calf, would be old enough to breed. Before haying time we would have another horse. The barn would be almost full again by next winter.

We heard Mother singing in the house. Father stopped and listened and I saw him smile. I saw the certainty even more clearly than before in his face. Then Mother called us and we went in to supper.

20

It isn't too difficult to plant corn with a hoe, once you've made up your mind to it. It's tedious work, and your arms get tired and your back aches; but the sun isn't too hot at corn-planting time, and there are lots of birds around, singing and looking for bugs and worms in the soil as you turn it up. We didn't have any crows to take the corn as fast as you planted it, and that was a help. Father and I took turns with the hoe. His hands weren't tough, as mine were, and they blistered the first afternoon. But he put on cotton flannel work gloves and kept at it.

Mother baked a cake for our birthdays, but we didn't take any time off. We kept at the corn planting. We had it down to a system by the second day. The one with the hoe chopped down, dug a hole with one swing and scooped out the dirt in the same motion, lifted the hoe and chopped the next hole, and the next, and the next. The other one, with a sack of corn slung around his shoulder, dropped a few kernels of corn in the hole, scuffed dirt over it with his foot, stepped on it to firm it, and went on to the next, and the next. We went right down the field, planting on the ridges between last year's old stalks, and we planted about four acres. Then we put in a row of pinto beans, just as we had the year before. And we left room to plant a short row of potatoes.

It took us most of the week, and before we were finished Louie had come to the upper camp with his flock. Two roustabouts from Gerrity's home ranch came with him, pitched a tent beside the windmill, and took turns sitting on the hillside above the camp with a .30-30 rifle handy. The men were guards, and there was trouble brewing. Before he went back to Brush, Father had a talk with Louie. Father didn't like the look of things.

Louie didn't know much more than we did. It was the trouble Jack Clothier had mentioned before he went to Wyoming. The cattlemen were being pinched for grass. The Lazy Four was especially hard hit by the drought the previous summer and it had lost quite a few cattle in the blizzardy winter. The Lazy Four boss blamed Gerrity and his sheep. And the situation was brought to a head by several minor things.

Two other cowboys besides Jack Clothier had quit at the Lazy Four. Three fiery young Texans had been hired to replace them. Times were changing, but the young Texans didn't know it. The day was close at hand when a cowboy would be just a farm hand on a horse; they thought the old days of hard-riding, gun-toting cowhands were still going strong.

Then, just at the start of lambing season, one of Gerrity's regular herders was kicked by a work horse in the barn and got a broken leg. Another regular herder quit to work for a man in Montana. Gerrity replaced them with two Mexican herders from New Mexico who could speak little English.

One of the new Texas cowboys, all dressed up in chaps and a six-shooter, met one of Gerrity's hands in Gary one Saturday just as lambing was starting. The cowboy called the sheep hand a Mexican. The sheep hand laughed at the cowboy and his six-gun. Although most cowboys and sheep herders still carried short-barreled .30-30 rifles to shoot coyotes, almost nobody carried a revolver. The cowboy had had a few drinks. He reached for his gun. The sheep hand rushed him, a shot was fired, the gun was knocked from the cowboy's hand, and the two of them went into the dust in a clawing, kneeing fist fight. A bystander pocketed the six-shooter.

The fight didn't amount to much, a black eye and a cut lip and a few scratches. Two husky homesteaders pulled the fighters apart. The cowboy demanded his gun, didn't get it, climbed on his horse, and rode away, shouting loud threats.

The next Saturday all three Texans went to Gary looking for trouble, but all Gerrity's men were busy with lambing. The cowboys shot a few tin cans, made a lot of noise, and rode away.

Lambing over, Gerrity, with a strange, stubborn blindness, sent his two Mexican herders with flocks to be grazed on the edge of the Lazy Four range. And, expecting trouble, he sent armed guards with all his flocks, including Louie's.

Father talked to Louie, who was a little frightened and full of threats. If the Lazy Four cowboys came to attack his camp he would shoot them, every one of them. He was a good shot, and he had a good rifle. He could take care of himself. If there was going to be a range war, he could handle his end of it.

Father came back and said to Mother and me, "I don't think there's going to be anything but loud talk. Whatever happens, there is no reason anything should happen here. We're not involved in any way." Mother agreed. So Father went back to Brush to work a few more weeks and get money enough to buy the other horse.

What was happening, of course, was beyond the control of the ranchmen. They didn't even see it. None of us realized it in those terms, but an era was coming to an end. The days of the big ranches and the open range were almost over. Previous waves of homesteaders had lonelied out or discouraged out or dried out, but this wave of settlement was going to stay. Rising land values and a rapidly expanding population in the Midwest were pushing farmers toward the marginal lands of the West. This movement was encouraged by a moist cycle just starting on the plains, a favorable weather cycle that was to continue with little interruption for ten or fifteen years.

Another factor, even more important and even less foreseeable, was the rumbling in the far-off Balkans. For years there had been small wars in the Balkans. This time a small war was to explode into World War I, which would be felt on the plains primarily as a wheat boom. Gang plows would move in, vast acreages of sod would be ripped up to grow two-dollar wheat. The plains would be opened to the winds of eventual drought and depression.

But those were matters for the years ahead. At the moment the ranchmen were being squeezed out of business by a shortage of free range. They were being slowly choked to death by the homesteaders and their strands of barbed wire. Most of the ranchmen, however, thought of homesteaders as a transient nuisance and waited for nature to drive them out, as it had before. Had the ranchmen chosen to do so, even then, they probably could have driven most of the homesteaders out by force. Instead, they turned on each other. The Lazy Four blamed Gerrity. The old, old cattle-sheep feud was revived.

Father went back to Brush, and two days later there was a prairie fire on the range of one of the Mexican herders. It smudged and smoldered only a mile or so, but it trapped and smothered fifty head of sheep. Less than a week later a similar fire on the other Mexican's range killed forty or fifty of his flock.

But fire wasn't the answer, and if it had been the timing was all wrong. If the Lazy Four wanted to burn Gerrity out of business the move should have been made the previous summer, when a prairie fire would have run for miles in the drought-sere grass. Such a fire would have been disastrous not only to Gerrity but to dozens of homesteaders, who would have lost houses, barns and precious hay.

The next move was a night raid. Raiders crept up in the darkness, somehow eluded the guards, opened the pens, whooped one Mexican's flock out across the flats. But they didn't start a real stampede. All but a dozen or so of the sheep were gathered the next day.

Louie by then was sure the next raid would be on his camp.

When there is trouble around, some people feel neglected if they aren't involved. They have to live a kind of awed and hopeful expectation of disaster. Louie didn't want to be shot or beaten, but he wanted to feel important enough to justify such a possibility. The next move, however, was also against the Mexican herders.

A slow-witted farmer whose wife had died in childbirth the previous fall and left him with five children lived in the edge of the sand hills north of Gerrity's big camp. The farmer's oldest child was a drab, frightened girl of fifteen. She often wandered in the sand hills, a girl even more slow-witted than her father. The cowboys started the rumor that she was visiting the Mexicans. Then they spread the story that the Mexicans had raped her. The girl denied it, but the father believed the story and declared he was going to kill "them damn Spicks."

The whole thing was undoubtedly a frame-up, but the cowboys had picked the wrong man. The farmer wasn't the kind to kill anyone. When a week passed without any action, three masked riders descended on the wagon of one Mexican herder in the darkness, trussed up the guard, trapped the herder in the wagon, castrated him, and burned the wagon.

At that point the sheriff rode into the picture. He came out with two deputies, questioned the maimed herder and arrested the three Mexican-hating young Texans. He took them to town, jailed them, and the law began its deliberate process of indictment, trial and conviction.

Nobody questioned the authority of the law. The boss of the Lazy Four didn't even bail out his cowboys. Once the sheriff stepped into the picture, the law was dominant, for there is an ingrained sense of the majesty and the ultimate justice of the law, of duly constituted authority, which runs through all our history, from the first establishment of a system of local self-government in Boston and Salem more than three centuries ago. True, the frontier and especially the western frontier, often had its vigilante rule before organized government was established; but it is significant that the vigilantes usually went through the motions of legal process, if only to justify dubious actions.

Our range war ended. Gerrity's other Mexican herder quit and took the first train back to New Mexico. Gerrity divided the abandoned flocks among his other herders and withdrew his ineffectual guards, Louie swallowed his disappointment, and June crept across the plains with its peaceful and plenteous warmth. Father bought another horse and came home, and we put up more hay than we had ever in our stack yard. We cut the volunteer rye. We hoed the corn. Mother's garden flourished. And Father and I helped Jake Farley build his new house, fighting flying ants and listening to Jake's stories.

But Jake was absorbed, most of the time, in his approaching marriage. "I wonder," he would ask, "if Mildred is going to like it out here. This country's a lot different from Iowa." And he would say, "I guess I ought to go to town and get some new furniture. Or do you think it would be all right if I painted up what I got?" And, over and over, he asked, "Do you suppose there will be a shivaree?"

Jake worried about the shivaree, in which neighbors gathered at the home of a newly wed couple, made a din, and demanded a treat. Jake was afraid of a shivaree, and he was even more afraid there wouldn't be one for him and Mildred. He dreaded it, and he couldn't face the social disgrace of being ignored.

We got the walls up, the roof on, the partitions in, and Jake mixed dobe mud and plastered the inside. And he kept worrying about the shivaree.

When the time came, everything went off all right. Jake's bride arrived in Brush on schedule. She was as old as Mother, a chubby blonde, shy, and as frightened as Jake was. Mother said, "She's nice. And she thinks the world of Jake." Mother and Father went to the preacher with them, and after the ceremony Jake took his bride down to the general store and said, "Buy anything you want. It's your wedding present."

Mildred bought fifteen dollars' worth of groceries, not another thing. Jake carried the boxes of groceries out to the wagon, helped Mildred in, and they drove out to the new sod house on his homestead.

There was a shivaree the next night. About twenty neighbors gathered, with cowbells and wash tubs and tin pans, and a couple of shotguns to punctuate the din. Jake was delighted and Mildred was relieved. She had spent all day baking cakes and, as she whispered to Mother, "I don't know what I'd have done with them if folks hadn't come!" Everybody crowded inside and admired the bride and the new house, and Mildred served coffee and cake. Then one man produced a mouth organ and played a tune, and all the menfolks and boys began carrying the furniture outdoors, even the cookstove. Once the house was cleared they began to square dance. They danced till two o'clock in the morning, then moved the furniture back in, put up the stove again, and went home.

The shivaree was the big social event of the summer. The next week the men gathered and began to build the school-house. There wasn't much time left, because school was to start the first of September. We were to have only a five-month term that year, but with interruptions for bad weather we knew it might stretch into February or even March.

There were only seven of us of school age, and all the other six lived over east. Four of them had arrived with their families the previous fall and I didn't know them. The other two of them were too young for me to play with even if I had wanted company or had time for it. The teacher, Miss Howard, was only nineteen and had finished high school in Denver the previous spring. Her seven pupils were scattered over five grades. Only three of us were boys, one a six-year-old first-grader, one a gangling youngster of sixteen, an inch taller than Miss Howard, and in the eighth grade.

I felt like a stranger in the group. Except for the sixteen-year-old eighth-grader, who had been doing a man's work since he was thirteen, they all seemed very young. They were still children. The oldest girl, who was in the sixth grade, had trouble reading words of more than two syllables, and the big boy in the eighth grade couldn't do long division. I was a schoolboy, and yet I was already reaching toward adulthood. Miss Howard soon learned what books I had read and fed me all the adult reading she could lay her hands on. Anything, I suppose, to keep me busy and interested. But because I had left school in Nebraska in the fourth grade, she had to start me in the fifth.

Our books were a strange assortment, probably dug out of a storeroom by a casually interested school board far away. I had a McGuffey reader and a blue-back geography whose map of the United States showed the whole area from eastern Kansas to the Rocky Mountains as "The Great American Desert." I went through my McGuffey reader in the first month and through the one for the next grade a few weeks later, memorizing dozens of poems and orations as I went. Miss Howard promoted me to the sixth grade, which simplified her work. That made three of us in the sixth grade and reduced the number of grades she was teaching to four. By Thanksgiving I was helping the big boy in the eighth grade with his arithmetic. That wasn't unusual in a one-room school, where those advanced in one subject often supplemented the teacher.

Miss Howard lived with the Hagens, over east. They had two children in school, and Miss Howard and the Hagen children drove to school in the Hagen buggy. The rest of us walked, except in bad weather, when I rode Mack. When the storms came, the blizzards that made travel dangerous, everyone knew there would be no school. We stayed at home and started school again when the storm was over.

We had the best Thanksgiving we'd ever had on the homestead. We still lived largely from the land, and we burned cow chips and sheep chips. Father and I kept meat on the table and we ate plenty of beans and cornmeal mush, but there was no sense of privation or hardship. Daisy's new calf had been a bull. We fattened it all fall and when the cold weather came just before Thanksgiving we butchered it and had young beef for the winter. Mother said, "With beef hanging where you can cut a steak any time, rabbit tastes a lot better, doesn't it? I guess it's human nature to want what you haven't got."

Christmas passed, and January was stormy. School dragged on till the last week in February. And then spring came again, a wet spring with good grass and a promise of good crops.

Our major troubles were past. After the decision had been made the previous spring, everything was easier. What problems we had didn't seem to crowd in so hard. Once it had been decided to stay and prove up on the homestead, there was a sense of freedom. We were staying because we wanted to, and that made all the difference. Now it was possible to look even further ahead, beyond the time when Father could prove up and get a patent, a deed to the land.

Father was not a farmer. He had found that out. He loved the Colorado plains, but now he knew that he wouldn't be content to spend the rest of his life digging a living from them. He had to make the move, take the homestead and prove up on it, to satisfy something within himself. We had about made a success of that venture. Now the question was: What next?

"What do you want to do?" Mother asked. It was a sunny April day with a spring wind blowing.

Instead of answering her question, Father said, "My father went to Nebraska and took land over near Vesta. But he didn't stay on that place. He farmed it till he got title, but all the time he was running a little blacksmith shop right on the place. Finally he moved to Sterling, where there was water for a mill, and started the mill and blacksmith shop. Most of the businesses in Sterling were started by folks who moved in from farms they had homesteaded. They sold out to farmers who came along after the first settlers."

"Do you want to move back to Nebraska?" Mother half smiled, knowing the answer.

"No! I like this new country, and you know it. We came to Colorado to stay."

"Maybe you'd like to move to Brush. It's a nice town."

Father shook his head. "Brush is a good town, but its big boom is about over. Besides, there are two newspapers there now."

Mother smiled. "Once a printer, always a printer."

"I guess so. Ink in my veins. Remember what L. A. Varner said when we left Sterling?" Mr. Varner was the man who taught Father the printer's trade. " 'Will,' he said, 'I'll give you just five years away from a print shop. Every printer I ever knew,' he said, 'thought he wanted to be a farmer.' "

Father rolled a cigarette and lit it and thought while he drew a lungful of smoke. "One of these days," he said, "I'll go look for a town. Somewhere here on the plains. I know what I want. Not too big a place, but a growing town. I'll either start a paper there or find a place with a run-down paper and buy it. We'll grow with the town. This is a growing country, and there are lots of good towns that are going to grow with it."

That was the germ of the idea, and it was in the frontier tradition. Conquest of the land was only part of pioneering. And there were all kinds of pioneers. Some were clerks and some were storekeepers and some were bankers, some were blacksmiths and some were printers. They built the towns and organized the commerce and the trade in the new land. And some were the restless folk who had to live their lives out on the fringes ahead of the permanent settlements, moving on as soon as towns grew up and neighbors arrived. Without their restlessness the United States would still be a narrow band of settlement along the Atlantic Coast. And without the pioneers turned tradesmen and artisans, the land would have become a rural backwater living by barter and handcraft.

Father and Mother talked, and all through their plans ran the bright thread of confidence. The things I had seen in Father's face and vaguely sensed, that afternoon when he said we were going to stay and prove up on the homestead, were in his words now. He could do whatever he wanted to do. There might be barriers, but there were ways over or through or around. The homestead years had convinced him of that. He and Mother had never lacked courage; now they had the confidence to go with it.

Spring stretched into summer. The last two dugouts in our area were replaced by sturdy sod houses. A dugout was always considered a temporary home, easy to abandon; when a man built a soddy he meant that he intended to stay. More and more miles of barbed wire fences were put up. More and more patches of sod corn were planted. The homesteaders were winning the quiet war for the plains.

The Lazy Four went bankrupt and was sold to a man from eastern Kansas. He fenced its deeded land and made no attempt to hold its open range. He stocked his fenced pastures with good beef cows and brought in two blooded white-face bulls, Herefords. Gerrity put out two fewer flocks than usual, and the flock he sent with Louie to the upper camp had only fifteen hundred head, half the usual number. Gerrity knew that the old order was changing.

There were still a few echoes of the old days. That summer a cowboy who had been fired from a ranch down south rode in to Gary, trying to drown his sorrows in a bottle, and pulled a gun and fired two wild shots in the direction of a group of farmers swapping stories beside the store. One of the farmers knocked him down with his fist, took away his gun, and carried him to the horse trough and dumped him in. The disgraced cowboy crawled out, dripping and considerably sobered, got on his horse, and rode away.

An era was ending. The country, as the old-timers said, was getting crowded. It was getting "all womaned up." A homesteader with enough credit to buy a wagonload of groceries from a wholesale house started another store six miles south of Gary, in an area that hadn't a house or a fence in sight when we first came. He called it Woodrow and established a post office there. The old trails, which were shortcuts across the flats, began to vanish and people drove on the section lines, a good deal of the time between fences.

And that summer Father proved up on the homestead and got his patent, his legal title to the land. I still have the original patent, number 363429, which granted to Will A. Borland and his heirs and assigns, "the north half of Section seventeen in Township one south of Range fifty-six west of the Sixth Principal Meridian, Colorado, containing three hundred twenty acres." It was issued by Woodrow Wilson, President of the United States.

The old era really ended there on the plains, it always seemed to me, when the government asked Con Hallahan to bid on carrying the mail from Brush to Gary and Woodrow by truck. Con read the request for bids and exclaimed, "By truck! If my wild horses aren't good enough to haul the mail, be damned to you!" And Con refused to bid. That was in 1915. There still wasn't a farmer or a homesteader south of Gary who owned an automobile or a truck, but a man near Brush bought a Model T truck and got the contract.

That was also the year, 1915, when we moved to Flagler. Father had found the growing town and the struggling newspaper he wanted. Flagler was a town of about 600 people situated on the Rock Island railroad ninety miles southeast of the homestead, almost in the center of the High Plains. It was a new town, only twenty-eight years old. The section foreman on the railroad there had helped lay the first rails west of Kansas across the plains. A handyman around town said he had ridden with Jim Bridger and Kit Carson. He probably had. Bridger had been dead only thirty-four years and Carson only forty-seven. The old Old West wasn't very far in the past.

Father bought the *Flagler News* and became a distinguished country editor. There, under him, I learned the printer's trade, just as I always knew he wanted me to. There I went to high school. And I went to the state university from there, along with the son of a man who had trailed a herd of longhorns up the Chisholm Trail from Texas and a boy whose father had once hunted buffalo. And I came to know that a frontier is never a place; it is a time and a way of life. I came to know that frontiers pass, but they endure in their people.